ART, MIMESIS AND THE AVANT-GARDE

Aspects of a philosophy of difference

Andrew Benjamin

London and New York

First published 1991
by Routledge
11 New Fetter Lane, London EC4P 4EE
Simultaneously published in the USA and Canada
by Routledge
a division of Routledge, Chapman and Hall, Inc.
29 West 35th Street, New York, NY 10001

Typeset in 10/12 Garamond by
Witwell Limited, Southport
Printed in Great Britain by
T J Press (Padstow) Ltd, Padstow, Cornwall

British Library Cataloguing in Publication Data
Benjamin, Andrew
Art, mimesis and the avant-garde: aspects of a philosophy
of difference.
1. Ontology. I. Title.

Library of Congress Cataloging in Publication Data
Benjamin, Andrew
Art, mimesis and the avant-garde: aspects of a philosophy of
difference/Andrew Benjamin.
p. cm.
Includes bibliographical references and index.
1. Aesthetics. 2. Avant-garde (Aesthetics). 3. Mimesis in art.
I. Title.
BH39.B3845 1991
111'. 85–dc20 91–47905

ISBN 0 415 06047 8 (hbk) 0 415 06627 1 (pbk)

Paperback cover illustration: 'The Jewish School
(drawing of a Golem)', R.B. Kitaj, 1980.
Marlborough Fine Art (London) Ltd.

CONTENTS

ACKNOWLEDGEMENTS

These texts written over the last few years, 1986–90, have appeared, often in earlier and even more hesitant versions, in a variety of books and journals. As such I would like to thank the following for allowing them to be reproduced: Academy Editions, Manchester University Press, Oxford Literary Review and Oxford University Press. It must be added that, because of the differences between the places of their initial publication, some texts will be more programmatic than didactic; more strategic than academic. Complexity arises once tone is no longer singular. Furthermore, it will be seen that while 'early' formulations are adapted and reworked, central preoccupations endure.

Writing on the visual arts is always hazardous. The use of illustrations does not diminish the risk, it merely changes the stakes. None the less I would like to thank all the individuals, galleries and museums as detailed in the list of illustrations on p.ix for permission to reproduce paintings. In particular the generosity and support of R.B. Kitaj must be acknowledged.

Finally, this book is for Jennifer, with whom many of these paintings were first seen, and the related projects initially elaborated.

ILLUSTRATIONS

INTRODUCTION: INAUGURATING REPETITION

Addressed here, despite the range of topics, is a particular *topos*. The *topos* in question concerns the attempt to rework and thereby to readdress the philosophical task in terms of the centrality of ontology. It is in relation to this centrality that art, mimesis and the avant-garde come to be presented. The conception of ontology at work here starts from a rethinking of ontological difference, a constitutive component of which will be the primacy of existence. However this does not mean that what is at stake is the specific historical presentation of existence, which, as the expression of its historicity, derives its force from its opposition to essence. It is rather that existence denotes, in the first place, more than the simple attribution of the fact of existence since it brings into play the articulation of existence within modes of being. The articulation is *necessary*. The analogy would be the impossibility of thinking being outside of the categories since being is categorial. This move neither effaces nor evades the question of being. On the contrary, it signals a reorientation within philosophical questioning. In the second place; as existence will involve modes of being, it will also denote the ontological rather than what is taken to be its opposite namely the merely empirical. Consequently, not only does the opposition between existence and essence come to be displaced, the posited universality of existence itself (as opposed to its primacy) is checked by its having been dispersed within differential modes of being. While the presence of dispersal works against universality it does not hinder let alone weaken the force of a differential ontology and its semantic and interpretive correlates.

For Heidegger, on the other hand, the difference marking onto-logical difference takes place between Being and beings. The task of fundamental ontology is generated by the distinctions enacted in one of Heidegger's proclaimed points of departure: 'The Being of beings *is*

1

itself not a being' ('*Das Sein des Seienden "ist" nicht selbst ein Seiendes*').[1] It is thus that the question of Being cannot be posed as though what was at stake was no more than the ontology of a given entity. The negation – the 'not' – breaks the standard identifications that, for Heidegger, are usually thought to direct the question of Being. In *Being and Time* the ontological priority of *Dasein* derives from this break since Being is already implicated in *Dasein*. There is therefore no need for an outward movement that would still the negation by reintroducing an identification (the identification of Being with an entity outside of itself). In a similar way the overcoming of misidentifications is central to the project of tracing 'Being to its own form of Appropriation' announced in *On Time and Being*.[2] Misidentification in this instance takes place as the thinking of Being 'in terms of beings as ideas, energia, actualitas . . .'.[3] In this latter text Heidegger describes his project in the following terms:

> The task of our thinking has been to trace Being to its own from Appropriation – by way of looking through true time without regard to the relation of Being to beings.[4]

Locating the site of difference between Being and beings gives rise to a specific construal of the philosophical task, that is, the priority of the question of Being, where Being comes into its own in its differentiation from beings. The reciprocal dimension is the devaluation of beings such that they become no more than the facts out of which the world is made for positivism. The two components – the question of Being and 'facts' – are interdependent. Their symbiosis generates the question of Being as the philosophical question. Related to the centrality of this singular question is an understanding of the history of philosophy as the continual attempt to pose this question where each attempt turns out to be part of a continual succumbing to the trap of identification.

There is no straightforward response to Heidegger's presentation of ontological difference and the consequent centrality of the question of Being. This is in part due to Heidegger's use of the texts comprising philosophy's history as part of the means by, and through, which his argument is advanced. Rather than attempt to plot a specific response to Heidegger the chapters to come will endeavour to present ontological difference differently. The question is how difference is to be understood? What will be suggested is that if modes of being, interarticulated with modes of time, are always present in terms of their divergence then there can be no question of Being *qua* Being – Being as differentiated – for there is no relation to the divergent that is not itself part of the divergent. It follows that there is no longer the problem of identification as the site of difference has changed. It has moved from the non-relation and hence location of difference as between Being and beings, to defining the relationship between modes of being. This shift has occurred because difference is henceforth differential rather than simply marking a negation or non-relation. What this will mean is the primacy of the already present and already plural ontologico-temporal. This presence, that which is present, is neither an already unified and hence pre-given totality nor does it function as an *arché*, rather, it marks that which is anoriginally differential.[5]

Whatever the complexity that may be at work here, it is the consequence of an inauguration – the attempted 'rethinking' – within the task of philosophy. The familiarity of the language – ontology, difference, identity – begins the repetition. It must be pointed out, of course, that the possibility of any attempted inauguration – of inaugurating itself – does not escape attention. It is dealt with here in terms of the avant-garde.

The attempt both to detail and argue for some of the elements of this inauguration forms part of the concerns of the first two chapters, 'Interpreting reflections: painting mirrors' and 'Spacing and distancing'. These details are given a more precise location in studies of specific paintings by Kitaj, Freud, Kiefer and Malevich, the architecture of Peter Eisenman and the writings of Roger Laporte. In addition to these studies highlighting the problematic nature of the relationship between philosophy and painting, architecture and literature they also serve to introduce the central topics of tradition, mimesis,[6] affirmation, interpretation and the avant-garde. This introduction – its scope and constitution – will be determined by the inauguration. In other words these topics come to be repeated within, and as, this particular formulation of the philosophical task.

The writings of Walter Benjamin form a fundamental part of any attempt to take up the interconnection between the topics of tradition and interpretation. Present here are two related approaches to the implicit philosophical dimension of those writings. Chapter 10, 'Tradition and experience', attempts to indicate the way Benjamin's work charts the limits of a particular conception of modernity, that is the present as a locus of loss. It is further suggested that this limit also delimits the possibility of a different philosophical endeavour. Part of the argument advanced in the ninth chapter, 'The decline of art: Benjamin's aura', is that this possibility is already inscribed in the temporal structure within which aspects of Benjamin's conception of the aura come to be articulated, as well as the way in which he distinguishes in 'The storyteller' between the temporality of the story and the temporality of information.[7]

The topics of the avant-garde and mimesis are pursued along different lines in Chapters 8 and 11, 'Pluralism the cosmopolitan and the avant-garde and Descartes' fable.' The former opens up some of the political implications of the avant-garde. In addition it takes up the question of the relationship between art and national identity. As such it forms part of a more general reworking of tradition. Descartes' description of the *Discours de la méthode* as a painting (*un tableau*) and a fable (*une fable*) provides the basis of a detailed investigation of the relationship between fiction and truth and in particular how truth is constrained by, and yet defined by or presented in terms of, always having to overcome the threat of fiction. Central to this investigation is Descartes' use of imitation and representation.

The final aspect at play here, explicitly though more often implicitly, concerns the work of Jacques Derrida and Jean-François Lyotard. It is clear that here their different, though at times related, philosophical undertakings and projects, are of central importance. The importance is marked by an initial acceptance of certain formulations and modes of approach. It is also present in terms of what could be taken as a response. The centrality attributed to ontology and time, coupled to the use and location of spacing are intended as a reply to Derrida. The formulation given to the avant-garde and the sublime are intended to engage with central aspects of Lyotard's recent work. It goes without saying that here engagement and response are marks of respect.

NOTES

1 M. Heidegger, *Being and Time*, trans. J. Macquarrie and E. Robinson (Basil Blackwell, Oxford, 1972), p. 26. Even though both the German and English editions have the 'is' emphasized, this needs to be understood as an attempt by Heidegger to give to the negative an ontologically positive character. As such this does not detract from the non-relation. All it does is remove it from the possibility of nothingness.

2 M. Heidegger, *On Time and Being*, trans. J. Stambaugh (Harper & Row, New York, 1972), p. 24.

3 ibid., p. 21.
4 ibid., p. 22.
5 The use of the term anoriginal and the related philosophical stance that is implicated in it are presented and discussed in later chapters. They continue a task announced in my *Translation and the Nature of Philosophy* (Routledge, London, 1989). See in particular the Introduction and chapter 6.
6 The problem with any attempt to deal with a topic as vast as mimesis is trying to take the range of its permutations into account. In what follows the conception of mimesis in question is the one that commences with Plato and comes to be linked to imitation and representation. Absent from these considerations is any systematic confrontation with what could be described as the Aristotelian heritage.
7 In W. Benjamin, *Illuminations*, trans. H. Zohn (Fontana, London, 1973). I have also taken up the question of the temporality of interpretation within Benjamin's work in *Translation and the Nature of Philosophy*, chapter 4.

1
INTERPRETING REFLECTIONS: PAINTING MIRRORS

DELIBERATIONS

Within the process of interpretation it is, at times, essential to distinguish between the specificity of a given interpretation and the object of interpretation itself. It is only by holding them apart (recognizing, of course, all the attendant risks and problems of this particular undertaking) that it will then be possible to focus attention on the nature of the object. What is at stake in this instance is not the object prior to interpretation as such, but rather the possibility of understanding both the place as well as the nature of the object within the actuality of interpretation, that is within the practice of interpretation.

Now one of the most difficult problems presented by the object of interpretation concerns the categories and concepts within which it is (or is to be) interpreted. There will be no attempt at this stage to distinguish in a systematic way between understanding and interpretation. Part of the reason for not doing this would be explicable in terms of the argument that *understanding* is itself already an interpretive category; one gesturing toward the posited centrality of the experiencing subject. Such a move would thereby serve to suggest that the practice and direction of interpretation had commenced. Interpretation, on the other hand, is intended as no more than a cover-all term designating the responses (those pertaining to experience as well as the discursive) to an object where that object exists, not *qua* simple material object (with whatever subsequent determinations which would then come to be added) but as an object of interpretation. Rather than attempting to deal in general terms with the issues raised by the inherently problematic nature of the object, a specific tack will be taken. If the broader approach were to have been pursued, then, at the very minimum, it would have been necessary to take tradition into consideration, not as a given but as itself a problem already implicated within any philosophical consideration of interpretation. Here, however, as has been suggested, the task is more limited as the focus of attention will be the figure:[1] its existence, the interpretive demands made by it and finally the confrontation of the two specific symbolic domains it engenders. The first is the domain of the figure proper – its implication within iconography and history – and the second is language: the figure of and within language.

Any approach to the figure within painting, or even to figurative painting, automatically confronts the problem of how the figure is to be interpreted. (The place of the figure within the metaphysical opposition between the literal and the figural cannot, as will be seen, be completely divorced from these considerations.) It is tempting to take the figure as that which figures within the frame; the figure thereby becoming an interpretive end-in-itself. If this path were followed the task of interpretation would be to represent the figure where the figure was itself conceived as a representation. Interpretation would thereby be the representation of representation. Such a conception of interpretation would have the inevitable consequence that the process (or practice) of interpretation would have thereby become that task whose object was to construct, either implicitly or explicitly, a homological relation between the object of interpretation and interpretation itself. One would still the other. Interpretation would thereby repeat interpretation; a repetition by, of and in the Same. The proliferation of prepositions expresses both the persistent presence as well as the determining effect of the Same.

Homology involves a fundamental link with representation. The link however is not a simple contingent connection. Indeed as is indicated by the term itself, homology provides a basic, if not intrinsic component of the ontology of representation. This means that within the terms of what tradition intends for representation (and the presence of that intention as itself, in part, constitutive of tradition), representation and the homological are, in effect, interarticulated. This interarticulation will serve to preclude any argument that privileges the heterological over the homological. In other words what could not take place within the parameters set by this inter-articulation is any argument that took dis-unity as an original presence rather than as a secondary effect. Original dis-unity would mark the presence of an origin – a site – that resisted synthesis. The move away from homology, as the move away from the dominance of tradition, a move whose presentation is, in part, the task being outlined here, will necessitate such a conception of the origin. Moreover it is precisely the reality of this possibility, both the move and the subsequent reworking of the origin, that demands a subsequent reconceptualization of the origin. The original as original disunity, and not as the simple opposite of unity will be rethought and rearticulated here in terms of what will henceforth be called *anoriginal heterogeneity*.

In outline what is at stake within this reworking and hence within anoriginal heterogeneity is the following. The origin presupposes a beginning – a point of departure – that has its own causes and consequences. Origins thus construed will always involve teleology (marked by the twofold presence of either an implicit or explicit *arché* and *telos*). There is, in addition, a specific temporal dimension at work within a traditional and metaphysical conception of the origin. Even though it is perhaps self-evident it is worth reiterating its particular determination. Within the origin as a traditional philosophical concept, whether implicitly or explicitly present, is the assumption of a beginning: the *arché* as an ontologically and temporally primitive point. Any departure from the origin presupposes the possibility of a return. (The return can figure as an explanation, interpretation, etc. An instance of this emerges from Descartes' argument in *La Recherche de la vérité*, that an understanding of the complex stems from tracing the movement from the complex to the simple and then back to the complex. It is this move that allows the complex to emerge as an object of knowledge.)[2] In addition time as sequential continuity has to be presupposed in order that this interpretive (or explanatory) process of departure, return and departure is, in fact, possible. What is found at the origin is a unified site whose unity is, once again, presupposed in order that it function as an origin. Plurality is only possible after the event: the original event as founding moment. It is this postulated original event therefore that could never be the moment in which the presupposition of unity founders. Indeed it has to be the case that this possibility is always excluded. This exclusion is complex since even though anoriginal heterogeneity cannot be thought within the concepts and categories of the dominant philosophical tradition, its exclusion and subsequent reaffirmation must incorporate, though not as dominant, exactly that which occasioned the initial exclusion.

Furthermore it must be remembered that the exclusion is not the result of an intentional or conscious act, rather it marks the limit of what metaphysics allows to be thought.

It is the presence, the actuality of 'original' dis-unity – its presence within as well as its constitution of the frame – that is signalled in the expression *anoriginal heterogeneity*. (The being of the event will become the event of, and within, becoming.)[3] What is assumed by it is that the object of interpretation can never be, *qua* object of interpretation, a unified site. Part of the becoming-object of the work of art will involve the recognition of a heterogeneity that, in precluding the possibility of unity, and thus in not being a founding moment can never, within the classical determinations of the word, function as an origin. And yet there is nothing prior to heterogeneity. 'Prior', in this instance, marks firstly the necessity of the impossibility of a temporality of continuity and thus secondly gives rise to the need to rethink time beyond such a conceptual constraint. In other words is signals a *reorientation* of the philosophical task. It is this reorientation that delimits this present endeavour.

Heterogeneity is descriptive of the mode of being of the object of interpretation. It is thus that the term anoriginal is used. It allows for the presentation of an origin that is not original: the impossible origin, hence the anoriginal. While there may be surface connections – mere similarities of formulation – between the anoriginal and elements of Derrida's work, the difference resides in the importance attributed here to ontology and hence the affirmed impossibility of escaping modes of existence. Ontology is not exhausted by metaphysics. Indeed ontology refers to the many ways in which things are: the plurality of modes of existence. (A plurality, it should be noted, that is anoriginally conflictual and thus differential.) Ontology, therefore, names the differential plurality of modes of being. There needs to be added to this description the additional point that modes of being are always already (hence anoriginally) interarticulated with modes of temporality. It is thus that it is possible to speak of specific 'ontologico-temporal concatenations'.

While a number of philosophers (though most notably Heidegger) have argued for the necessary interconnection of being and time, this usually takes place in terms of a distinction between the singularity of Being and the plurality of beings. In *An Introduction to Metaphysics*, after suggesting a number of examples in which 'is' comes to be used, Heidegger goes on to add that 'Being discloses itself to us in a diversity of ways'.[4] What needs to be noted in this description is the distinction in terms of singular and plural between 'Being' and 'beings'. Being is from the start singular and then comes to be disclosed within 'diversity'. Even though the precise nature of this singularity resists simple summation it is none the less clear that the distinction drawn by Heidegger has an implicit conception of movement and therefore of direction within it. The move from singularity to plurality both occasions and allows for Heidegger's construal of the philosophical task to appear. It will involve the attempt to recover that singularity in the wake of the actuality of diversity and subsequent loss of the meaning of being. (It should be remembered, for example, that Heidegger, in his work on Nietzsche, describes the present within which his philosophical task is both conceived and enacted as one that is 'indifferent to Being'.) While it is the case that recovery, or even the attempt to do the same, will, for Heidegger, necessitate a futural direction, inscribed within both the philosophical task and the move from an original singularity to a subsequent plurality is an implicit teleology (the move from a postulated *arché* to a *telos* determined as the future) that provides the task and the movement with their conditions of existence. In other words the relationship between singularity and plurality ('diversity') and the philosophical task that it sanctions depends upon an implicit, and hence unstated, teleological dimension. A dimension that sanctions the movement of interpretation: recovery and retrieval.

The position presented here in terms of anoriginal heterogeneity seeks to deny the viability of the distinction, within being (within a generalized ontology), between the singular and the plural, while at the same time maintaining the centrality of ontology. There is no necessary connection between a plurality of modes of being and a postulated – either as present or not – conception of being as without exception singular. Indeed it is possible to go further and suggest that there is no reason to think that the plurality of specific beings necessarily even suggests the existence of such a connection. Consequently arguing for this connection would have to presuppose that plurality harboured the Same rather than marking a plurality that was anoriginally differential.[5]

In formulating the structure of what he calls 'the question of Being' in the Introduction to *Being and Time*,[6] Heidegger, after distinguishing Being from 'entities' (*Das Sein des Seienden 'ist' nicht selbst ein Seiendes*), goes on to make the following claim:

Being as that which is asked about must be exhibited in a way of its own, essentially different from the way in which entities are discovered. Accordingly what is found out by asking the question – the meaning of Being – also demands that it be conceived in a way of its own, essentially contrasting with the concepts in which entities acquire their determinate significations.

While resisting the commitment to the implicit empiricism that Heidegger seems to suggest would stem from refusing the distinction between Being and entities, it remains the case that the very presuppositions of Heidegger's argument are precisely those against which the philosophical import of the ontological dimensions of anoriginal heterogeneity is directed. The singular pronouns within which Heideggerian Being is announced are, within this general reorientation of the philosophical task, to be refused. There is no singular question of 'the meaning of Being' that can be posed independently of modes of being. Here the modes are not the modes of something which is independent of, though perhaps present in, the modes themselves. There is therefore no question of Being *qua* Being, there is simply the plurality of questions pertaining to the plurality of ways in which things are. The question of Being will always give way to questions pertaining to beings. And thus posing as independent 'the question of Being', asking it such that it 'contrasts' with questions which address modes of being, is itself only possible if the unity and singularity of Being precedes, though proceeds through, the 'diversity' of beings.

There is an important semantic dimension at work here. It is in part founded on the necessary interconnection of semantics and ontology (the differential plurality of meaning and being). Reworking ontology, as the term has been deployed here, away from Heidegger and the 'question of Being', will mean taking up the semantics of anoriginal heterogeneity. What is being resisted is the idea that a word can ever have a singular and unique determination that exists independently of different uses but which none the less shows itself within those differences. Once again, this would be to posit a distinction between a secondary plurality and an original unity such that what was original showed itself within that plurality while never being coextensive with it. The original would always unfold within an oscillation between 'revealing and concealing'. In opposition to this semantic frame the semantics of heterogeneity entail that what is named by the word ontology (i.e. being) – though this will be true to different degrees for all words – is from the start potentially conflictual and plural. The start here is the anoriginal.[7] There is therefore no meaning of being outside of this anoriginal differential plurality. The possibility of thinking the *difference* between the unique and separate question of Heidegger's Being and the task here adumbrated, provides one possibility for a philosophy that cannot be formulated or reformulated in Heideggerian terms. Moving beyond Heidegger's formulation of 'the question of Being' would mean that philosophy, rather than taking the Same as central, would henceforth be or become a philosophy of difference. However not difference as a series of variations within or of the Same but one where difference was differential.[8] The Same does not simply pertain to the uniqueness of the question of Being for Heidegger, it figures within, and as part of, the dominant tradition that comprises the history of philosophy. A philosophy of difference is only possible therefore to the extent that, firstly, the centrality of ontology is retained and, secondly, that ontology be thought beyond both the confines of the relationship between the singular and the plural on the one hand and the reign of the Same on the other.

FIGURES

There is a direct consequence of any attempt to rethink or reconsider the figure in light of a generalized though not as yet specified subversion of the Same. It is that a specific interpretation which took heterogeneity as anoriginal would still have to confront representation; it would still be constrained by it – however, no longer with representation providing the possibility of interpretation but conversely with the possibility of interpretation from now on involving the necessity of having to displace – to re-place – representation. It would thereby follow that neither the figure within the tableau nor even the more conventional figures within paintings, could be interpreted in terms (concepts and categories) that were dominated by, and hence which also articulated, the specific ontologico-temporal concatenation proper to representation. It must not be forgotten that here propriety, the proper, resides within a given object of interpretation's intentional logic.

Intentional logic is the self-identification of that task or project that a specific text, painting – in short an object of interpretation – sets out to enact. The object (text, painting, etc.) is, within this logic, envisaged as the site as well as itself being the manifestation of the task as enacted. Enactment, within the ambit of an object's intentional logic, is always intended to be coextensive with the object's self-identified task. The term 'task' can, of course, be deployed outside of the domain of intentional logic. The outside here would mean that while the assumption that a task was enacted would remain, and indeed would have to be assumed, what could never be assumed and hence what would always have to be left open is the coextensivity itself. The term/word 'task' is thereby redeemed since it can henceforth be redeployed in terms of the philosophical possibilities generated by anoriginal heterogeneity. Consequently the object of interpretation could never be absolutely coextensive with the task isolated or identified by intentional logic. In addition it could never be homological. That is why, eventually, the expression 'object of interpretation' will have to give way to one that incorporates within it the move from a philosophy of being to one that takes the ontology of becoming as central. In other words the object will become, and as such the object will come to be reworked in terms of the becoming-object of the object of interpretation.

In relation to representation the intentional logic of a particular object will limit the object within the demand (a demand within a purported self-referentiality) that it be interpreted as in fact a representation. It would thereby be the case that the object would have to be interpreted in terms of the opposition between the inside and the outside, where the possibility of interpretation lay within and was thus provided by that opposition. The object of interpretation would be constituted as an object in terms of its relation to that which lay outside of it. However this formulation needs greater clarification – since even though the object exists *qua* object because of its relation to an outside, this presupposes – as well as being presupposed by – a conception of the object (the inside) as unified, that is as homological. This has to be the case in order that it can sustain such a relationship with that which is outside it. The necessity at work here further attests to the interarticulation of representation and the homological. Leaving representation to one side – and thereby allowing the tension that marks interpretation within heterology to endure – will mean that different ontologico-temporal considerations will have to come into play. They will emerge, as was suggested, within the possibility

14

of the becoming-object of the work of art. The becoming-object, in no longer being situated within the opposition between the inside and the outside, will demand a rethinking of the figure. The demands stemming from the becoming-object cannot, if taken more generally, be limited simply to the figure.

These considerations need to be taken a step further. Here a way towards the figure will be provided by the mirror. The mirror reflects. It reflects more than that which is reflected in it. It takes what is outside and in providing the surface and frame can hold and thus re-present it inside. Reflection and representation are not reducible to each other. None the less the mirror enacts that temporal simultaneity and exactness of production – of re-production – such that it functions as almost the ideal type of representation. The mirror mirrors the perfection underpinning the ontological aspirations of representation. It constructs the perfect homological relation between inside and outside. What appears within the frame is the 'same' as that which is outside it. And yet one is a reflection of the other.

The mirror, as a material object, lends itself to its own inscription into the frame. It can thus form part of the painting and thereby part of the interpretive field. The inclusion of the mirror is however far from unproblematic since the mirror is not just the simple site of reflection. There is more at play. For it would now seem that the conditions underlying the figural as a representation can be incorporated into the tableau. The mirror presents, within the representation, a ruse, for it introduces onto and into the surface a disruption of the surface. It creates, as will be argued, a space within the field of the painting over which mastery can never be asserted. Whether it be the detached, though attentive, gaze created by Giovanni Bellini in *The Young Woman at her Toilet* or the delicious and perhaps ironic gaze within Balthus' *Les Beaux Jours*, or the complexity of reflection within either Bacon's *Portrait of George Dyer in a Mirror*, or Lucian Freud's self-portrait, *Interior with Hand Mirror*[9] in each instance mirroring, or rather the inscription of mirroring within the painting's own field, can be viewed in terms of the mirror functioning as an interpretive *mise-en-abyme*.

What is intended by the term *mise-en-abyme* here is that the mirror within the painting, linked as it is to the mirror as ideal form (itself mirroring the ideality of representation within reflection) serves to structure the possibility of interpretation in advance of the act of interpretation itself. Richard Rand describes the *mise-en-abyme* in the following terms:

> [It] is meant to designate the way in which the operation of reading and writing are represented in the text, and in advance, as it were, of any other possible reading. In ways that the reader can never bypass, the role of the reader is perpetually spelled out beforehand; and if the reader ever hopes to come forth with a new reading, he or she must as an essential preliminary, read off the reading lesson already at work in the work at hand.[10]

Here indeed it would be possible to go a step further and argue that the mirror's inscription within the interpretive field of painting allows for claims to be made about the interpretation of the figural as such. The mirror as *mise-en-abyme* will need to be sketched in great detail. It should not be forgotten however that there is a larger though more general point that is being made here, namely, that the use of terms, names, the proper names of paintings and painters, the conceptual terminology pertaining to aesthetics as well as to the philosophy of art, will need to be revaluated within the terms that will come to be set after having taken into consideration, from within interpretation, perhaps even as it, the task of interpretation itself. The presence of the *mise-en-abyme* provides this opportunity since it is the moment when interpretation can be seen as taking itself as its own object within the practice of interpretation, thus giving rise to a state of affairs in which any straightforward distinction between subject and object is called into question. It should be self-evident that this does not take place prior to any confrontation with the work of art, but as interpretation (interpretation in and as interpretation). If the suggestion of the already present *mise-en-abyme* is viewed as providing a beginning, and as such provides a particular determination, then the question that emerges as central concerns not the determination *qua* determination but its specific content within what the *mise-en-abyme* generates as the already determined dimension of the present task. It goes without saying that the recognition of this state of affairs is already a move both within and as interpretation. In addition the split between the implicit 'to be determined' and the explicit 'already determined' inscribes the impossibility of homology and the resistance to a repetition governed by the Same, into the conception (and enactment) of interpretation.

In order both to amplify these opening moves and clarify how the figure is to be understood, given the reorientation of the task at hand, the lead offered by certain elements at work in the way in which Lyotard formulates the distinction between the 'figurative' and the 'figural' will be taken. In *Discours Figure* he distinguishes between them in the following way. The term 'figurative' indicates the possibility of deriving the pictorial object from its 'real' model by a continual translation. The trace on the figurative tableau is a non-arbitrary trace. Figurativity is therefore a property relative to the relation of the plastic object with that which it represents. Figurativity disappears if the tableau no longer has the function of representing. If, that is, it is itself the object.[11] The figurative and figurativity are in Lyotard's presentation part of what in more general terms can be described as the opposition between the literal and the figural. They thereby open up the question of mimesis. The move within his work from the figurative to the figure allows for an understanding of the object beyond the confines and the purview of mimesis. It is precisely this possibility that is of central importance. Not only therefore does the value of his distinction between the figurative and the figure lie in its providing an initial vocabulary within which to situate the now redefined philosophical task. His formulation also draws attention to the dependence that the figurative has on representation. The mirror will allow for an understanding of the becoming-object of the tableau. Taking Lyotard's reworking of the figure away from representation, where the figure of the mirror would only mark the presence elsewhere of the 'real' mirror, will mean that the mirror, from now on, will be able to function, if only to begin with, as the *mise-en-abyme*. The reality of the mirror, the mirror as real, will henceforth be elsewhere, in no longer being interpretation within a more generalized becoming-object of the object of interpretation.

MIRRORS

Mirrors figure within paintings. They are present within the frame. And yet prior to any attempt to address this figure (these figures) the problems residing within the mirror must be confronted. On a more general level these problems are captured as well as held within the impossibility of giving a single and fixed determination to the words: 'painting mirrors'. The question that must be answered is, of what are

17

these words descriptive? Answering this question will involve paying specific attention to the 'what' of the what. The mirror brings with it the history of reflection. A vital part of that history has been the antagonism constructed by philosophy for art; this antagonism is encountered within, if not as, mimesis. The visual arts have always been, from within the terms set by this particular philosophical tradition, struggling with an ideal type that can never be fulfilled. The mirror is from the start conceded as an impossibility. And yet it positions art within an equally impossible situation. Mimesis, representation and the figurative do at the same time acknowledge the ideal and its impossibility. It should be noted that these three terms are deployed within writings on art and not within the work of art itself.

The desire for art first enacted within Plato's *Republic* and which is then silently repeated within the concepts and categories handed down by the dominant tradition within philosophy and within which the work of art is conventionally presented, demanded of art a homology between the inside and the outside that art could never sustain. It was thus that this homology moved away from the literal and became figural. The figural necessitates an outside, a literality, and yet sanctions and defines art as the trace left in crossing the bar that separates and joins, silently or not, the *re* and the *presentation*. Even though the history of mimesis is not reducible to Platonism – and hence the difference between Plato, Aristotle and Neo-Platonic conceptions of mimesis and the way access to beauty is provided even within Greek philosophical thought needs to be acknowledged – what comes to be repeated within the history of mimesis is a fundamental opposition between the inside and the outside, an opposition articulated within homology. This repetition of the Same as the tradition of mimesis means that the reference to Plato will have to be followed.

Of the many reasons why the detail of Plato's own presentations is important two specific aspects are central here. The first is that the Platonic conception of mimesis has dominated the way in which art is invariably presented. (Especially in so far as it is the inside/outside opposition that determines, in advance, the interpretation of the figure.) Overcoming the dominance of mimesis means overcoming the Platonic inheritance. Mimesis could always be present within the figurative (though only on the level of intentional logic) but is not to be understood in the terms that it itself presents. The homological moves to the heterological. The dominance of Platonism was recognized by Nietzsche who defined, in part, his philosophical task in terms of the need to 'overturn Platonism'. This overturning is not a reversal of the opposition between the physical and the ideal out of which the structure of Platonism is constructed. Mere reversal is simple nihilism, and understood as such by Nietzsche. It is rather that the overturning posits the possibility of a philosophical adventure that, while retaining – housing – the tradition, is no longer explicable within the concepts and categories handed down as tradition. That is why the project of the revaluation of values needs to be linked to this projected overturning. Clearly what is of vital importance here is the attempt to specify what is at stake in any projected overturning of Platonism. The second reason for taking up Platonism is that the function or role of mimesis within the Platonic texts is far from straightforward. It can be argued that within the dialogues there are at least two approaches to mimesis. Their analysis must, therefore, form an integral part of any attempt to rethink the figure beyond the confines of the tradition – beyond the confines of mimesis and representation.

There are two different presentations of mimesis that are of interest here. An example of the first can be found in the *Cratylus*. The other will be taken from the 'celebrated' discussion of art in Book X of *The Republic*. The first concerns the relationship between the name and the named. The significance of this example lies in the fact that Socrates describes this relationship between name and named as mimetic. Consequently the theory of signification advanced within the *Cratylus* is from the very start mimetic. Mimesis is not an interpretive attribution. It is inscribed within the dialogue's intentional logic. Within the *Cratylus* naming and therefore signifying involve a mimetic showing. Consequently the question to be addressed is what is shown within a correct instance of naming? In other words when a name is used correctly, what is presented via and as mimesis? It is vital to note, even at this stage, that in regards to naming – the mimetic activity naming – truth is possible. Understanding why is contingent upon recognizing what is being named within the naming relation.

The second presentation of mimesis concerns painting. In formulating his argument Socrates poses a specific question (*Republic* 598b). It is advanced within two sets of oppositions. They provide the terms in which painting as mimesis is, within the Platonism of the

Republic, to be understood.

> To which is painting directed in every case, to the imitation or
> reality as it is, or of appearance as it appears? It is an imitation
> of a phantasm/image/presentation or of the truth?[12]

As a preliminary move the oppositions must be more clearly
identified. The first is between 'reality' and 'the appearance as it
appears'; and the second between 'truth' and the 'phantasm/image'.
In Greek these distinctions are in the first case:

reality	τὸ ὄν
appearance as it appears	τὸ φαινόμενον, ὡς φαίνεται

In the second they are:

truth	ἀλήθεια
phantasma/image	φάντασμα

It is already clear from the formulation of the second that truth
(except in a negative sense) cannot pertain to painting. The 'image'
can neither be nor bear the truth. Consequently the initial question
that has to be asked in relation to these two different uses of the term
mimesis is, why in the case of the *Cratylus* can a mimetic relation be
true and why is this possibility excluded in the case of painting? There
is a direct answer to this question. It is that a name where used
correctly does not name 'the appearance as it appears' but rather the
presence (παρούσια) of the essential being (οὐσια) of the named
within the appearance, that is a name names, when used correctly, the
reality of the thing. There is however something else at play here.

In the *Cratylus* both the correct as well as the incorrect relation
between the name and the named are described by Plato as mimetic. It
is worth paying particular attention to this passage (*Cratylus* 430b–
430d). The first point made within it concerns the description of the
name *qua* name as an imitation: 'the name (τὸ ὄνομα) is an imitation
(μίμημα) of the thing named'. Without at this stage taking up the
question or status of the thing (τοῦ πράγματος) what is at least clear
is that the naming relation is articulated within mimesis and that the
name is mimetic. The next stage of the argument involves Socrates
getting Cratylus to agree that, in addition, paintings are imitations of

'things'. None the less, the significant element here is that what is imitated is, in each case, different. Socrates then asks further and more testing questions. (It is clear, however, that they are questions that take place within mimesis. They are not questions for mimesis, let alone a questioning of it.) He is concerned to know whether or not the imitations, paintings and names, can be applied to that which they imitate. Given their separation, can they be brought together again? Can one be made to stand for the other again? To these questions Cratylus assents. He has assented, that is, to the viability of the bringing together of the imitation and that which has been imitated. What emerges here however is an additional element. Over and above the imitation and that which is imitated there is the 'assignment', or 'application'. Socrates goes on to pose an additional question in relation to it. He continues by asking, 'can we assign the likeness of the man to the man, and that of the woman to the woman?' Once again the reply must be in the affirmative. It is none the less worth noting what is going on in this question. Socrates is indicating, once more, that there is a secondary move involving the application of one to the other; of the imitation to the imitated. It is already assumed that the relation is mimetic. Moreover it is also already assumed that the 'likeness' is an imitation. What is at stake here is the 'assigning'. In addition, as is indicated by Socrates' next question, it is possible to assign incorrectly. It would be incorrect, for example, to attribute the likeness of the man to the woman. This allows for the formulation of what occurs within correct assigning. It is the one that attributes 'to each what belongs to it as it is like (τὸ ὅμοιον) it'. After having made this point Socrates sums up his overall position.

> I call that kind of assignment in the case of both imitations –
> paintings and names – correct, and in the case of names not only
> correct but true; and the other kind, which gives and applies the
> unlike I call incorrect and in the case of names false.   (430d)

Analysing this passage in light of what has already been discussed will take us to the central issue: the possibility of a positing of, and within, mimesis.

The first thing to note is that, once again, both paintings and names are imitations. Correctness and truth inhere in the assignment. Paintings can only ever be correct, while names may be both correct and true. Incorrectness and falsehood on the other hand only pertain to the assignment of unlike imitations. One question to emerge from this is what is involved in likeness and unlikeness? It arises because, as is clear from this presentation, mimesis itself is not the object of criticism. (Indeed, how could it be when it defines the nature of the relationship between name and named, object and copy?) It is rather that within the general area of mimesis there is the possibility of truth as well as falsity. Correctness and truth occur not by nature – there is neither a natural nor a simply arbitrary relation between name and named – they are both brought about by assignment, by the one who assigns.

Truth therefore is descriptive of the correct mimetic relation in regard to names. What comes to be named within the correct relation is the οὐσια or essential being of the named: its 'reality'. Truth (ἀλήθεια) refers to a relation: an assignment within the domain of naming. It does not, here at least, refer to presence or the process of presencing *tout court*. Rather truth pertains to οὐσια and its presence within the naming relation in which it is the named. The specificity of truth is clear. The truth of naming makes it possible to turn to paintings in the *Cratylus*.

Paintings are imitations. Within them 'like' (τὸ ὅμοιον) can be attributed to 'like'. The skill of the painter would be defined thereby. What the painting cannot present is the essential being (οὐσια, τὸ ὄν) of that which is presented. What paintings are constrained to present therefore, is, using the formulation of the *Republic*, 'the appearance as it appears'. Within Platonism knowledge of appearance does not entail knowledge of essential being (οὐσια, τὸ ὄν). The painting thereby emerges as the imitation of an image. It is the mimetic representation of an image or presentation (φάντασμα). Naming and painting do not differ merely in that the first admits of truth while the second does not. Nor is it simply that they are similar because they are both mimetic. The twofold nature of mimesis, within at least these dialogues, is defined by the nature of truth.

Now truth (ἀλήθεια) is, as was mentioned, relational. Furthermore truth involved essential being. It necessitated, in other words, a homological relation between those elements of which it is comprised. It is the complex relationship between mimesis, truth as relational within mimesis, homology and essential being (reality, τὸ ὄν, οὐσια) that must now be taken up. It is only by undertaking this task that the interdependence of all of these elements will emerge (as well as providing a path towards the mirror). In addition it will serve to indicate the possibility of maintaining mimesis (retaining representation) – its taking place within the frame – but no longer allowing it to provide the criterion in terms of which the frame exists as an object of interpretation. Their retention within the domain of interpretation, while at the same time being outside and hence precluded from the possibility of interpretive dominance, is precisely that which is at stake in the becoming-object of the object of interpretation.

Within the presentation of mimesis in the *Cratylus* and the *Republic*, the defining characteristic of artistic representation is that it cannot present the truth. None the less within artistic mimesis there is a sense of propriety: of the proper. At an earlier stage in the *Republic* (in particular Book III) Plato admits of the possibility of telling stories that present the true nature of kingship, bravery, etc., and those stories which deny it. Essential to this argument is the commitment to there being an essential nature proper to these states. Therefore a story or narrative that presented the proper would, by definition, construct a homological relation between the unity of the referent (unity in terms of its nature and propriety) and the story being told. It does not follow from this that the story has to be the same in each instance. Sameness does not pertain to the presentation as such but to its basic meaning.

The presentation of the proper has to be discerned. Hence within the language of Platonism the proper was the ὑπόνοια or inner meaning which came to be discerned as allegory. The ambiguity of the term ὑπόνοια and the particular sense of propriety that it engenders can be traced in a number of different ways. One would chart a path from the *Republic* 379d, to Plutarch's *Quomodo Adolescens Poetas Audire Debeat*, 19e, via Xenophon's *Banquet* 3.6, a path that would establish the link between mimesis and pedagogy. What emerges despite the complexity is the recognition that beneath a particular story there was its essential and singular inner meaning. In straightforward Platonic terms it is possible to argue that it was exactly this meaning that escaped the rhapsodes in their knowledge of poetry. (If the Platonic dimension were to be followed in great detail it would be essential to take into consideration the distinction, drawn in the *Phaedrus*, between the 'good' and the 'bad' rhetoric. In addition it would be essential to examine the interrelationship between memory, knowledge and meaning presented in the *Ion*).

In general, however, it is still possible to argue that allegory arises from within a mimetic presentation which, while not bounded by truth, maintains the same structural and ontological relation as the one provided by the interconnection of truth and mimesis. This is clear if the distinctions between reality and appearance, truth and image (φάντασμα) which are generated in the *Republic* are examined. The proper story is one that aims to present that which is proper to the subject in question. Like must be attributed to like. Even though the risk within a story is that propriety may not be recognized, it can, none the less, still be present. Hence literature, the poetic, the visual arts – understood as mimetic from within the purview of mimesis – become inherently unstable entities since the recognition of truth is no longer assured. It is mediate rather than immediate. It is the shift from the immediate to the mediate that introduces intentionality and via it morality in the realm of the aesthetic, since the guarantee of truth while internal to the mimetic relation will depend upon the intention of the creator as well as the intention of the narrator. Hence the importance of the one who 'assigns'. The centrality of intention is implicitly inscribed therefore within the mimetic tradition and thereby repeated within the opposition between the inside and the outside.

The recognition involved in the case of mimesis is of the proper, either of the truth or of propriety. (The correct assignment is, in the *Cratylus* 430d, described as both 'correct and true' (τῷ ὀρθὴν καὶ ἀληθῆ.) It is therefore either the recognition that the name has, in fact, named essential being, or that the particular story has presented the proper such that it may be seen as it is. In the first case the recognition is immediate. It is seen as knowledge from the position of knowledge. In the second case the recognition is mediated via the need for interpretation. It should not be forgotten that while these examples differ they both involve the opposition between the literal and the figural. In the case of interpretation what is assumed is that the homological relationship between content and presentation is not self-evident but is construed within the process of interpretation.[13] The meaning – the content – has the same ontological status as the literal in so far as it is self-identical and unified. The lack of stability refers therefore to the failure of interpretation to construct the homology; or more dangerously to misconduct it. In this latter case interpretation is misidentification. Before taking up Plato's conception of truth, at least as it appears in the passages under consideration, it is worth noting that built into this conception of interpretation are three elements all of which must be ontologically the same in order for interpretation itself to be both proper and viable.

In the first place there must be a homological relation between the presentation and that which is presented (the homology is not sameness as absolute identity but the sameness generated and sustained by propriety). In the second place the interpretation must both uncover this relation and at the same time neither alter nor restrict it within the act of interpretation. The ontological homology demanded by the first can only be discovered (as the interpretive act) if the relationship between interpretation, the object of interpretation and that which the interpretation yields are all homological. Here of course the homological can be understood as a syntactic ontology that will bear and allow for a difference of expression. In other words the repetition of a given ὑπόνοια does not necessitate that the same story always be told. (Sameness is not identity, or at the very least is not automatically reducible to identity.) It does however demand that the Same be told in each story.

The recognition of the truth, as opposed to propriety, is immediate. The mediating presence of interpretation is unnecessary. Even though the name was mimetic and that truth involved a mimetic relation, its recognition was always temporally commensurate within its being cognized. Recognition and cognition were one and the same. This coextensivity demanded that the unity of the named be presented, and absolutely presented, by the unity of the name. The specific ontologico-temporal concatenation at work here is complex. There is absolute immediacy in so far as the unity of re-cognition is concerned. However within Platonism the relationship between name and named independently of the recognition cannot be described in this way. It involves the relationship between the transcendental and the instant. (However within Platonism the recognition of that relation is, from the position of ἐπιστήμη, immediate.) For these concerns this latter point is not central. The important issue is that re-cognition differs from interpretation in so far as the first is immediate while the second is mediate.

Now even though the separateness of truth and propriety soon became blurred in the interconnected history of mimesis and allegory, the heritage handed on by these terms demands that within a given presentation there remains the possibility of establishing the unity and singular nature of that which is not presented as such but which none the less is the presentation's 'inner meaning'. This is allegorical interpretation. It also forms the basis of the conventional practice and understanding of translation. An integral part of the conditions of existence of both these activities when construed within mimetic terms is their articulation of – while also being articulated within – the oppositions between, on the one hand, the inside and the outside and on the other the literal and the figural. In addition, this particular conception of allegory and mimesis gives rise to a specific conception of complexity and plurality. It is one where, as has been suggested above, plurality becomes the differing ways of presenting the same inner meaning (ὑπόνοια). Plurality therefore will always be effaced by the homology both uncovered and demanded by interpretation.

Complexity can be explained in a similar way. The complex would involve complexity within an allegorical structure. While it is true to suggest that allegory means that what is present points to the existence of something other than itself and that therefore there is never pure presence, this on its own is insufficient as an account of allegory. What needs to be identified with greater clarity is the postulated non-present. In other words simply delineating between presence and non-presence is not on its own a sufficient account of allegory because there are many ways in which such a relationship can be structured. Allegory is neither simple nor unified. In the case of Platonism, indeed within the dominant tradition, the non-present involves ontological and semantic unity. Interpretation as the move from presence to non-presence assumes and gives rise to the homology inherent within these unities. Once again they are all interarticulated. Complexity therefore refers to the difficulty of moving from the present to the non-present. It does not however engender a move away from homology. The existence of complexity will mean that the possibility of interpretation – here interpretation rather than being generalized is understood as the enactment of the homological relation, the discovery and enactment of semantic unity, etc., – will have become increasingly both more remote and complex.

The most important conclusion to emerge from this cursory consideration of complexity is that it is now no longer possible to posit complexity (and this point will also be true for other similar terms such as 'difficulty' and 'plurality') as though it were an end in itself. Complexity does not have a singular determination, but is itself open to a number of possible, and therefore potentially conflictual, determinations. Complexity can be located within the Platonic tradition; it can however be located beyond that tradition. What would be repeated within that beyond was the structure of presence and non-presence. However its repetition would not involve a repetition of the specific determination tradition gives to that structure. It is precisely in this way that it is possible to have a repetition within which what is repeated comes to be repeated for the first time. It also allows for an understanding of how that which is dominant can come to be located within the new – the beyond – without it dominating, in terms of concepts and categories, the specificity of the beyond. The tradition of mimesis is one that demands homology both within the object as well as within interpretation. It should of course be remembered that homology involves a claim made from within the mimetic tradition about objects of interpretation. Consequently the importance of starting with the mimetic within Platonism is that it allows for greater consideration to be given to what would have to be at play in any reconsideration of the figure, where that reconsideration – rethinking, rearticulation – took place within the frame provided by the affirmation of anoriginal heterogeneity. (The repetition of the 're' will itself demand to be rethought, since it is reinscribed within a more general reworking of repetition.)

The pause – pausing within and as an opening – will allow for a reintroduction of the problems that would come to the fore if what were at work here was no more than a gestural and hence un-questioned repetition of Nietzsche's task, that is the overturning of Platonism. The difficulty with the terminology of 'overturning', 'beyond', 'departure', etc., is that they all seem to suggest an absolute break. It is precisely the absoluteness of this break that is impossible. Tradition understood as the determination in advance can always be refused. The overturning therefore is linked to refusal. However, refusal conceived in and for itself is no more than mere negativity. The negativity must involve the generative. This is not to say that the negativity itself can never be generative. It is rather that refusal – and the overturning – need to give rise to an interplay of both refusal and generation. One is not the other. None the less both will be present. They will take place within the same time, where time is proper to the object in question and furthermore where the singularity of time harbours the potential for a plurality of times.

Overturning Platonism does in this instance amount to a projected resistance to viewing mimesis as that which provides the means by which the work of art (or the generalized object of interpretation) are themselves to be interpreted. This will also be the case even for those works which are, on the level of their own intentional logic, mimetic. This is of course not to assume that mimesis within Plato is stable and cannot be read as involving that which will render impossible the project established by its own intentional logic. Rather, intentional logic is taken as central here. Doing no more than showing the impossibility of the enactment of the task established by intentional logic goes no further than introducing a different form of negativity. Accepting intentional logic, even through recognizing its potential impossibility, will allow for the interplay of refusal and generation. The impossible possibility of the projection of mimesis by intentional logic needs careful consideration. The justification of the use of an expression such as 'impossible possibility' will need considerable argument. (This cannot be undertaken here.) It would be in sum that the work of art or object of interpretation is always to be understood as anoriginally heterogeneous in spite of, or even despite, the projected presence of mimesis. The projection whether or not it is attributed to the object by interpretation or given to the object within its own terms will come to be overturned. The already alluded-to interplay of refusal and generation needs can be expressed in terms of what has been called interpretive differential plurality.

The meaning of 'interpretive' is not intended to be problematic. It simply attests to the presence of the object within interpretation. The object, thereby positioned, is thus neither merely material nor ideal. Constructing it as the object of interpretation removes it from any straightforward articulation within this metaphysical opposition; the either/or of tradition. The plurality marks the inherent in-exhaustibility of the object of interpretation within the process of interpretation. It provides a further reason why the object is in a continual state of becoming and why the ontology of becoming (rather than that of either stasis or being) generates the ontological dimension, the mode of being, of anoriginal heterogeneity. Positing an interpretation within that becoming does no more than establish an interpretive context. It introduces a pragmatic dimension in so far as it yields the event or pragma given within and as a specific interpretation: as the event of interpretation. The pragma or event defines and delimits a fixed and finite meaning and yet it does not exhaust the potential for meaning. Even though the pragma is fixed within a more general impossibility of absolute fixedness it is still the case that there is a mode of being proper to it. The pragma is within becoming.

Finally the use of the term 'differential' is meant to indicate that the differences generated by plurality are not structured by the Same.

Positing difference within and as the repetition of the Same would deprive difference of value. The introduction of value means that these differences are potentially, if not actually, conflictual. It should always be remembered that an object of interpretation sustains interpretive differential plurality. Indeed it could be suggested that this state of affairs is exactly what defines an object of interpretation. It is its *conditio sine qua non*. The object is, in sum, always the site of conflict. Conflict is anoriginal. Conflict is therefore another way of naming anoriginal dis-unity. It is a name that refers to a twofold and fundamental conflict within the history of philosophy which even though it cannot be discussed in detail none the less needs to be mentioned. It should be noted that the 'name' names original dis-unity.

The first element concerns the important interrelationship between conflict and harmony within Heraclitus. It is an interrelationship that lends itself not just to a generalization but to the possibility of the redemption of a philosophy of difference. The second is related in that it concerns what can be described as the anoriginal conflict between Plato and Heraclitus. (The fact that it is a description means that it involves interpretation.) The generalization of these initial conflicts means, as a consequence, that they allow for an interpretation of the history of philosophy as itself anoriginally conflictual. The founding (remembering the paradox of *founds*) conflict is alluded to by Nietzsche in *On the Genealogy of Morals*: 'Plato against Homer, that is the whole, the genuine antagonism.'[14] Here the proper names of Homer and Heraclitus are interchanged in so far as both mark the anoriginal conflict with Platonism – a conflict the possibility of which can never be precluded even in attempts by, for example, Hegel and Heidegger to think the history of philosophy in terms of a philosophy of the absolute (the history of philosophy as either the history of Being or the history of the self-becoming of Spirit). It is thus that the history of philosophy will sanction its own reinterpretation in which the heterogeneous is taken as primary. With this move the philosophy of the absolute has become impossible. No longer can the particular be thought within the whole – within totality – now it is thought within a general field of dispersion. Interpretations, claims, will have fixity only in that they are events: pragmas. The plurality of difference as differential means that the ethical and the political have to be rethought in relation to the pragma. They are inscribed within the differential nature of difference. A further philosophical task is thereby identified.

29

In order to continue this reflection it is essential to move to the frame of paintings themselves. Once again not in terms of an undifferentiated generality but within the borders constructed by the presence within the frame of the mirror mirroring its presence as an interpretive *mise-en-abyme*. Focusing attention on the mirror and hence on reflection raises though perhaps will also allow for a way to avoid the problem of exemplarity.

Paintings by Bacon and Bellini to which attention will be paid – *The Portrait of George Dyer in a Mirror* and *Lady at her Toilet* – are not examples of a more general claim. Indeed they are not examples at all. As has already been suggested the relationship between an oeuvre, painters, specific paintings (individual frames of reference) and the concepts and categories of interpretation, all come to be rethought and hence re-expressed within that move which locates-relocates anoriginal heterogeneity as primary. It becomes the origin within, though also constructing, the paradox of origins. The paintings rather than being examples are themselves already objects of interpretation within the preceding. It will be argued that their interpretation demands, since it occasions, the reflection on reflection. It figures as a figure in advance. The advance here is not tradition but the *mise-en-abyme*. Each has a different temporality and mode of being. It is not therefore the determination in advance but rather a pause; an opening.

These paintings are therefore good examples. However they are not examples in the sense of being particulars, where such a designation stems from a given position within the absolute. They themselves instantiate precisely that of which they are examples. The 'that' will always be a paradoxical self-referentiality. The paradox marks the incomplete completeness of self-reference. The difficulty of establishing a fixed definite relationship between the mode of interpretation and the object of interpretation is compounded here in two different though related ways. The first involves the paradox within self-reference. Given the positing of anoriginal dis-unity then this will mean that the site of reference could never be unified such that it resulted in a completion within the self-referential. The reason why this is the case is that reference, even self-reference will also be a reflection – perhaps even a self-reflection – in which an interpretive or semantic mastery is no longer a possible option. (Clearly reflection and reference are not only reciprocal terms, they are also interchangeable.) The second

30

involves a change in register which is here marked by the necessary difference firstly between mode and object, and secondly between media. These two differences, even taken on their own, mark the necessary tension within interpretation given the twofold impossibility of a projected homology.[15]

PAINTINGS

The first step that must be taken concerns the identification of the mirror within the frame. The inclusion of mirror inscribes the outside within the inside. What comes to be enacted therefore by this inscription is the removal of the opposition between the inside and the outside from its position of dominance. This serves, at the very least, to check the interpretive strength harboured by the opposition. From the position of a specific intentional logic it can always be suggested that reflection within the frame – both mirroring in the tableau as well as the mirror in the frame – attempts to enact the ideal. Mimesis posits reflection, and hence the mirror, as central. And yet the description of centrality is not on its own sufficient. There are at least two ways in which it can be understood. The first concerns the desire, located within intentional logic, for the mirror to enact the ideal itself. In other words for the painting to repeat that which is handed down to painting in order that it be repeated. In this instance it would comprise the presentation within the tableau, that is within the frame, of the distinction between the inside and the outside. Intentional logic also locates the point of impossibility: the moment where (and when) the task it sets is presented as an impossible possibility. This state of affairs has already been suggested when it was argued that the mirror introduces a ruse into the frame. It disrupts the surface in its self-presentation within and as the surface. This interplay of disruption and presentation is held within the frame; that is within a general presentation. It is thus the frame can be viewed as framing, for and from the position of interpretation, a paradox.

The paradox emerges despite intentional logic. The desire for the mirror, the desire that it itself mirrors, is only possible if the mirror can be seen as both abandoning its ideality while at the same time reflecting that ideality. In either instance it functions beyond any ready rearticulation within the dominant presence of mimesis (for example, opposition between the inside and the outside), while at the

31

same time presenting that opposition as that within which it is, or desires to be, thus interpreted. Within the ideal the mirror gives, and gives onto the world. The world is given and is given back by the mirror. The ruse wrecks this ideality. The mirror is neither cracked nor does its tain emerge as that which dominates and therefore maintains the possibility of interpretation. The situation is both far simpler and yet more complex since there is within any reflection always more than what is reflected. It is the more, the simple addition, that introduces the complexity into reflection. Again, more comes to be reflected.

The other sense in which the mirror comes to be inscribed marks the presence of tradition ('reflection', inside/outside, literal/figural, etc.) while maintaining it beyond the reach of its own dominance. This opens up the space of refusal and generation. In moving to the paintings themselves it is essential to reiterate the point already made; namely that they are not particular instances of a general claim. It is rather that the general points are already interpretations, that is they are already implicit claims about the paintings, which are in turn made possible by the already located presence of the *mise-en-abyme*. Finally it should be noted that the domain in which exemplarity occurs or is posed as a problem is one where the relationship between mode of interpretation and object of interpretation is thought to be both unproblematic and able to be expressed in terms of homology. In other words the relationship between mode and object is thought to enact the ideal posited by mimesis. Interpretation thereby takes the form of a pure and unmediated presentation of content. The inside and outside would be coextensive. It is this possibility that is suggested by the mirror. And yet it is the mirror as ruse that in suggesting it undermines it.

Now, the problematic status of this 'ideal' within the work of art has already been suggested. It becomes problematic within the attempt to found the homogeneous and thus within the reciprocal attempt to express that founding moment in terms of an original exclusion of the heterogeneous. This figures quite dramatically in Bacon's painting, *Portrait of George Dyer in a Mirror*. The split head within the mirror mirrors and yet what comes to be viewed of that which is mirrored – the head outside the mirror – is not the same as the mirrored head. There is more involved here than the mere splitting of the self. This is not to deny that it emerges at this precise moment. For here the interplay between correspondence and non-

Plate 1 'Portrait of George Dyer in a Mirror', Francis Bacon, 1967–8, oil on canvas

correspondence – the reflection that both does and does not reflect – has to be dealt with from outside the interpretive ambit sanctioned and sustained by representation. Otherwise the work becomes a negativity, though not one opposed to positivity. Negativity would be understood simply as failure. The frame frames therefore what can only be described as an ineliminable heterogeneity that was – and this is the function, in this instance, of the mirror as *mise-en-abyme* – always already there.

Interpreting the mirror within this particular work necessitates allowing the process of interpretation to begin from within the affirmed acceptance of the domain of refusal and generation. Undertaking this task can commence by the attempt to answer the question: What does the mirror retain? This question admits of at least two possible types of interrelated answer. The first concerns the specificity of the mirror mirroring a mirror within the frame. The second relates to the mirror as figure. However it does so as a figure that positions itself beyond a reality given within the opposition between the literal and the figural. The first of these answers pertains to the two heads (the head mirrored) and therefore opens up the problem of the self. While the second represents and repeats, beyond the domination of the Same, the stakes of the figure.

In relation to the second of these answers what emerges as essential is the presence of the mirror. The difficulty is that if the mirror locates, but is not located within, the interpretive oppositions of tradition then how is that presence to be understood? The force of anoriginal heterogeneity resides precisely in its capacity to provide an answer to this question. If the oppositions marking tradition were at work, then the mirror within the painting, the frame of interpretation, would be understood as the presentation inside of that which lay outside the frame. The mirror functioning as a mirror within the frame would re-enact that opposition. The mirror as figure and therefore in figuring beyond that opposition, thereby refers to its presence while no longer being reducible to it. The mirror as figure marks the presence of the interplay of refusal and generation. It is therefore, and of necessity, beyond synthesis. It is anoriginally heterogeneous. The consequence of this is that the mirror can be redeployed without the restrictions imposed by tradition. The 'without', as is also the case in relation to the 'beyond', is not intended to be an absolute. Reference to tradition enables there to be a repetition within which something happens for the first time. The existence of an origin that marks the impossible possibility of self-reference expresses the reality of the mirror as an entity resisting absolute expression, and hence absolute incorporation into any one determination. It is none the less always itself where that 'itself' is anoriginally heterogeneous. Existence as plurality takes place beyond the interarticulation of essence and existence.

The specific mirror, the mirror mirroring the head, needs to be interpreted in relation to the mirror as figure. It is not the case that now the mirror has ceased to be a figure. It is simply that the figure has a specific determination. Once again it is important to begin by noticing that within the frame the mirror is not presented within reflection. It does of course also reflect. It is both same and different. It is this which allows the mirror, the figure in the mirror and the figure before the mirror, to be interpreted outside of both deception and distortion. Arguing that the mirror has distorted is a claim whose force resides in its being that other possibility inscribed within mimesis. Distortion would be a failure, decreed as such, by the non-reproduction of the proper. In this instance interpreting the complex interrelationship between mirror and mirrored as a distortion would involve an interpretive commitment to the existence of a true self that had become distorted. The painting would thereby be interpreted as the presentation of the corruption of self. This possibility is precluded by the presence of the mirror as figure as well as the particularity of the mirror. If the painting, on the level of intentional logic, intended to present either distortion or propriety, then either of these possibilities, given that one is simply the reverse side of the other, would have necessitated the presence of the mirror as the locus of true reflection. (The intriguing consequences that would flow from an interpretation of the expression 'mirror image' must be noted even though they cannot be pursued here.)

Within the painting the presentation of the head in the mirror and the head outside of the mirror is such that it is neither a true reflection nor an absolute non-reflection. The mirror resisting reflection *in toto*, thereby re-poses the question of the self and of what appears within reflection in a way that can no longer be presented within the terms provided either by metaphysical philosophy of reflection or the tradition of humanism. Identifying the importance of these two questions as in the frame, but then to think of them as preliminary to a full interpretation of the frame, would be to articulate the possibility of interpretation in terms, once again, of establishing a homological relation between mode and object. The identification of these questions is, in part, the interpretation of the painting. The asking and answering of questions is a projected completion that takes place within discursive writing. The figure figures.

Staying with the painting and thus to continue the process of interpretation one final element must be noted. It concerns the affirmed presence of anoriginal heterogeneity. The mirror attempts and enacts that which from the start – hence anoriginally – resists a totality dominated by the Same. It is thus that it must be distinguished from other objects of interpretation which, on the level of intentional logic, aspire to a repetition of and within the Same. In moving from the level of intentional logic to the object *qua* object the impossibility of the realization of this logic can always be discerned. Even if all objects of interpretation are anoriginally heterogeneous and therefore involve interpretive differential plurality, it remains the case that it is still necessary to distinguish between the objects that affirm heterogeneity and those which seek, vainly, to exclude it. It is within the terms set by this distinction that it is possible to redeem the concept of the avant-garde.

Another way of interpreting the painting, the play of mirror and figure (including the mirror as figure), would be to argue in a more general way that here the presence of the mirror works to enact precisely what cannot take place within the relationship between the inside and the outside. The work therefore becomes object. The surface is no longer a simulacrum. There are two reasons why this is the case. The first is that the mirror breaks the unity of the surface. The second is slightly more complex and hence more intriguing. Reflection within the frame rids it of any pretence. The shadowy likeness that is the simulacrum is replaced by the clarity of reflection. However this needs to be taken in conjunction with a more general absence of any deception. Deception as an interpretive category drops out of consideration. The frame frames its own work. It is not a substitute, not even for itself. The interpretation of the mirror is sanctioned by the mirror. These claims, coupled to the one advanced above, are interpretations of Francis Bacon's painting *Portrait of George Dyer in a Mirror*.

On a literal level the mirror may involve different levels of possible reflection. Indeed the mirror can be viewed as constructing different levels of reflection within the frame. In the case of Bacon this involves the use of one mirror. The young woman in Bellini's painting *Lady at her Toilet* observes herself in a hand mirror. On the wall above the bed on which she is sitting is another mirror. In it one (the observer) can see the reflection of the back of her head. One (the observer) can see what she cannot. She however has a view of herself that the observer cannot share. She sees what one cannot. No matter what is said about the painting, what can never be described (and here described should be given its full semantic rein) is what she sees. Moreover she must remain oblivious to what the observer sees. The two mirrors open up the possibility of an interpretation that has to a significant degree been located, situated, in advance: the mirrors as a twofold *mise-en-abyme*. This site of an impossible reduction – the impossibility of reduction and hence of domination – turns the frame from a mere instance of history or even a commodity into an object of interpretation, thereby reincorporating both history and the commodity (for example from *paragone* to patronage) within the object having become the object of interpretation. They are not exterior to the object determining, in their exteriority, both the possibility and the manner of interpretation.

The interplay of mirrors within this frame brings to the fore the possibility of homology. This time it is advanced in terms of mastery. Mastery will be the absolute presence of the object given to interpretation and thus as given within interpretation. Mastery and the absolute both demand and engender a particular conception of truth. It is that the object in being singular and unique can be known absolutely such that the expression of the object's truth precludes the possibility of a further assertion about the object if that assertion were to be a claim concerning either knowledge or truth. It is this interplay of truth, knowledge, mastery and the absolute to which the play of mirrors within the frame can be interpreted as alluding. The allusion does at the same time, due to the particularity of the mirrors, and the position of the woman's eyes, mark that which is eluded. The elusion does not generate illusion. If this were the case it would be simply the assertion of fiction over truth. What has been checked by the allusion is precisely the constraint of this particular metaphysical opposition. The presentation of the impossibility of mastery takes place within that reference to its possibility in which that possibility is both affirmed and denied. The complex texture of affirmation and denial and thus of the impossible possibility of mastery further reinforces the sense in which the object is the site of the anoriginal possibility for interpretive plurality, the plurality of heterogeneity within which difference is always differential.

37

The object is, in general therefore no longer a simple homogeneous object. Its plurality constructs it as always already heterogeneous. Viewed and hence understood within the purview of the becoming-object of the work of art this heterogeneity has, in the preceding, been identified within the play of mirrors. (It goes without saying that it is at play elsewhere; such are its stakes.) Be they Bacon's, Bellini's (or those of Freud or Balthus whose mirrors must be discussed further at a later date), what the mirror brings into play are precisely those considerations fundamental to the interpretation not of figurative art as opposed to abstract, but the interpretation of art as figural.

The work of art – the object of interpretation – that is, that which is divided, split, antagonistic – in other words a heterogeneous site – is a totality only in the sense that it is the belonging together of differences. The same and the different at one and the same time can never be assimilated except in terms having to deny precisely this initial heterogeneity. This is, of course, yet another way of expressing or re-expressing the problem of the relationship between discourses on art and art itself; discourse and object. Any attempt to reduce the work of art – the object of interpretation – to a place in a tradition, a history, a country is to refuse firstly the possibility of an interpretation that resists precisely these reductions. (This is not to deny, of course, the presence of tradition, history and nation. It is rather the nature of their presence within the frame of interpretation that is central.) Secondly the possibility of this reduction is predicated on denying anoriginal heterogeneity. The work of art is always already heterogeneous.

Finally it must be remembered that works of art that seek to assert and reassert heterogeneity are affirmative. To put this another way it can be suggested that works of art whose intentional logic resists automatic assimilation and which are thus enacted within the interplay of refusal and generation can be interpreted as affirmative. Here lies the possibility of rethinking the connection of aesthetics and politics. It draws a connection between the possibility within art and the interpretation of art and hence the repetition of that possibility within the political. This is not to argue either that aesthetics should be made political or that the political should be aestheticized (it is not as though the specific designation of these terms is sufficiently understood to know exactly what is at play in such a projected relationship). It is rather that what comes to be provided here is a way of understanding the possibility of a movement in which what comes to be repeated, in its refusal and in its creative potential, can be interpreted and understood as progress.

NOTES

1 The reconsideration of the figure has played a fundamental role in recent philosophical writing on art. The path opened by J.-F. Lyotard's *Discours Figure* (Editions Klincksieck, Paris, 1971) – one which has in part influenced the approach taken in this paper – is of tremendous importance. In addition attention should be paid to Deleuze's study of Francis Bacon, *Francis Bacon: Logique de la Sensation* (Editions de la Différence, Paris, 1981). Part of this reconsideration must involve 'tradition' as the term provided in and for philosophy and within which to take up the question of history. In sum tradition is understood here as the determination in advance. It is a determination involving not just great complexity but also power. The positing of tradition occupies a place within the relationship of dominance and subordination.

2 The movement from the complex to the simple and then back to the complex has pedagogical implications. It is within this light worth rereading, for example, the 'avis' to the Port-Royal *Logique ou l'art de penser*, in order to trace the interconnection between Cartesian method and education. The reference to *La Recherche de la vérité par la lumière naturelle* is to René Descartes, *Oeuvres Philosophiques*, ed F. Alquié, vol. II, Editions Garnier, Paris 1973).

3 This formulation has been adopted in order to indicate that the 'event' does not fall outside ontology. The event 'is'. The question of the mode of being proper to the event needs to be posed anew and within the recognition of the inherent plurality of modes of being.

4 M. Heidegger, *An Introduction to Metaphysics*, trans. R. Mannheim (Yale University Press, New Haven, 1959), p. 91.

5 The idea of plurality harbouring the Same is first systematically articulated in the philosophical work of German idealism. A clear example can be found in Schelling's *System of Transcendental Idealism*, trans. P. Heath (University Press of Virginia, Charlottesville, 1978). Schelling's conception of self-consciousness as historical means that philosophy is 'a history of self-consciousness, having various epochs and by means of it that one absolute synthesis is successively put together' (p. 50). The particular is included within the absolute. Another example emerges from the nature of Hegel's critique, in the *Difference* essay, of Reinhold's conception of the history of philosophy. For Hegel the fault lay in Reinhold's inability to think the particular within the universal and thus to see that past philosophical systems were all integrated (and not 'idiosyncratic') because they were all forms taken by Reason. This is a structure that is repeated throughout Hegel's writings. Indeed his critique of Schelling in the preface to the *Phenomenology of Spirit*, is situated within a philosophy of the absolute in so far as it refers to the fact that for Hegel Schelling's way of presenting the relationship between the

ART, MIMESIS AND THE AVANT-GARDE

particular and the absolute ended up effacing the individual particularity of the particular. The point was therefore that for Hegel Schelling's failure did not lie in the task he had set himself but the way in which it came to be enacted.

6 M. Heidegger, *Being and Time*, trans. J. Macquarrie and E. Robinson (Basil Blackwell, Oxford, 1972), p. 26. The claim being made in this specific instance concerns the Heidegger of *Being and Time*. It is not advanced, here, as a general claim about his overall philosophical position. Indeed it is difficult to generalize about the way the question of Being comes to be posed in Heidegger's work. It is clear that a shift takes place between *Being and Time* and the later explication/presentation of Being in terms of *Geschick*.

7 I have tried to develop what has here been called this semantic 'dimension' in *Translation and the Nature of Philosophy: A New Theory of Words* (Routledge, London, 1989).

8 It is in precisely these terms that it is possible to begin sketching a philosophical distinction between liberalism and pluralism. Liberalism cannot allow for a conception of difference that involves the conflict of value. This is the provenance of pluralism.

9 I have analysed this particular painting in Chapter 3. In addition, Francis Bacon's preoccupation with mirrors must be noted. This particular painting is one of a number in which mirrors figure.

10 For a more detailed discussion of the *mise-en-abyme* see R. Rand's introduction to his translation of J. Derrida's *Signsponge* (Columbia University Press, New York; 1984).

11 J.-F. Lyotard, *Discours Figure*, p. 211. For an important discussion of this aspect of Lyotard's work see G. Bennington, 'Lyotard: from discourse and figure to experimentation and event', *Paragraph*, 6 (1985), pp. 19–27.

12 All references to Plato are to the Loeb Editions. On occasion the translations have been slightly modified.

13 There is an interesting reversal that occurs here. The position advanced by Plato can be read as an exact inversion of the implicit conception of interpretation that can be extracted from the Heraclitean fragments. Within the fragments in general, and as part of the critique of knowledge based on sense-perception established in fragment I, it is argued that access to the reality of things (for example everything taking place κατα τὸν λόγον) only occurs if the need for interpretation is taken as primary. Immediacy is unique to the senses. The point can be developed by beginning with fragment XXXIII (Kahn's edition, *The Art and Thought of Heraclitus*, Cambridge University Press, Cambridge, 1979) and then by tracing the specific ontologico-temporal dimensions proper to 'stating', 'hiding' and 'signifying'. I have begun such a task in 'Time and interpretation in Heraclitus', in A. Benjamin (ed.), *Post-Structuralist Classics*, Routledge, London, 1988.

14 F. Nietzsche, *On the Genealogy of Morals*, trans. W. Kaufman, Vintage Books, New York, 1966, 111. 25, page 154.

15 The temptation that marks any attempt to write on the work of Bacon involves allowing Bacon's own words to illuminate the frame of inter-

40

pretation. The recorded interviews provided in *Interviews with Francis Bacon*, Thames and Hudson, London, 1985, form one of the most important documents in contemporary art. The difficulty emerges once there is a move away from simple history or biography, such that the interviews figure as themselves potential objects of interpretation. Indeed it is possible to go further and suggest that they bring to the fore a specific interpretive problem. It is of course the same problem that haunts the relationship between, for example, the artistic and poetic works of Michelangelo, or the notebooks and paintings of Leonardo. In each case the problem lies in plotting the relationship between writing (the discursive) and the figural. Is the painting an exemplary instance of a discursive claim? Or does the written form illuminate and resolve interpretive problems within the framed figure? It should be clear from the start that the difficulty with these questions – and they are only two of a large number of such questions – lies in their presentation of an unresolved understanding of both the figure and the text as themselves objects of interpretation. In sum therefore this entire paper can be read as itself presenting a series of considerations all of which are preliminary to any serious attempt to answer these questions. It is possible to make this problem more specific. In the interviews it is clear that Bacon is preoccupied with the question of experience. He asks, for example, 'how can this thing be made so that you catch the mystery of appearance within the mystery of the making?' (p. 105). The emphasis on the problem of appearance also emerges in one of his descriptions of his own work: 'And the way I try to bring appearance about makes one question all the time what appearance is at all. The longer you work, the more the mystery deepens of what appearance is, or how can what is called appearance be made in another medium' (p. 118). Here Bacon has himself identified the larger problem. The way in which appearance may be questioned within writing is going to be fundamentally different (if only because of the change of medium) to the way it is questioned within a painting. It is precisely this difference that constructs the nature of the relationship between the interviews and the paintings. It is one that gestures at a connection which in being established must also be effaced, if what is essential is an interpretation of the painting; the figure of the figure.

2
SPACING AND DISTANCING

Even if the two poles of absolute and relative are resisted, space and distance can still be said to take place between two points. Here however reciprocity is also at work since their separate existence as points is itself dependent upon space and distance. This is not intended to be a geometrical claim, for the points in question function as no more than markers of that separation and, thereby, of that which is separated. The relationship between these 'points' could be envisaged as one of radical separation, two points in chronological time; or interdependent separation, self and other; or even one to be overcome, the separation between mode and object of interpretation. In each instance distance and space are essential. How then are they to be understood? The question is one of a beginning; of developing an approach to space.[1]

The problem of reflecting on space – its becoming an object of either thought or reflection – is, that from its inception, such an act will have to involve a twofold spacing. The first spacing is the one that can always be said to exist between thought and its object (even though the actual mode of existence in question remains to be clarified). The second emerges because this primary spacing is reproduced; though now as the object itself. Spacing would seem to have been doubled; moreover this doubling would then have to function as a precondition for any attempt to think space. It is clear that just from these elementary considerations a number of complex issues have come to the fore. However at this point of departure they do not concern space as such; though they do *already* concern the possibility of any postulated 'space as such'. The initial difficulties that must be confronted are those inherent in the formulation of spacing. Even this expression is problematic for what is at stake here is not space as a given but the philosophical consequences of tracing the preconditions of an already presupposed space. The presupposition may only ever be present in terms of a given formulation, one which can always be denied within an explanation. The possibility of a denial of distance – its having been reworked within a totality – cannot overcome the initial recognition of doubling. However, as a beginning this is to do no more than offer a tentative approach. All that has been presented thus far is the inevitability of the inscription of spacing within the activity that seeks to take it (spacing) as an object. Now within the 'stakes' of spacing it could be conjectured that the two elements of central importance are distance and relation (though it must be added that these are not radically distinct or isolatable elements; they interconnect). Part of the value of the second – relation – is that it has the capacity to allow for the introduction of the ethical. In order to return to the initial problem of the doubling of space it will be essential to begin with distance. It will prove impossible to effect a radical separation between distance and relation.

The distance between elements is a fundamental component of the constitution of their specificity. The door and the window are held apart. The floor and the ceiling are distanced. Corners emerge out of the interplay of the meeting and distancing of walls. The wall works to divide. The staircase, while joining floors, none the less marks their distance. This takes place in a way that differs from the manner in which two floors are joined and distanced by walls. The constitution of the house necessitates distance. In addition it demands the experience of that distance. The experience of dwelling is, though in an as yet to be specified way, premised upon the experience of distance. (Distance need not, of course, be limited to the architectural. Both Buber and Heidegger have, in their own ways, tried to demonstrate that distance is a decisive element in the constitution of the being of being human.)[2]

What then is the experience of distance? Is it no more than the experience of a relation, albeit one that generates specific identities? The problem of experience cannot be posed as though it took place prior to spacing and distance. Experience is always going to involve a division between the experiencing subject and the object of experience. This distinction is not a heuristic primitive since it is still possible to ask the question of the conditions of possibility of experience itself. Now, however, as opposed to the doubling of space that takes place within the attempt to reflect upon it – that is space existing as an object of thought – what is at play here is slightly different. The difference will reside in the nature of the distinction that can be drawn between experience and interpretation. This distinction can never be absolute since both take place in relation to tradition. And yet neither is it completely defined by tradition and thus relative. There is a further dimension here, namely that any understanding of experience is going to involve the activity of interpretation. The difference is rather that interpretation as an act – as a philosophical task – will, of necessity, involve different onto-logical and temporal considerations than those at work within experience; even in an 'interpretation' of experience. The unfolding of these considerations will be traced. An initial marker can however be found in the presence within experience of the living out, or the lived actualization, of tradition. Experience is that which takes place within the bodily and cognitive encounter of the world of experience. The question then of the experience of distance will refer, though always only ever in part, to the reality of experience.

Demanding that experience be allowed the further description of 'lived' is not to link experience to an unproblematic and thereby simply posited empirical existence (the empirical understood as involving a purported unmediated givenness to consciousness). It is exactly in these terms that the empirical is thus already an 'inter-pretive' term. Hence there is no straightforward suggestion of an opposition between interpretation understood as discursive and there-fore of experience as lived (that is as non-discursive). It is rather that experience and interpretation involve different relations both to history (or in philosophical terms to tradition) and to the present.[3]

Now distance seems to bring with it a choice. It is not as simple as the alternative between closure and openness. The choice, here, is more difficult to define. It concerns the nature of the relation. Consequently it resides in the possibility of a distinction between a relation in which distance comes to be effaced and one in which, while it is maintained – one where distance endures – distance is exper-ienced in the absence, though not as the absence, of totality, and more significantly within the vanishing of teleology. (This absence must be clarified since it is not just non-presence: that would be the logic of the either/or.) In other words distance comes to be experienced as always involving the ineliminable presence of an otherness that can never be overcome in the struggle for synthesis. The real problem here will always concern the possibility of precisely this type of experience. The distance in which distance comes to be effaced is one articulated within and thus expressed – also experienced – in terms of teleology. It is in this way that experience becomes predictive experience. What emerges therefore as a fundamental component of these considerations is the predictive.

The temporality of prediction involves a split – a spacing – between a now in which the prediction is advanced and a future: one having a specific nature. In the first instance it is open awaiting the realization of the prediction. It then closes, enclosing what had been held apart, when the prediction comes to be realized. The awaiting that 'attends' prediction defines and directs both the possibility of experience and the specific object that comes to be experienced. The spacing of prediction therefore is one that involves both an opening and a closure. Space – distance – is effaced in the realization. As a consequence spacing, understood as a site of potential plurality, is denied by the progressive realization demanded by teleology. It would, of course, be far too hasty to conflate prediction and teleology. It is best to leave the specificity of prediction – the predictive – open and cite instances.

In outline it can be suggested that the philosophical strategy associated with the Hegelian element within German idealism is another instance of a predictive philosophical strategy.[4] Here the predictive involves an Absolute that encloses; enclosing while defining the nature of the differences within it in so far as the absolute – its actualization – provides the conditions of existence for any speculative identity. The movement towards the experience of the I=I of Absolute self-consciousness encloses, and will have *already* enclosed, the history of experience. The actuality of philosophy, in Hegelian terms, perhaps even the actuality of experience itself, occurs within the closure that marks the realization of the absolute as the absolute. The distance established within teleological prediction or within the attempted realization of the absolute, understood as taking place with the experience of the absolute *qua* absolute, is overcome in the synthesizing realization of the predictive. In other words predictive experience will, in the process of its coming to be realized, close the initial distance and thereby exclude any need to take up the question of the relation. (The ethical potential is thus denied.) The problematic element is the housing of non-predictive experience. The problem is compounded, for within concrete space teleology emerges in terms of function. The predictive and function are interarticulated. It is the distance between wall and window, between the experiencing subject and the object of experience, that comes to be effaced when the house is experienced in terms of function. The conditions of possibility for this type of experience are to be found in the tradition in which unity and totality are taken as prior and as having totality. Distance is overcome in a synthesis. The held-apart, the distanced, are henceforth rearticulated within a totality. The counter move is not to take the elements of distance in their radical individuality (once again this would repeat the nihilistic gesture of attempting to counter totality with the assertion of unmediated singularity or individuality), but rather to dwell on the possibility of thinking unity or totality beyond the determination of synthesis and therefore beyond a projected or posited essence and thus in terms of the possibility of unity/totality being the belonging together of the different; a fundamental and constitutive part of which will be distance. Distance will thereby emerge as an anoriginal presence. The anoriginal is the mark of an original dis-unity. Instead of taking distance and spacing as an opening up of that which had hitherto been a unity, they will be taken a primary; as anoriginal. The issues at play here rather than being stated in advance will come to be worked out.

It is only once the move of reworking identity and difference is made in terms of the anoriginal that the ethical/political problem of relation can be investigated. The reason for this being the case is that the relation, as a relation between the different, can itself only emerge with the distancing of the possibility of synthesis and the effacement of distance. It is a process whose work is to rearticulate and repeat its own presence thereby yielding the anoriginal presence of distance, which in turn generates the relation as a relation. Relation will provide a way of approaching the belonging together of the divergent. Recognizing the possibility that relation rather than being imposed after the event can be argued for as always anoriginally present. It is always possible that a relation between the different can come to be reworked in terms of sameness. In fact a great deal of ethical and political argument will depend upon this being the case; for example positions involving a *post hoc* solidarity. The important point is however that the move to sameness takes place in relation to anoriginal difference. Sameness will occur out of difference. Sameness, unity and totality will involve a pragmatic dimension; moves in a game. Therefore difference and identity, their specificity and the 'difference' between them will have to be rethought beyond the confines of tradition. Rethinking and tradition will themselves be

47

distanced from each other. Finally the mark of the anoriginal will always figure within the secondary sameness checking any claims of absolute synthesis or totality. Thinking difference will depend upon the anoriginal.

Having come this far it is now the question of how to understand the distinction between the predictive and the non-predictive that is of fundamental importance. Not just because of possible answers but because of the very formulation of the question. The distinction between the predictive and the non-predictive is not, despite surface appearances, (and in spite of the implicit irony) either a simple binary opposition, or a distinction articulated in terms set by the logic of the either/or. If it were – if, that is, the distinction involved a straight-forward oscillation between the positive and the negative – then the distance opened by the distinction would itself have vanished. The already suggested distinction between experience and interpretation is central here. In order, therefore, to analyse further the nature of the relation between the predictive and the non-predictive it will be essential to investigate some of the ways in which experience and interpretation can be differentiated. What is at stake is their distance.

It has already been suggested that the distinction between interpre-tation and experience lies in their differing relations to tradition and the present. Tradition is not a univocal term since there are differing and marginal traditions, and yet tradition intends to be univocal. There is, none the less, a dominant tradition. It is precisely in terms of this dominance (taking the interplay of margins and intentionality into consideration) that tradition can be understood as a determi-nation in advance. The foreclosing of the future within such an understanding of tradition is necessary if there is to be an adequate conception of change and experimentation since they will come to be defined by tradition, and yet in the process will come to redefine tradition itself. The determination in advance is the articulation of a repetition governed and dominated by the Same. Understanding tradition in this way gives rise to a conception of change/experi-mentation in which what comes to be presented – what takes place as a founding moment – is an original repetition. The Same does not mean absolute identity. What it refers to here is a repetition of conditions of existence, and thus of the possibility of thought.

The distinction between a repetition of and within the Same, and an original repetition, brings into consideration the problem of history and in particular the history of thinking, that is the history of philosophy. As has been indicated, what is intended by the Same here is not the repetition of the same, identical mode of thought, but rather the Same as itself a unifying process that determines what can be thought. It does not follow that this determination is necessarily successful. It is a determination on the level of intentional logic;[5] that is one that takes place in relation to the dominant tradition's self-conception. (It is this 'self-conception' that provides access to what has already been designated as the present, since the present can be understood as the moment implicated in the formulation of the philosophical task. The 'moment' – not the present moment but rather the 'moment' of the present, the epochal present – will be inscribed within the task and, in so far as it is applicable, generate the concepts of past and future proper to that task.) The original repetition, while situated within the same chronological time as the present of tradition, displaces itself. It pluralizes the time that is the present, establishes a distance – a space – such that the displacement of, for example, the original repetition, cannot be reduced to the present of tradition, while, none the less occupying a place within the same chronological present. It is thus that there will be an inevitable connection between chronology and the present of tradition. The connection will not admit of any type of reduction. It will, however, allow the original repetition to be dated. Spacing will be constitutive and thus involve anoriginal presence. It is the anoriginal nature of spacing that will relocate the ethical.[6] Its locus will become an already existent relation. The mode of being proper to this 'existence' is problematic. It is not actual existence. It will involve a presence which while present is not actualized as such. This is primordial presence. (Delimiting the specificity and the ontology of primordial presence remains to be done.)

The relationship between interpretation and tradition needs to be re-expressed in terms of the relationship between a dominant mode of interpretation and the philosophical task of interpretation. Setting up the distinction in this way allows for the inclusion and consideration of the presence of repetition and the effacing of distance. The particular self-conception of the philosophical task of interpretation that seeks conformity with the modes of thinking handed down as tradition will attempt to overcome the distinction between mode and object of interpretation. Within these terms the task of interpretation will have been completed to the extent that a homology between mode and object has been established. Homology will mark the attempt to exclude distance. Difference can always be thought within homology; however, it is a difference that is sustained by the Same. Difference will always take place 'after'. It will have to announce the twofold priority of unity and identity. Here, on the other hand, identity will always precede difference. Difference and spacing are therefore continually at work within thinking. The thinking of tradition can be viewed as parasitic upon anoriginal presence despite the fact that it works to exclude it. The thinking of tradition, therefore, as well as the possibility of identity, will be premised upon an anoriginal spacing that comes to be excluded and effaced within the attempt to realize the tasks that tradition sets for itself and which are thus fundamental to its own identity or self-conception.

While interpretation generates complex problems, the most complex, in this instance, concerns experience. Consequently what must now be investigated is how the present and tradition figure within experience. There will always be an analogical relationship between interpretation and experience. What is at play here however is not the analogue – that is, not the similarity – but the way in which they differ. As an approach to experience it is essential to draw an important distinction between two types of experience. The first concerns those experiences that can be made objects of reflection. The second are the experiences that fail to be noticed; that is to figure within consciousness – in other words, experiences of which there can be no actual memory. (Memory is not simply a negative characteristic since it is obvious that memory will play a fundamental role in the first type of experience.) While there are importantly different reasons why there may be no memory of a given experience – the differences will range from indifference to repression – emphasis here will be given to the first type. It is, perhaps, already clear that the move from experience to reflection could be thought to be another expression – though perhaps a reworked one – of the distinction, and therefore of the relation, between experience and interpretation.[7]

It is essential to recognize that there must be a unity in experience. This would occur in a similar way to there being a unity in perception. The 'all' that is experienced must be experienced in its totality. While this is the case, to remain at this level is to fall into the trap of offering no more than a phenomenological description. What must be investigated are the conditions of possibility for the unity of experience. One argument would be that time provides the answer. The experience or perception of the 'all' takes place at the same time: an argument that is for example pursued by Husserl.[8] Its unity therefore is temporal. The temporality of the experiencing subject would be identical with the object of experience. This would, in addition, define the relations between the elements of the percept, or object of experience, in temporal terms. The relations between X, Y and Z, assuming that X, Y and Z form the given object of experience or perception, would exist because they were in that particular set of spatial relations at the same point in *time*. To the extent that this particular argument is followed, perception and experience will not just involve a temporal simultaneity; their existence will be defined by it. This is, of course, far from sufficient, for the question of how this unity emerges as a unity cannot be answered by recourse to time on its own, for time (in the sense that time has been used in the above) will never address the question of the 'what' of experience or perception. The 'what' of the object is not commensurate with the existence of the object *qua* temporal entity. The 'what' is precisely what the object is.

The nature of the 'what' cannot be separated from the more general problem of the conditions of existence. The reason why this is the case is that objects of experience are always experienced in terms of this 'what'. Either the 'what' is unproblematic or it remains as a 'what' that is as yet to be determined. This state of the as-yet-to-be-determined can, in the main, be resolved by attention to detail, sharper focus, greater clarity, etc. None the less there will be a stage when the as-yet-to-be-determined will have a qualitatively different nature. It is this stage that will be of specific interest since it delimits what can be called avant-garde or limit experiences. Such experiences will call upon thinking and thus to that extent will demand philosophy.

The status of the object of experience or perception is not explicable in terms of its objectivity – its pure being as object. Indeed it is possible to go further and suggest that except in those cases in which the object is indistinct or out of focus (or other similar states of affairs) what comes to be experienced or perceived is never pure objectivity. The 'what' of the object intrudes into the experience or perception to the extent that meaning occurs. The absence of meaning – the incomprehensibility of the perception or the experience – can only be explained by the object having retained its objectivity and not having attained its 'whatness'. The consequence of this is that the existence of the object as no more than object entails that its specificity has yet to be determined; it fails to signify beyond objectivity and hence it is yet to mean. The further problem that emerges here concerns shared experiences or perceptions. It is on one level clear that the 'same' object of experience or percept has been experienced or perceived but this will only be strictly true in terms of the objectivity of the object. When what is at issue is the exact nature of the experience or perception then that which comes to be addressed is its meaning: its 'whatness'. It is at this point that disagreement and conflict occurs. The possibility of such an 'occurrence' is grounded in the fact that it does not follow that the experience or perception of the 'same' object will entail an agreement in regards to its 'whatness'. It is here that a link between experience and meaning can be established. Experience does not occur in terms, as it were, of its own pure objectivity. Experience will exist in relation both to the object and to that which makes possible the experience of the object as a meaningful object, namely tradition. Moreover it is the interconnection between experience and meaning that will allow for an explanation of conflicts and disagreements.

The link between experience and meaning takes place in relation to tradition and the present. As has been suggested, what is intended by the present is neither the instant, the *nunc stans*, nor is it the pure temporal moment within chronological time. The present is the 'time' of the self-conception of the philosophical task. It is therefore the self-conception of the age – an age that is itself described within the formulation of the task. The reciprocity here is inescapable. What it marks is the recognition that any age will always define itself in its own terms. (This self-description only reinforces the radical separation of the time of the present; that is epochal time and chronological time.) However, this description will not be one that it gives to itself but rather it is a description that is announced in the actual formulation of the philosophical task. It will occur therefore both within the conception of the task and also within the ontological and temporal preconditions at work within that task. These preconditions need not be explicit. Indeed their implicit presence often serves to check the realization of the self-sustained task. It will always be essential to add that the present will not be a unified site; there will none the less always be a dominant self-conception. The repetition of this dominance is tradition. That is the reason why tradition can be defined as the determination in advance.

The relationship between this repetition and experience involves a conception of meaning or understanding as precisely this determination in advance. It is possible to go further and suggest that the pre-existence of the categories of the understanding, being those through which any 'new' experience or perception is understood, will entail that within meaning and understanding, tradition acting in terms of rules – and hence enacting rules – will have a regulative function. Such rules will determine what can be understood and what can mean: have meaning. (This determination takes place as tradition working through and as the understanding.) The legislative function is the presence of dominance. There is an important corollary here – one that concerns the concept of the avant-garde since it involves what is generally understood as 'resistance' to tradition.

The interplay of meaning and tradition could give rise to a conception of the resistance to dominance as the assertion of non-meaning (the constraint of the primacy of meaning yielding such a response). The basis of such an argument would be the presence of the possibility of meaning residing in the determination in advance. Meanings, for which the future was always determined, and to that extent never really futural, would be countered by the promulgation, at the instant, of purported non-meaning. It is thus that comprehension here is confronted by the perpetual impossibility of comprehension. However it is precisely because of the relationship between the understanding and meaning that the contrary will be the case. The avant-garde is not simple negativity. If it were it would have the status of non-meaning. However, since non-meaning falls within the purview of the understanding it cannot mark its limit. The limit will not be an absolute but rather exist as a site of tension at which in spite of the presence of the understanding it can no longer be said to dominate. The closure of homology and tradition opens. The determination in advance no longer determines in advance. Even though they are present the understanding and tradition would have become displaced – replaced by their representation as either displacement or as displaced. This twofold possibility marks a process. The inescapable presence of the understanding – that is the historicality of the possibility of meaning and comprehension, the understanding as tradition – entails that what passes as 'resistance' will always have to be defined in relation to tradition and more importantly to the self-conception of tradition; its present. Finally, therefore, resistance on its own will no longer be an adequate description of the avant-garde project. Resistance becomes nihilism; pure negation devoid of even dialectical mediation. It therefore cannot be thought to mark the moment at which the understanding and tradition no longer either dominate or delimit the possibility of meaning, thought and experience.

This potential, the possibility of the avant-garde, will be connected – while not being reducible to – the imagination and hence to the aesthetic. One of the reasons the exclusivity of the imagination is not an option is the capacity for an experience of the as-yet-to-be-determined to generate reflection. Reflection, in this instance, will emerge at the limit of the understanding – in other words at that point at which distance is maintained; namely at the point where the percept, object of experience, etc., is such that it cannot be automatically assimilated to, and hence only be explicable within, the terms decreed by the determination in advance. Experience can be made the object of reflection, but here however the possibility for meaning, understanding, depends upon reflection. Reflection in this latter sense will always differ, in the way it operates, from the understanding, since its practice marks not only the understanding's limit as was suggested, but is at the same time the limit of tradition. One consequence of this is that it draws an important connection between understanding and tradition within experience. A further possible division within experience is established by the presence of the limit. On the one hand there is the experience of/at the limit. On the other, there is the capacity for a re-experience which would amount to a renewed holding-apart of experience and object of experience, thereby overcoming the automatic assimilation, and thus, finally, of allowing spacing. The renewed holding-apart would be a form of original repetition. The doubling of spacing would no longer be a paradox – or logical contradiction – but rather the actuality, the reality, of thinking at the limit. While this opens up themes that will have to be explored in greater detail elsewhere, it will allow for greater precision in examining the distinction between interpretation and experience.

When a non-limit experience has been made an object of reflection, then what takes place is a retracing of how the meaning or comprehensibility of that experience is established. What comes to be noted is its conformity to the understanding and thus to tradition. Within the attempt to reveal the precise determination of the 'what' of experience, the 'retracing' will both reopen and close the distance between the original experience and object of experience and their subsequent presence within reflection. The experience will be of a conformity or a homology. These characteristics are not intrinsic to the object. They delimit the relationship between the object – its 'whatness' – and that in terms of which this 'whatness' is determined, namely, the understanding and tradition. This is the nature of predictive experience. It is not as though the 'whatness' could be experienced in another way if it is to have either meaning or comprehension within the experience. Once again this is not intended to preclude the possibility that, either in terms of re-experience or reflection, the 'whatness' could come to have a different and perhaps even conflictual determination. It is simply that in so far as the interrelationship between understanding, tradition and meaning is concerned, the 'whatness' – in relation to non-limit experiences – is determined in advance. Within such experiences distance can only be said to figure in its being effaced. It is with the emergence of the question of re-experience that the homological nature of experience can be opened up. Distance and spacing become reinscribed. Plurality would seem to intrude. Experience gives way to interpretation. Re-experience is the potential at work with tradition that the understanding need not dominate. While the possibility of re-experience need not involve an original repetition, the fact that it can means that harboured within the present is a past which will not be re-presented but will be presented anew.

One of the defining elements of the non-limit experience is homology and thus the absence of plurality in relation to the 'whatness' of the object. Once the move towards re-experience and reflection are made then this unity becomes pluralized. The potential for plurality will always lie in the reworking of the 'whatness' of the object. It is, of course, exactly this reworking of the 'whatness' that cannot take place as experience. The possibility of this reworking is not to be located in the object of experience *per se* but in the possibility of thinking beyond the determinations of the understanding and tradition in relation to the object. Here the analogy with interpretation comes into play. Interpretation can always involve homology. The difference is, however, that while homology may be an aim it is not the precondition for interpretation. The precondition lies elsewhere. The problem at this stage is not with the activity of interpretation but the way in which plurality figures – in a positive and negative sense – within that act. This will be another way of distinguishing between interpretation and experience.

Interpretation will involve distance. Spacing does not become an integral part of the activity of interpretation; it is a constitutive element. The temporality of interpretation concerns both the specific act of interpretation as well as the capacity either for different interpretations or for reinterpretation. The potential is inscribed within the object and as such may figure within the interpretation itself. The interpretation that demands homology – a unity between subject and object – must fail to address or try to exclude that element that cannot be reincorporated: that is, to use Walter Benjamin's terms, the potential 'afterlife' of the object. The specificity of the 'afterlife' can never be fully determined in advance. To the extent that it is, the future becomes present; to the extent that it is not, the future potential resides in the present. It is therefore futural in the sense that it is always yet to be determined. The problematic aspect of this argument concerns the claim that this potential is inscribed within the object and that hence it may come to figure within the process of interpretation. This needs to be understood as involving the following considerations.

The desire for homology can be viewed as a desire for that unity or totality within which the truth of the object comes to be established via the act of interpretation. Truth, in this sense, marks the closure of distance. It is here that an otherness prior to both unity and totality – an otherness that founds the initial desire – comes into play. The primacy of becoming over stasis will form an integral part of the mode of being proper to this otherness. The recognition of the anoriginal will entail that the distance between mode and object of interpretation can never be fully overcome. Truth is no longer an option. The result will be that the force or viability of an interpretation will have to be judged in a different way. Judgement thereby returns as a philosophical problem. A fundamental part of this will be the consequences of holding a given interpretation: consequences stemming from its presuppositions and implications.

The next consideration will flow from the recognition that the tension accompanying a conception of the object as anoriginally heterogeneous means that attention will need to be paid to style. Style and project will be both distanced and related. There will therefore be neither an absolute difference nor complete commensurability. Homology as the dictat of tradition will founder on the primordial presence of spacing. Attention to spacing opens up the critical dimension within the object: one, it must be added, that the object's intentional logic may always seek to deny.

The final consideration is that the plurality inherent within interpretation can only emerge within the practice of interpretation. This emergence, once again, needs to be understood in both a positive and negative sense. The lack of a direct comparison with experience resides in the temporality proper to each. Experience will always involve a cognitive assimilation of the object. If this does not occur then experience gives way to reflection. There will none the less be those limit experiences in which what comes to be experienced is the presence of an ineliminable distance between subject and object. This presence can only even be grasped after the event. It is in this way that temporal deferral becomes an essential element of limit experiences. Having reached this stage it is now possible to return, albeit briefly, to the problem of relation.

Between any two 'points' not only will there be distance, there will also be a relation. Distance and relation are to that extent inter-articulated. One does not precede the other. The mode of being proper to this relation is complex. A relation will always involve distancing and spacing. It is however only if the held-apart is taken as held-apart that relation emerges as central. If the constitutive elements are given priority then individuality would be thought to take place prior to relation. This precedence is based, not on the original elements of relation, but on effacing the initial relation that constitutes the elements in their individuality. The initial constitutive relation is therefore primordially present since its being present does not of necessity depend upon its having been actualized. The primordially present relation works to reinforce the description of a relation that involves anoriginal heterogeneity. The relation both holds apart and brings the held-apart together. The significant element is that this process does not work to assimilate the constitutive distance between same and other. The absence of assimilation is the absence of homogeneity. The relation sustains a difference outside of synthesis. It is only once relation is held as a primordial presence marking anoriginal heterogeneity that the question of how the relation is to be understood, such that the belonging together of the different is able both to take place and be maintained, can come to be posed. The question of the relation pertains equally to the ethical as well as aesthetic realm. In this instance it is the aesthetic that is of primary interest.

Relation is important within aesthetics because its centrality will yield an approach to the object that does not take the relation between subject and object as a totality but as the interplay of identity and difference; of same and other. This generates a different object. The question of how relation is to be understood is, for example, a fundamental question within architectural thinking once the domination of functionalism and determinism no longer takes place. The centrality of relation will mean that the task of interpretation will no longer be conceived in terms of the need to establish a homological relation between subject and object. One consequence of this is that what is thereby allowed to come to the fore are those elements within the object that would not sanction either totality within the object – the object would no longer be approached as though it were a synthetic unity, or a totality based on the overcoming or effacing of relation, the held-apart, existing between subject and object. Anoriginal heterogeneity therefore will play a central role within interpretation. Interpretation will henceforth work otherwise.

The distance between philosophy and architecture and their relation, the spacing within the building with its own plural in-built relations, are themselves to be approached, from within philosophy, in terms of the held-apart: the primordially present held-apart. It is only in this way that distinction *qua* distinction can come to figure within interpretation, re-experience and reflection.

NOTES

1 The impetus for writing this chapter came in part from trying to think through some of the ways in which philosophy and architecture may be thought to connect, and how experience and the understanding would figure within it. And in part in response to rereading John Sallis's important and fascinating book *Spacings – of Reason and Imagination* (University of Chicago Press, Chicago, 1987).

2 The way this occurs in Buber and Heidegger is complex and will be treated in greater detail at a later stage. In sum it concerns Buber's paper 'Distance and relation' in *The Knowledge of Man* (Humanities Press International, Atlantic Highlands, NJ, 1988); and elements of Heidegger's commentary on Sophocles' *Antigone* in *An Introduction to Metaphysics* (Yale University Press, New Haven, 1985).

3 This term is, in part, clarified in the remainder of the essay. In sum both the present and tradition provide a way of thinking philosophically about history.

4 These far too cursory lines presuppose a certain reading of Hegel. They privilege the *Phenomenology of Spirit* and, it can be argued, concern Hegel's project in the form that it comes to be announced in that work.

5 As was indicated earlier, by intentional logic what is meant is the self-identification of that particular task or project that a given object of interpretation sets out to enact. See p. 14.

6 I have tried to develop some of the considerations involved in this 'relocation' in 'The place of the ethical', *Irish Philosophical Journal*, no. 5, 1988.

7 These comments on the relationship between memory and experience are skeletal and stand in need of a great deal of expansion and elaboration. Part of such an undertaking would involve taking up the distinction drawn, though in different ways, by Buber and Walter Benjamin between *'Erfahrung'* and *'Erlebnis'*.

8 In have in mind here Husserl's analysis of experience in the first part of *Experience and Judgement.*

3
BETRAYING FACES: LUCIAN FREUD'S SELF-PORTRAITS

PREAMBLE, REPRESENTATION

The self-portrait cannot help but raise the question of its own status. Clearly it falls within the purview of representation in so far as it re-presents. And yet does representation delimit its specificity and describe what is unique to it? Part of the difficulty in dealing with the self-portrait or indeed with 'representation' in general stems from the growing recognition of the inability of representation to provide an adequate interpretive mode in which to analyse paintings (if not all purported 'representations').

Representation involves presence. It gives presence to what had hitherto not been presented. It is of course this formulation that marks the problem representation poses for itself. Any representation must lack authenticity in its striving to be authentic. A painting of a bowl of oranges can never be the same as a bowl of oranges. Consequently a representation must try and capture an essential quality. The representation must recognize the impossibility of camera-work and try therefore to present the reality of the object. If the reality cannot be captured by the camera then it is neither simply the empirical nor the material but also the essential (an essential quality which, as shall be seen, has materiality).[1] Linked to the essential is the question of authenticity. The strength of a painting, its force, when determined within the ambit of representation, is to be judged in relation to the essential, not just in relation to the object itself. Representation in this sense brings with it two referents. The first is the object *qua* object, and the second is the essential quality of the object. If interpretation remains within the field of representation then the interplay between object and essence must, in the strictest sense possible, comprise the locus and practice of interpretation. The frame becomes therefore the site of that interplay.

How then does this interplay work within the frame presenting a self-portrait? Here the representation is of a unique self both as object and as essence. The self-portrait within representation is constrained to present the 'I' as it is. (This constraint operates equally within interpretation as well as providing the *intentional logic* of a particular self-portrait.) Appearance must give way to reality and yet of course the reality must appear. Prior to taking up the self-portrait – of portraying that which is unique to it – a detour needs to be made. What is at stake within both representations and interpretations enacted within representation is a specific semantic economy. Coming to terms with that economy is to come to terms with the possibility of its having been displaced. Its replacement figures as much in works of art as it does in interpretation.

The semantic economy at the heart of representation can in general terms be understood as involving a straightforward relationship between signifier and signified. The signifier can be viewed as representing the signified. Their unity is then the sign. The possibility of unity is based on the assumed essential homogeneity of the signified. The sign in its unity must represent the singularity of the signified. It is thus that authenticity is interpolated into the relationship between the elements of the sign. Even though the signifier and the signified can never be the same, there is, none the less, a boundary which when transgressed would render the relation-ship inauthentic. The relationship between signifier and signified would have become improper. It is precisely this conception of the sign that emerges within the aspirations of seventeenth-century philosophical thought and which comes to define, either in retrospect or actually, elements of both Classicism and Modernism.[2] Its break-down, which can be traced in a number of different domains and which has a plurality of forms, provides the conditions of possibility for the move away from the semantics of Modernism. This movement is, in sum, that which follows in the wake of the growing impossibility of any straightforward relationship between signifier and signified; resulting within the present in the necessary irrecoverability of a unified and self-identical signified.[3]

The crisis of modernity therefore is the recognition of the irreconcilable split within the sign (a split, which, retrospectively it is possible to argue has always already been there). This irreconcilability has occasioned precisely that melancholia that marks the art, literature, philosophy, interpretation, etc., that remain trapped within the confines of modernity. The impossible possibility of the sign need not however give rise to interpretations and works of art that are organized around a past that has been lost, a present where the loss comes to be experienced, and a future in which loss may be overcome by its having been redeemed. Ironically it is possible to redeem the crisis itself while at the same time allowing loss to reappear. However it would no longer appear as that which determines the present but rather as something to be determined within the present. Modernism has not failed; it has, on the contrary, reached its limit. The presence of this limit is attested to by arguments for and against its having been reached. The nature of this limit and what it delimits must be briefly noted since at stake here are major claims both about the actuality of works of art as well as the practice of interpretation.

Fundamental to modernism is the presupposed unity or homogeneity of the object of interpretation. Such a conception of the object works within the assumption that the object is on an ontological level compatible with the self-image of the mode of interpretation or philosophical inquiry. Indeed this is the demand of the dominant tradition within the history of philosophy. Unity was given to the object of interpretation (here the work of art) by the unity (though only unity as self-image) deployed within both interpretation and philosophical inquiry. Excluded from both therefore was the very possibility of overdetermination or heterogeneity.[4] The work of art could only frame the singularity of intent. There is however, an affirmative dimension of the crisis of modernism. In a sense it results from the nature of the crisis itself (even though it does, at the same time call into question the term 'crisis). To use a different formulation, the crisis of modernism can be described as resulting from the impossibility of sustaining the homogeneous and therefore of excluding heterogeneity. The affirmative is situated within this gap. However its situation does not occasion nostalgia.

The affirmative has two important aspects. The first is that it allows for an interpretation of works enacted within the desire for unity (given the rider that the desire can no longer structure the method and direction of the interpretation of such works). The second is that it sanctions a distinction which can be drawn between works attempting what, to use Derrida's formulation, can be described as a 'nihilistic repetition' of unity, homogeneity and pure presence, and works which take place within the recognition of the futility and impossibility of that attempt. These latter works are not avant-garde in the sense that they simply involve a rejection of tradition. In fact the language of acceptance and rejection is here, in this instance, inappropriate. A more accurate way of expressing the designation avant-garde concerns repetition. The refusal to repeat does not delimit the painting's concern. However the recognition of the refusal of the repetition of the same would comprise the opening move in any interpretation. These cursory comments and tentatively drawn distinctions can serve to provide a space in which to locate a number of Lucian Freud's self-portraits. These paintings can be divided such that they enact the division that marks the consequences of the crisis of modernism.

Perhaps as a way of starting it would be best to deal with the obvious objection. What makes it obvious is that it arises from the premises that identify the crisis itself. It can be argued that if the present is structured by the impossibility of establishing a fixed and unified relationship between the signifier and the signified, then, given that a self-portrait could only ever enact the desire for presence and hence of a stable and fixed relationship between signifier and signified, it would have to follow that the self-portrait had become an impossible state of affairs. It would be the supreme example of the repetition of the desire for unity. It is of course this desire that has been shown to be of necessity unfulfillable. The reply to this objection is contained in the divide that can be established between the two groups of self-portraits, and therefore in the possibility of an affirmative self-portrait. It needs to be specified in advance that a detailed interpretation of paintings whose intentional logic indicated the desire for presence and unity would show how such a logic failed to rid the canvas of heterogeneity.

FACING PAINTINGS

The eye attracts and is attracted. The interlocking eyes – gazing out, gazing in – introduce a visual simultaneity. Whose eyes gaze out? In Freud's painting *Man's Head (Self-Portrait)*, 1963, his own open eye captures and is captured. However there is nothing in the painting – in the frame – except for the title which is outside of the frame that marks it out as a self-portrait. It is similar in style and execution to a number of portraits. In spite of its power it leaves unquestioned the practice of painting self-portraits. Its intentional logic involves a pure presentation which, while intended to represent the self who painted it, might as well be a simple portrait. The portrait as genre is here repeated as and within a self-portrait.

While this repetition becomes increasingly less stable it is none the less possible to include *Reflection (Self-Portrait)*, 1981/2, and *Reflection (Self-Portrait)*, 1983, within the parameters it constructs. The lack of stability arises not just from the always already heterogeneous nature of painting, but here, specifically, because of the type of application and use of paint – the techniques of scraping and building – works to undermine the intentional logic.

Freud's fascination with paint is clear from his own explanation of why he uses Cremnitz white as the 'basic pigment of flesh'. 'I wouldn't use Cremnitz on anything that was not alive. I use it for flesh, or even on the hairs of a dog, but never for instance, on a woman's dress. It is simply a code.'[5] It would be worth pursuing the consequences of his techniques of scraping paint. It works to create a dense, thick surface that, amongst other things, draws attention to the surface as painting. The consequence of focusing attention on the painting (as the mark of an activity) is that it calls into question the assumed temporality of representation. This occurs in two specific ways. The givenness, or pure presence, inscribed within the intentional logic of the representational self-portrait (that is the self-portrait conceived as representation) is mediated and thus checked by the paint-work. The mediation introduces the first moment of temporal alterity and engenders the second since it is to the extent that representation is mediated that the frame starts to en-frame the heterogeneous. It therefore gives rise to and sanctions a reworking – similar to the Freudian *Nachträglichkeit* – in which the original homogeneity is reworked in terms of an always already heterogeneous content. This reinvestment renders the original no longer the same as itself. It is the second way in which the temporality of representation is questioned. The absence of the need for such a reworking is another way of describing affirmation. It is in terms of three specific paintings that affirmation will be discussed. It should be added however that they would need to be complemented by *Two Irishmen in W.11*, 1984/5, and *Painter and Model*, 1986/7, since they both form an integral part of Freud's dwelling, within painting, on the activity of painting itself. In the case of his painting, *Portrait of the Two Irishmen*, the painting inscribes the activity of painting – the partly finished canvases – within the frame. Hence the painting becomes a painting

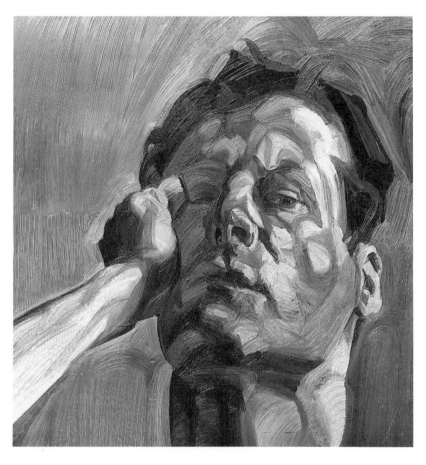

Plate 2 'Man's head (self portrait)', Lucian Freud, 1963, oil on canvas.

of portraiture, the process, rather than the simple presentation of a portrait, stasis. In the case of *Painter and Model* the paint used by the framed painter and the paint used to paint this event of painting become one and the same while remaining distinct. The distinction between subject and object is maintained and in being maintained comes to be denied. The distinction blurs.

The first of the 'self-portraits' which will be considered in slightly greater detail is from 1967–8, *Interior with Plant, Reflection Listening*. The second is a painting from 1967, *Interior with Hand Mirror*, and finally an earlier painting *Reflection with Two Children* of 1965. All of these paintings are catalogued as self-portraits. In each instance reflection either figures within the painting or forms part of its name. It is the way in which reflection is deployed within these paintings that serves to differentiate them from the other group. One of the aspects that marked the other paintings was the repetition of portraiture within and as self-portrait. It should not be thought however that the 'affirmative' group do not portray. It is rather that their portrayal takes over the portrait but refuses to let the representational conception of portrait, self-portrait, sign, etc., attempt to dominate the frame. The frame en-frames the event of questioning. These three paintings do not need to be reworked in order to trace their attempt to question what a self-portrait is. This questioning works to redefine in advance of any possible answer. The question shifts from who is being portrayed, to what is being betrayed within the portrayal.

Interior with Plant. Reflection Listening, (Self-Portrait) is of particular interest in this regard. It is tempting to focus on the dislocated body that seems to emerge incomplete from behind a plant which is thereby made preposterous. The body lacks centrality. It is there where it should not be. How is dislocation to be understood, however? Here this question is made more dramatic if it is joined to the more fundamental one, namely how is dislocation – the displaced – to be identified? The answer to this latter question is unproblematic. Identification is the consequence of sight, vision, of seeing the body there where it should not be; of viewing its lack of completion; of recognizing the impossible scale of man and plant. The eye reveals. Once the eye is focused on the 'self-portrait', on the face, then what is revealed is precisely that mode of cognition that displaces the centrality of the eye. The eye therefore is drawn to what cannot be seen. It moves ineluctably to the representation of that which is inherently unrepresentable, namely sound. The eye in focusing on

Plate 3 'Interior with plant, reflection listening (self portrait)', Lucian Freud, 1967–8, oil on canvas.

listening – on the cupped ear – confronts what it cannot confront. It is not just that the link between painting and vision, and hence between painting and representation, is thereby checked. There is far more here than a simple refusal. This painting sustains the possibility of the self-portrait but enacts it within an unending questioning of its own activity. In looking at this self-portrait, in looking at the ear, in hoping to 'hear' the painting, the question of the self-portrait itself is being asked. It is possible to take these preliminary deliberations a step further by concentrating on reflection within *Reflection with Two Children*.

Reflection involves the desire for a temporality of simultaneity. The desired look is reflected at the same time as the look takes place. The mirror is therefore thought to be the site of an absolute but momentary return. (The mirror in *Interior with Hand Mirror* plays, as will be argued further on, a fundamental role in ridding the frame of the domination of reflection.) In the painting under consideration reflection, while named by the title, seems to be impossible. The frame in containing two frames casts doubt on the viability of reflection by its affirmation of the impossibility of the temporality of simultaneity.

The entire frame – the one that bears the title – contains within it a secondary frame. It is this secondary frame that frames Freud and is thereby the self-portrait. The thick brown line does not simply break the frame in two, thus introducing two different perspectives; it also breaks the temporality of simultaneity by pluralizing time within the entire frame. What comes to be portrayed – portrayed within a self-portrait – is the plurality.

The two children, who form part of the self-portrait because they are named in its title, do not occupy the specific frame of the self-portrait. They are outside that frame. They do not, however, by themselves construct that outside. They are positioned there by the framing brown line. The line is important because it does not reduce the difference between Freud, as the subject of the self-portrait, and the children, as part of the self-portrait's subject, to an otherness defined in terms of a difference from the same. Difference therefore within this painting is not presented (represented) in terms of a simple self/other distinction. Within the frame – the entire frame – difference is differential because it involves plurality; a heterogeneous plurality that resists synthesis.[6] This particular 'reflection' in breaking with reflection opens up a rethinking, within painting, of time, of self/

Plate 4 'Reflection with two children (self portrait)', Lucian Freud, 1965, oil on canvas.

other, of plurality and of difference. It is tempting to see this 'reflection' that resists reflection as ethical. In addition it is also clear in what way the painting is affirmative in its presentation of heterogeneity. Indeed it poses a problem for a reductive interpretation that, in its desire for simultaneity and representation, would have to preclude – if not occlude – the affirmative that is en-framed; here, en-framed by a doubling within a more general frame.

Reflection as an impossible possibility also figures within *Interior with Hand Mirror*. Reflection is absent from the title. None the less it figures within the painting. The mirror is the site of reflection. It is held in place by a window frame. Here the frame is not the transparent window; the window onto and hence framing the world. The window, while being a frame, does not, in any straightforward sense, frame. It is not transparent and thus involves neither an inside nor an outside. It neither gives onto a world nor encloses (en-frames) one. Within the general frame (the one bearing the title) and between the window frames there is another frame.

The mirror can only ever frame the transitory. What it holds and returns must be present. If the mirror were to frame, it would necessitate an eternal present in which the temporality of simultaneity could unfold without end. Within the mirror, reflected by it, is Freud's face. The mirror frames the self-portrait. The irony is that his eyes are shut. The unending backward and forward movement demanded by the temporality of simultaneity ends. The shut eyes mean that the reciprocity is broken. Reflection reflects into the closed and empty eyes. The logic within which the mirror is articulated not only works to break the power of reflection, but at the same time renders impossible any attempt to use either the categories of reflection or representation as means by which to interpret *Interior with Hand Mirror*. The mirror as frame cannot be viewed in isolation. Within the general frame the mirror no longer functions as a mirror. It is this functional refusal that links it to the window.

The window both by name and function involves framing. The window should present a world; frame it, divide it and thereby allow access to it. While the mirror sustains reflection, the window should picture the world. Here, in this painting, the mirror not reflecting and the window not picturing seem to be captured by its title. The window has not become the mark of an enclosure but of a foreclosure. The opposition between the inside and the outside has been foreclosed. It is now only displayed. The window has become a pure frame. It holds

71

Plate 5 'Interior with hand mirror', Lucian Freud, 1967, oil on canvas.

the hand mirror. Between its own frames is the hand mirror as frame. The window therefore frames an interior with a hand mirror.

The overall result gives rise to a chaos of framing. The logic of each frame is called into question by what it en-frames. The overall frame cannot contain a self-portrait as representation. The window frames neither frame nor en-frame. They hold a frame that cannot hold what it frames – except if the mirror is stilled, so that in being presented as a mirror it cannot function as a mirror but rather as a frame which does hold. This excess within framing manifests a series of inter-dependent frames. The collapse of the functional and therefore of the reduction of frame to function is that which allows this particular moment of framing to take place.

At play therefore within different frames is the recognition of the possibility of the self-portrait that, in being possible, serves to undermine the possibility of a self-portrait framed by representation, that is, by presence. Once again, though, the additional point needs to be made that *Interior with Hand Mirror* is not reducible to a refusal of repetition. The refusal, as has been suggested, opens up the possibility of interpretation in so far as it frees the painting from any teleological determination. Teleology demands the exclusion of heterogeneity. Its inclusion as always already present inverts the demand and precludes the possibility of ever being able to reduce a work of art, either from the start or at the end, to a *telos*. The doubling and redoubling of a framing beyond function does in the moment of its presentation demand a response to its own portrayal. If, as was argued, the question to address is, 'What is betrayed in the portrayal?', the answer must be generated by the paradox within the *betrayal*; the word 'betrayal'. Here at the same time there is a showing and a denial; there is an honesty despite itself as well as treason. The word *betrayal* betrays plurality – semantic differential plurality – and therefore can never be reduced either to a simple oneness, or a unity, or a representation, or pure presence, or simultaneity, etc. This is of course precisely what is portrayed in betrayal and therefore what is betrayed in the portrayal.

The divide within Lucian Freud's self-portraits establishes the specificity of the proper name at the same time as taking its unifying power from it. These self-portraits, if taken as a whole, betray – show and deny – the self-portrait. This betrayal is not the ruin of evaluation. Indeed the distinction between a repetition bounded by the Same and a repetition involving difference and hence affirmation opens the way for a revaluation of value and allows for the redemption of evaluation itself. Value and evaluation can be redeemed and hence linked to aesthetic judgement to the extent that there is an interconnected redemption of the avant-garde (both in relation to the 'object' as well as to experience).

NOTES

1 The critique of the camera as providing the model for representation is exemplified in Zola's writings in art. For Zola the camera could not capture what he described as 'la vie avec son mécanisme complet'. E. Zola, *Mon Salon, Manet, Ecrits sur L'Art* (Flammarion, Paris, 1970), p. 335.
2 The irreconcilable split between the signifier and the signified marks, for example, the advent of psychoanalysis. I have tried to trace this move in 'The overflow of words; from Breuer to Freud', in *New Formations*, no. 5, 1988.
3 Foucault has offered an important analysis of the development of this particular structure of signification within what he calls the 'Classical episteme'. See *Les Mots et Les Choses* (Gallimard, Paris, 1966), pp. 60–92.
4 While it cannot be pursued it is worthwhile noting that this exclusion has both an ontological and temporal dimension. In regards to time what cannot figure within the frame is a plurality of times.
5 Quoted in R. Hughes, 'On Lucian Freud', in *Lucian Freud Paintings* (British Council, London, 1987), p. 22.
6 I have discussed this conception of pluralism in Chapter 8, 'Pluralism, the cosmopolitan and the avant garde'.

4

PRESENT REMEMBRANCE: ANSELM KIEFER'S *ICONOCLASTIC CONTROVERSY*

The question of memory, the presence of a past – its reality and possibility – cannot be posed outside of tradition. And yet far from giving the question a fixity, such a location, while accurate, only serves to compound the question's problematic nature. Tradition lacks a specific determination. Tradition can be incorporated within history – it may even be 'history' – none the less neither tradition nor history is thereby finally determined and allocated a semantic and heuristic structure. There are further difficulties since memory, tradition, history do not simply encounter the problem of time, they have a specific temporal dimension at work within them and hence proper to them. Each is unthinkable without time. (This will be true even in the weak sense that their being thought will always contain within it, either implicitly or explicitly, a temporal dimension.) Rather than attempting to give greater specificity to these complex interrelationships in advance, they will be allowed to emerge within a consideration of the interpretive problems posed by Anselm Kiefer's work *Iconoclastic Controversy*.[1]

Kiefer's title names the painting. It is a title which is thought to exhibit Kiefer's concern with history. Within his own history the title has been repeated and thus could be construed as naming a preoccupation. In addition, of course, the title also names the dilemma at the heart of titles; the arguments within and over the image. The difficulty for interpretation – perhaps also as an interpretation – that emerges even within these opening and tentative deliberations is twofold. The first is the problematic nature of the naming relation (the relationship between name and named). The second is connected to the first since it stems from that element within any representation (and therefore within mimesis), that yields the possibility of representation at the same time as calling into question the viability of

75

Plate 6 'Bilderstreit', Anselm Kiefer, 1980

representation; that is, of permanently establishing and fixing the relationship between the representation and the represented. This takes place within the terms – the conditions of possibility – which are set by representation for itself. This particular element is succinctly captured in the following question: can the painting, *Iconoclastic Controversy*, be viewed as a representation of the Iconoclast controversy? If it were to be asked 'What is the Iconoclast controversy?' ('What is named by the term "Iconoclasm"?'), then the twofold problem, already identified above, would have been merely repeated.

The factual co-ordinates of Iconoclasm are relatively straight-forward.[2] The ban on the production of religious images was imposed by Emperor Leo III in 730 AD. It was challenged and altered at the Second Council of Nicaea and finally overturned in 843. The latter part of the period coincided with a struggle for power between Empress Irene and her son Constantine. The ban concerned religious images rather than secular ones. During the period in question painting, engraving and the illustrating of manuscripts were practised, as was the construction of mosaics. Indeed abstraction flourished. While it is always possible to fill out the factual detail of Iconoclasm this would neither address nor answer the question of whether or not it was this 'detail' that was named by the painting's title and therefore which was represented within the frame. If this gap between title and history endures then the simple recitation of the factual, while providing an adumbration of elements, will, of necessity, fail to allow for a significant interpretive approach to the frame. The shadow of images endures. It is possible to go further and suggest that what seems to emerge here is a rift for which there is no obvious bridge since, no matter how much information was amassed concerning Iconoclasm, it would always fail to form the interpretation. In fact, though perhaps ironically, it is precisely this problem that already informs interpretation since it brings to the fore the question of history, of access to the past and therefore of memory. It is for these reasons that it is essential to return to the difficulties posed by naming and representation. History – understood in this instance as the 'detail' of the past – does not provide any direct access to history as a problem within interpretation and thus as a figure within the frame.[3] The emergence of naming and representation as problems does not take place in isolation. They are brought into play by the frame and by its name. It is, however, as always, more complex. In order to trace this complexity it will be necessary to approach these problems under two different headings – 'Representation titles' and 'Memory history'. These headings – titles – will contain, as an ineliminable presence within them, an oscillation between their adjectival, nominal and verbal forms.

REPRESENTATION TITLES

The question of titles is an element of the larger problem of naming.[4] What is demanded and expected of a title, however, is different from the demands and expectations made of name. None the less while the naming relation is more rigorous than the one at work within the title, it is still the case that the title does in some sense still name. The painting is entitled to a name which then comes to be its title. (The legal and moral aspect of titles and entitlement should not be overlooked.) The title designates the frame in at least two senses. Firstly it allows it to be named within any discussion; be that discussion legal, aesthetic, referential, or even the opening moves within an interpretation. In this sense the title names the frame; the tableau. It is not, as yet, intended to name what is framed. This will be the second designation. The first is exact. It exemplifies the accuracy demanded by the conventions of citation. (The viability and the possibility of the fulfilment of this demand is a separate issue.) The question that must be answered is: what takes place in the move from the title as designating the tableau – the painting *qua* material object – to its designating the painting *qua* object of interpretation? This shift in register is not a simple redescription of the 'same' entity. The painting as material object involves fixity. Its being is exhausted in and by its objectivity, its 'everydayness'. The object of interpretation will lack exhaustion as it is continually open to reinterpretation. This is why it is preferable to speak of the continual becoming-object of the object of interpretation. It is within this shift – this fundamental change in the nature of the object – that the title as designating the content of the frame needs to be approached. (In sum the painting is no longer a simple commodity – cultural or economic – but an object of interpretation. This gives rise to the further problem of specifying the relationship between commodity and object of interpretation, given that one is no longer reducible to the other.)

It is however in relation to the becoming-object that the question of representation and titles becomes more complicated. The reason for this is straightforward. What is at stake here is that if the object of interpretation is the site of interpretation as well as the site of the continual possibility of reinterpretation, then it follows that the title – any title – can always be read as designating the actuality of interpretation in addition to this inherent possibility within any actual interpretation (where the actual is defined as the present, that is the locus of the task of interpretation and from which it comes to be enacted). This split within presence, between actual and primordial presence, must be noted. Primordial presence is the mode of being proper to that which was described above as the 'inherent possibility' within the actual for subsequent and hence future interpretations. The relationship between the actual and the primordial is not that of an either/or, since the trace of one works with a determining sense within the other.

Now it is clear that the title cannot be thus interpreted within intentionality – that is in relation both to what is intended for the title and to what the title itself intends. It is rather that the interpretation of the title, the interpretation of the frame and the interpretation of the relationship between title and frame, all sanction this reworking of the title's function. The intriguing element here is that while this is a general claim about titles it is also possible to argue that the title *Iconoclastic Controversy*, the content of the frame, and the relation between them work to bring to the fore the already present inscription of these considerations within the frame of *Iconoclastic Controversy*. In sum, therefore, beginning to interpret the frame, the painting, *Iconoclastic Controversy*, involves recognizing that part of its content is this enacted rethinking of titles. This does not occur in addition to its content but as part of its content; as it. (It goes without saying that, at this stage, it is its content thus interpreted.) There are important implications of this inscription for an understanding of memory and history. Prior to taking up this task, however, it is vital to plot the way this inscription takes place.

The ostensible issue within Iconoclasm was the worship of images. There is a sense therefore in which this historical moment, even though it is coupled to the division between the eastern and western church, and the more general question of power within the Byzantine empire, is also an integral moment within the history of mimesis. (These two moments are not mutually exclusive.) The problem raised by the worship of images refers on the one hand to the Judaic and Islamic traditions in which God could not be made present, while on

the other it invokes the Platonic argument that a mimetic presentation within both the visual arts and literature, by definition, is always
going to be unable to present the 'reality', or 'essential being' (τὸ ὄν,
οὐσία) of the represented. When the argument concerning the limits
of mimesis concerned a trivial example – the 'bridle' in the *Republic*
(Book X) – then the significance of the limits lay within mimesis
itself and not with the example. In the case of God however there are
different stakes. The particularity of what figures within the example
is of central importance here.

The problem of the presentation of God has its origins as well as its
conditions of existence in Platonism. When, for example, Augustine
in *The Confessions* (Book XI, vii) poses the question of how God's
word can be represented because it takes place at one and the same
time, and therefore cannot be articulated within the temporality
proper to human speech, he is drawing on the distinction established
by Plato between the ontology and temporality proper to the 'Forms'
(Platonic 'ideas'), and the ontology and temporality proper to the
domain in which things come into existence and pass away. The
problem generated by the Platonic conception of mimesis is that it
may lead to transgressions against God. This is a risk that is both
sustained and generated by mimesis. Understood as a moment within
another history, namely the history of mimesis, Iconoclasm will
involve therefore, at the very minimum, two additional elements.

The first is that it has to be assumed that what is not present has a
fixed reality which by definition cannot be represented as itself, that is
presented in itself. And secondly that the purported representations
of God led the 'faithful' to conflate the image with the reality. Once
again this is precisely the problem Plato identified within mimesis. (It
informs, for example, the careful consideration in *Republic*, Books II
and III, of which stories should be told to children, thereby raising the
more general problem of the moral instability of fables – their
capacity to deceive as well as to inform.)[5] The important element is
not God as such but the non-present; the projected presentation of
non-presence. For once the presence of Iconoclasm comes to be
inscribed within the frame titled *Iconoclastic Controversy* it is then
possible to interpret this non-present as history. In addition the
presentation of history – the coming to presence of the non-present –
would seem to involve a painting that was enacted as memory, that is
as an act of remembrance. As with any beginning the specificity of
these terms is far from clear. What must be pursued therefore is not

simply the relationship between history and memory, but rather a reworking of memory and remembrance such that they could in the end be situated beyond presence; in other words reinscribed in order that they be maintained – be present – but not as purveyors of presence.

MEMORY HISTORY

The inscription of the problem of non-presence within the frame indicates that the question at hand concerns how the presence of that non-presence is to be understood. This problem is not reducible to establishing the possibility of a remembrance in which the non-present becomes present. (However, as shall be seen, remembrance brings with it the questions of what is remembered and for whom?) Iconoclasm was a movement that resisted this possibility though it was a resistance formulated within mimesis. The *Iconoclastic Controversy* as a title does not name a problem within mimesis. Rather the past does not emerge out of the ambit of mimesis, but on the contrary as a problem for mimesis. Therefore the criteria of interpretation cannot themselves be articulated within mimesis. There are wider implications as the painting, in addition, poses the question of the possibility of history – the coming to presence of the non-present – even of history as the narrative of continuity given the nature of that history.

The frame itself contains a number of important components that can be seen as enacting these considerations. The first is the combination of media, that is photography and paint. It is often assumed that it is the presence of mixed media within the frame to which the painting's title makes reference. Or at least that the title questions the 'reliability' of the photograph. It is extremely unlikely that these possibilities on their own could account for the relationship between title and contents; let alone the inscription of the title's dilemma (the dilemma of the title) into the frame itself. The way towards an understanding of the co-presence of both photography and painting is provided firstly by the presence of the palette outlined in black, and secondly by the words written in the bottom right corner, *Bilder-Streit* (the title entitled).

The palette figures in a number of Kiefer's paintings. There are at times slight variations. In *Icarus – March Sand*, for example, the palette has a wing. This painting also involves a combination of media and, in addition, its title is written within the field of the painting. Invariably within his work the palette exists in outline only. The palette therefore can be interpreted as being at the same time both empty and full. This is especially the case in *Iconoclastic Controversy*. It is empty of its specific content and yet is filled by what it outlines. The paradoxical palette is both a part and yet apart. The palette opens a rift within the frame that the painting does not try to heal. It is precisely the presence of the 'a part/apart' that indicates the impossibility of a retrieval or recovery of a past which is no longer present, while at the same time allowing for an engagement with that past. The present within this paradox becomes the site – the witness – to a continual remembrance. It is however one where remembering demands neither the continuity of narrative nor of tradition. (The temporal dimension that is displaced, as well as the one that emerges in its place, pose interpretive questions of considerable importance.) The rift, the holding apart, that signifies without mimesis – apart from mimesis and therefore without a fixed and determined signified (the represented) – is the possibility which, while not being contained within Iconoclasm, is none the less the risk within mimesis that mimesis itself attempts either to restrict via the introduction of truth or circumvent via what could be described here as a generalized iconoclasm. It is in this sense that the palette is connected to the words that also stage, by entitling it, the argument over images; *Bilder-Streit*.

The frame, the painting *Iconoclastic Controversy*, has therefore inscribed within it – 'within it' becomes, of course, 'as it' – a questioning, if not reworking of titles and of representation. The presence of this activity within the frame works to reinforce the rift opened by the palette since both suggest that, on one level at least, neither representation, nor mimesis are adequate to the task of providing an interpretation of the painting. Indeed this emerges, in part, as an interpretation of the painting. In other words the problems of interpretation, mimesis, etc., are not anterior to the painting but take place within the frame. They do have a specificity. The point is that history, memory, remembrance, etc., do not just happen, they form part of a tradition; a dominant tradition. Power and therefore both dominance and subordination are integral parts of tradition. Contests, even a controversy, that take place within the tradition concern dominance. It is the way in which the tradition has come to dominate, taken in conjunction with the consequences of that dominance, that it becomes essential to house tradition, but not within the house of tradition.

In *Iconoclastic Controversy* the presences of the tanks and the wall gathered within the paradoxical palette form a part of historical continuity and yet are at the same time held apart from it. They thereby signal the necessity that emerges when history, memory and tradition can no longer be thought within representation and mimesis; that is, within the very terms that tradition demands that they be thought. What also emerges is time, since the temporality proper to memory and continuity is the temporality of the ordered sequence. A break within that sequence – a rift – can always be healed by memory. Memory is understood as creating a narrative within the temporality of sequential continuity, a homology within the frame that establishes interpretation as homological. Memory creates unity. It is this conception of memory that the painting suggests is no longer possible. Memory is not to be linked to the past. The painting gestures towards a present remembrance; a witness to the rift. The rift itself is in general the mark of the irreducible and ineliminable presence of anoriginal heterogeneity.

This task – present remembrance – is most often undertaken within Kiefer's work by deploying figures and events from 'history'. However each use works in a particular way such that it calls into question the possibility of its own use as the creator of a true history in which the past comes to be either retrieved or restored. There is an important additional point that emerges here. (The 'here' still involves the interpretation of *Iconoclastic Controversy.*) The irrecoverability attests to the possibility of interpretation where the presence of an irrecoverable origin entails that in the practice of interpretation the figure is no longer reducible to an event that is outside. The inside and the outside both figure within the frame. The distinction is thereby removed from a position of interpretive dominance. This is not a denial of history but rather an affirmation of the essentially heterological nature of the object of interpretation. Here it is the work of art.

The task of present remembrance needs to be understood as affirmative since it opens up the possibility of thinking the temporality of the rift and in addition of developing a conception of tradition as rift. Tradition and time (though only the time of tradition) now have a determination. It is, of course, one that is not handed down within and as tradition. The determination is the rift. It is in sum the actualization of the risk within mimesis.

NOTES

1 This chapter takes up, but does not complete, an interpretation of Kiefer's work that was begun in *What is Deconstruction?* (Academy Editions, London, 1988), pp. 50–4. See, in addition, my 'Kiefer's Approaches' in A. Benjamin and P. Osborne (eds) *Thinking Art. Beyond Traditional Aesthetics* (ICA Documents, London, 1991.)

2 Even this claim, without of course being misleading, is problematic since the primary sources are themselves split between the opposing factions. The majority of conventional histories are torn between the east and the west. For an overview see E. J. Martin, *A History of the Iconoclastic Controversy* (SPCK, London, 1930). A general discussion of the arts of the period is provided by David Talbot Rice in *Byzantine Art* (Pelican Books, London, 1954).

3 I am not denying the importance of evidence and the factual content of history. Indeed it is at times essential to have access to such material. A clear example concerns the polemic around the 'existence' of the death camps. The two points that emerge here are different. The first point involves the recognition that evidence can never exist *in vacuo* but is deployed and redeployed and thus ordered within the different, and at times, conflicting narratives in which it appears. The second is significantly more complex. It refers to the problem of representation (and hence mimesis) in the sense that it refers to the problem of understanding what it is that is presented in the present as history. The question is: what form does the presence of the past take? Moreover, is it constrained to take a particular form? The question therefore does not concern the 'that' of history – its content – but history itself. The point at issue here is whether or not Kiefer's painting raises these questions from within its content; or, more radically, are these questions its content. It is precisely the tension between these two possibilities that will be explored in this chapter.

4 I have discussed the problem of naming in *Translation and the Nature of Philosophy: A New Theory of Words* (Routledge, London, 1989). See in particular chapter 6.

5 I have tried to take up the question of deception and its relation to fables in Chapter 11, 'Descartes' fable: the *Discours de la méthode*'.

5
KITAJ AND THE QUESTION OF JEWISH IDENTITY

One of the major difficulties that confronts any attempt to dwell on the problem of Jewish identity lies in the relationship between that identity and the history of anti-semitism. Is Jewish identity the identity given to Judaism and hence to the Jew by that history, or is there an affirmative conception that seeks to overcome the continual historical enactment of anti-semitism? While there is a straight-forward theological answer to this question it is one that is con-strained to ignore even a dialectical relationship with anti-semitism. It is therefore one that does not confront the contemporary reality of the problem. A way into this apparent dilemma is provided by one of Christian thought's most dramatic presentations of the Jew; the allegorical figure of the synagogue. Its importance lies in the fact that it presents the logic in terms of which the question of Jewish identity is answered by Christianity. It is of course an answer that is intimately connected to anti-semitism. It is precisely in terms of the identity-giving frame constructed by the logic of the synagogue that Kitaj's preoccupation with Jewish identity needs to be situated. It also provides a way of assessing some of the critical writings that surround Kitaj's paintings; or at least those paintings concerned with the Jew. It will also be suggested that the question of identity is a larger concern in Kitaj's work.

Prior, however, to any discussion of the figure of the synagogue it is essential to construct the logic in which it is articulated. Two important instances of the enactment of this logic can be found in St Augustine's descriptions of the Jew:

> Because the Jews reckoned . . . that they would fulfil all due observances by their own efforts they stumbled at the stumbling block and the rock of scandal, and they did not acknowledge the

grace of Christ. For they accepted the Law which would render them transgressors but could not absolve them from their transgressions.[1]

They are like the carpenters of Noah's ark who built the boat but who themselves perished in the deluge. They are like the markers indicating a route they cannot follow. They are like the blind man with a lantern who shows the way to others but who does not see it himself.[2]

The Jews are caught, as these passage from Augustine indicate, within an inescapable double bind. They are necessary for the very possibility of Christian thought. Were it not for their having shown the way, built the ark, etc., then those for whom these tasks were done would have got lost or would have perished. Necessity is however also at work on another level. It is as essential that Jews be excluded in order that what they are taken to have begun may continue. This curious logic which includes only then to exclude is the logic of the synagogue. It inscribes Jews within a law that positions them as its inevitable and persistent transgressors.

The figure of the synagogue is Christian thought's representation of the Jew. The woman with her broken spear and her eyes blindfolded is the allegory of the Old Testament. She who, while carrying the truth, had to fail to see it as such. Furthermore she was unable to see that what she prophesied was fulfilled by the coming of Christ. The logic of the synagogue is continually at work within Christian thought. It constructs the identity of the Jew within it. Logic and identity are here linked to the inevitability of blindness. Blindness is at the same time moral and epistemological. In other words it is not just that the 'eye' is privileged, both really and metaphorically, within the history of philosophy.[3] It is also the case that blindness has a moral dimension. It is this dimension that is signalled in John 12:41, 'Sin is to remain in the darkness.' The Jew is positioned by the logic of the synagogue to remain without sight. Indeed Christianity depends upon the Jew as transgressor. The irony is that what is in fact really fundamental to revealed religion is not the one who sees but the one who does not. The force of sight does not exist in itself but resides in the necessity of a perpetual blindness. The blindness of one sustains the in-sight of the other.

Now, it will emerge that what is at stake here is a choice between the eye and the ear. It is by no means a simple choice. The eye is inscribed within the logic of the synagogue. The blind Jew is the inevitable transgressor. The eye brings with it moments of epistemological closure. While it is to open up a theme that cannot be adequately pursued here, it must none the less be noted that the relationship between sight, knowledge and the ethical is not only present in theological texts. It is an interplay that marks the history of philosophy; a history which includes Plato's allegory of the cave as well as Heidegger's complex description of truth as 'lighting' (*Lichtung*). Despite Heidegger's attempt to free himself from the Greek philosophical heritage he still conceives of truth and untruth in terms of light and darkness. Opposed to the '*Lichtung*' is 'untruth as errancy' (*Die Un-wahrheit als die Irre*). Describing untruth as errancy is to situate it within the opposition between light and dark, '*Irren*' as wandering is a departure from light as it is also a departure from the place.[4] The relationship between light and darkness, truth and error, involves two conceptual oppositions that give a place to the Jew but only to the Jew as transgressor. The Jew remains the Other in order that the Same remain the Same. Otherness therefore does not pertain to self-identity but to an identity giving designation that in coming from outside serves to guarantee that from which the designation proceeds.

The logic of the synagogue therefore constructs the Jew as continually enclosed within an epistemic foreclosure. Expressed in economic terms the prevailing eye can be linked to the payment of a debt. The ear is open. It resists foreclosure. It is not by chance that Emmanuel Levinas constructs openness in terms of a different economic model:

> The speeches of the Torah are not a debt; because a debt can be paid, while what we have to work with here is something that is *always* [*toujours*] to be paid).[5]   (My emphasis)

The '*toujours*' (always) marks the implicit impossibility of an end and hence of the fixity secured by sight. The overcoming of an ontology of stasis locates the Judaic response beyond the logic of the synagogue. The ear is open. Sin is no longer inscribed within it. The openness can be generalized. In a recent paper Jean-François Lyotard alludes to an unending listening in his discussion of Freud's paper *Analysis Terminable and Interminable*.[6] Despite moments of great significance within any analysis – within any giving of the ear – the analysis remains as potentially without end. What emerges here as infinitely deferred is the revelatory connection between the signifier and the signified. Interpretation is always taking place. At play within this opening is the refusal of representation and images as interpretive ends in themselves. The eye fixes. The ear is always open. It is always already open. Resolving the problem of developing an affirmative conception of Jewish identity must involve a dialectical interplay between the eye and ear. In other words it must situate itself within a space opened by the logic of the synagogue and hence one involving images and representation; the space of the eye. At the same time it must open that space; move beyond it by opening up the other space of the deferred end opened by the ear. This space positions the painting as a site of what can be called an interpretive differential plurality. In this instance what will emerge from the paintings under consideration is the co-presence of two different and incompatible fields of interpretation. The painting's interpretation will arise from the interplay – the tension – between them. One is not reducible to the other. One excludes the other and yet both are necessary if the interplay between the eye and the ear is to be allowed to unfold. At stake here is the possibility of a space of paradox. As will be suggested a number of Kitaj's paintings can be situated within this space.

Of the many critics who refer to Kitaj's preoccupation with Judaism all refer to the importance within his work of references either to anti-semitism or to the Holocaust. In a recent study Juliet Steyn argues quiet correctly that for Kitaj, 'Jewishness is an issue which he refuses to separate from anti-semitism.'[7] In a sense this is true, though it is not enough. What is important is the nature of the refusal. Even his own writings are not sufficient to answer this question. He poses his existence as a Jewish artist within a series of questions. He says of Jewishness: 'Can it be a force one declares in one's art? Would it be a force one intends for one's art? Would it be a force others attribute for better or for worse?'[8]

One immediate response to these questions is that for Kitaj, for the painting, and contrary to what Steyn and others argue, Judaism is not presented simply in terms of the images of the Holocaust. They are present but there is more. If Jewish identity were nothing other than the identity handed down by the history of anti-semitism then Steyn would be correct to argue that Kitaj's presentation of Judaism is reducible to creating a symbol through which and in which the Jewish experience can be encapsulated. His image is a chimney – the chimney at Auschwitz.[9] Escaping this reductive and self-enclosed conception of

Jewish identity necessitates detailing the space where the mirror image of the Jew as transgressor – namely the Jew as transgressed against – is mediated by the possibility of an affirmative conception of identity. Even if the latter is the continually always as-yet-to-be-determined conception of the Jew. Kitaj's own questions, in not admitting of immediate answers, gesture toward answers that are not yet. The questions opens. The hasty answer encloses Kitaj within the logic of the synagogue.

It is perhaps best to begin with his painting *The Jew Etc.* In representational terms it consists of a man sitting in a railway carriage. Rather than sitting back he is leaning forward. In place of the passivity of contemplation there is the activity of thought. He is wearing a hearing-aid. Each of these elements deserves careful consideration. This is especially the case as the 'same' figure also appears in the earlier work *If Not, Not.*

The train marks at the same time the transportation of Jews to the death camps and the Jew as the wanderer. The train therefore becomes the space of differential plurality. It lends itself to two different interpretations which, even though they are related, cannot be reduced one to the other. The relation between them is the mediation between enclosure and overcoming. Wandering defers the answer. The Jew remains within the open question. Even the Holocaust cannot close the question of Jewish identity. It is precisely in relation to this that the distinction between contemplation and thought needs to be situated. Within the terms of Augustinian Christianity, the answer to the question of human identity emerges from the contemplative act in which the individual is seen as the image of God. Here identity is constructed in terms of an image which functions as an interpretive end in itself. The answer to the question closes. Finitude as opposed to openness. The eye as opposed to the ear.

As the Christian Bible may be closed, the Torah is continually open. Arguing, however that the Jews are the people of the book is meaningless unless the status of that book is qualified. It is precisely in terms of this act of qualification that the work of the French writer Edmond Jabès can be situated. It is a situating that defies the propriety of the place: 'This absence of place, as it were, I claim. It confirms that the book is my only habitat, the first and also the final. Place of a vaster non-place where I live.'[10] The wandering Jew, alluded to in these lines by Jabès, takes place within a process which in philosophical terms privileges becoming over being. It is this privilege that is captured, presented, by the train. It is thus that the train cannot be reduced to a simple image of the Holocaust. It is moreover the reason why the Jew sits at the edge of the seat projected towards a future whose nature is yet to be determined. This is the Messianic within Judaism. It is within these terms that the intriguing hearing-aid must be understood. While there may be important biographical reasons why the Jew is presented in such a way, any interpretation of it must be situated within the logic of the painting.

What then is the function of the hearing-aid? Does it denote a weakness or inability? The hearing-aid attracts our attention. The eye of the viewer is drawn to it. The eye is drawn to the ear. The eye confronts listening. The hearing-aid mediates this attention. At the same time therefore attention becomes focused on the ear and yet the ear appears weakened. The hearing-aid overcomes the weakened ear and in so doing underlines the importance of the ear within Judaism. Its necessity is reinforced by the presence of the hearing-aid. There is a dramatic sense in which were the Jew to be deaf then the possibility of an affirmative conception of Jewish identity would, as a consequence, be threatened. The hearing-aid therefore marks what is emerging as essential to any preoccupation with Jewish identity. In the same way as the train is the site both of the Holocaust and the primacy of process and the futural, the hearing-aid marks vulnerability and hence positions the Jew as victim. The Jew is, however, more than merely the transgressed against. Accepting just this description is to remain entrapped within the logic of the synagogue. The hearing-aid takes the Jew beyond any status reducible to that of victim. At the same time, however, it marks the necessity of recognizing the history of anti-semitism and hence the history of the Jew as victim. The hearing-aid like the train is the site of an interpretive differential plurality. Here it is the site of two interpretations both of which must endure, while at the same time refusing the possibility of one being reduced to the other. The hearing-aid and the train open the space of the heterological. It would be in relation to the space of paradox that it would be possible to begin an interpretation of *If Not, Not* and *Cecil Court, London WC2 (The Refugees)*. In this instance I want to concentrate on the first of these paintings; saving a discussion of the other one for a future date.

If Not, Not is a difficult and complex work. Various interpretive grids have been offered. Kitaj himself has suggested that it is based on

Plate 7 'If Not, Not', R. B. Kitaj, 1975–6, oil on canvas.

Eliot's *The Waste Land*. Joe Shannon has drawn a comparison between it and Brueghel's *The Triumph of Death*. In both paintings the sky is an orange black. Shannon describes this as creating 'a world's-end phantasia'. It is difficult to give this comparison a great deal of credence. While Shannon is right to identify the presence of 'connections', paying them too much attention is at the very least problematic, if not in the end misleading. The black and orange of Brueghel's sky is in fact the triumph of death – the death within Christian redemption. In *If Not, Not* death is not triumphant, nor does it redeem in a Christian sense. *If Not, Not* demands – indeed the title demands – that respect be paid to Judaism, a respect that will allow to Judaism an existence stemming not from its interpolation into Christian thought – even Christian philosophical thought – but rather from the interplay of sameness and difference that is self-sustaining.

Now, the top of the painting presents death. Around the stark symmetry of the entrance to the concentration camp is the black smoke. Once again the painting is not reducible to this image. Even though the camp's entrance seems to stand above, almost beckoning, its presence within the frame is mediated by other elements within it. At the bottom there lies a body. The foot is bare. The absence of a boot would seem to suggest that death was the consequence of struggle; here death triumphed over the will to survive. Next to the body, being lifted and comforted is the Jew; Kitaj's Jew. Between the body and the Jew at the bottom of the painting, and the entrance to the concentration camp at the top, is one of Kitaj's most dramatic biblical references. As Abraham was about to sacrifice Isaac in response to God's word the angel intervened causing Isaac to be saved, Abraham saw a ram caught in a tree. The ram was sacrificed and presented to God as a burnt offering instead of Isaac.

Between the two deaths Kitaj has situated the possibility of redemption through sacrifice. And yet even this is insufficient as a description since the deaths are not the same. The body is the presence of the presence of death. The concentration camp and the smoke are the presence of an absence. It is an absence that checks the power of the image. The image can only present the absence. The absence is itself unsayable. Above the Jew is a bed containing an adult and a child. Here survival has become secularized. In the bed the sacrifice yields a life. The Jew in the foreground is dressed, he is male, he is being lifted up and in rising from the ground he has turned and is looking up. He is being raised by a woman who is not clothed and whose features are light rather than grey. She is lifting from above. The contrast between them reinforces their differences while it maintains their relation. Sameness and difference presented as one – as co-present – will demand a specific form of philosophical thinking in which it is possible to generate an ontology of difference: one where difference, rather than involving a self-articulation within, and as, similitude, will itself be differential. It is precisely the need to understand difference as differential that emerges from the painting. It is however a recognition that must have larger implications.[11]

In *If Not, Not*, beneath the horror of Auschwitz, beneath the reference to the biblical necessity for sacrifice, to the side of the presence of death, the Same and Other look into each other's face. This look is the possibility of the ethical. It is also the possibility of art in so far as the work of art is that which always looks back. Once again, despite this cursory and tentative – tentative because it is only a beginning – interpretation, not of the painting as such, but of elements within it, what emerged was the interplay between life and death. Survival and sacrifice; one not reducible to the other and yet both present. Doubled within presence they mark the frame as a heterological site.

It is also in terms of non-reducibility and hence of the heterological that another of his paintings can be situated. His 1980 painting *The Jewish School (Drawing a Golem)* is, as commentators have pointed out, based on the anti-semitic engraving *Die Judenschule* by G. E. Optiz. Marco Livingstone has offered an important interpretation of this painting in his monograph on Kitaj:

> The Jewish School . . . transforms what in the original source was merely a swipe at the alleged anarchy of Jewish behaviour into a metaphor of the Jews' inability to defend themselves adequately against their persecutors.[12]

Livingstone bases his interpretation on the transformation that occurs from the original. In the original there is a boy drawing on the blackboard. In Kitaj's version the drawing is of a golem. From this Livingstone concludes that the 'golem . . . is incomplete; he will not come to life in time to save them'. Here again the Jew is the victim. Is this all that Kitaj's painting presents?

The first thing to note is that the golem is coming to life. The legs have moved beyond representation and into life. The torso, the head

Plate 8 'The Jewish School (drawing of a Golem)', R. B. Kitaj, 1980.

and the arms are still representational and yet are on the threshold of life. The golem, however, as a figure within the Judaic folk tradition can be both good and bad. As with all human creation it can be harmful as well as beneficial. The golem need neither save nor defend. There is, moreover, an additional element of fundamental importance, as Gershom Scholem points out: 'The creation of a Golem is . . . in some way an affirmation of the productive and creative power of Man. It repeats on however small a scale, the work of creation.[13] As the golem is coming to life Kitaj's painting enacts exactly this affirmation. This is not, however, to deny Livingstone's point that the golem did not save the Jews. It simply indicates that it is not sufficient. It refuses to allow the painting to be a space of paradox.

Kitaj has transformed Optiz's engraving so that it affirms the creative power of the Jew which is always, like the golem in the painting, in the process of coming to life; creation as the continual renewal. Indeed the fact that the golem is presented as moving from representation into life is of even greater significance. It makes more dramatic the limit of representations by focusing on the question of how it is that the golem can be imbued with life. Within the folkloric tradition it was a result of placing the written name of God into the golem's mouth. Here life is a consequence of writing rather than figural representation. The child drawing on the board affirms the power of writing. Of the many other points that can be made, perhaps the next most significant is that the process of coming alive – a process enacted by the painting – contains a futural dimension, namely the transformation of the golem presented as incomplete gestures at its own completion. The gesture towards completion is Messianic in that it is a gesture towards the future. Once again this is to identify a preoccupation with the Messianic within Kitaj's work. The golem presented in the painting as always coming to life invokes a different hope; one alluded to by Jabès when he wrote, 'L'espoir est à la page prochaine.' This is why for the Jew the book can never end. The ear must always be open.

The child drawing on the blackboard could indeed be the most supreme autobiographical gesture. In announcing the importance of the futural and in affirming human creative power it reinforces the fact that the question of Jewish identity is one to be negotiated. It is neither handed down nor reducible to the history of anti-semitism. Part of this futural negotiation involves the refusal by the Jew to be the Same. In fact it is the claim for universality that also works to rob the Jew of any specific and different identity. Since universalizing works to exclude the Jew, the import of the demand made by critics that Kitaj should be concerned with universals must be understood for what it is.[14]

Situating at least these paintings within the space of the heterological entails that conceptions of identity which demand universality and which stem from the heritage of the Enlightenment are no longer applicable. Part of the present must be a concern with an identity that is no longer reducible to the Same. Rather than privileging identity over difference, difference must be understood as already potentially in place. In the case of Jewish identity, when it is a question posed beyond the logic of the synagogue, and hence beyond the identity given to the Jew, what emerges as central is the space of paradox – space that contains the past but which moves toward the future; the space of process rather than stasis. Thinking this space is the concern of philosophy in the wake of the Enlightenment.

NOTES

1 St Augustine, *On the Psalms*, trans. and annotated by Dame Scholastica Hebgin and Dame Felicitas Currigan (London, 1961), vol. 11.
2 Quoted in B. Blumenkranz, *Le Juif médiéval au miroir de l'art chrétien* (Paris, 1972), p. 47.
3 The importance of the 'eye' and visual imagery in connection with both moral and epistemological claims has been shown by J. Derrida in a number of his texts.
4 M. Heidegger, 'Vom Wesen der Wahrheit', in *Wegmarken* (Klostermann, Frankfurt, 1978). See pp. 193–6.
5 E. Levinas, *L'au-delà du verset* (Editions de Minuit, Paris, 1982), p. 89.
6 See J.-F. Lyotard, 'Rewriting modernity', *SubStance*, no. 54, 1988. Lyotard develops the relationship between the eye and the ear in 'Figure Foreclosed', in *The Lyotard Reader* (Blackwell, Oxford, 1989).
7 Katy Deepwell and Juliet Steyn, 'Readings of the Jewish artist in late modernism', *Art Monthly*, February 1988, no. 133, p. 8.
8 'A Passion', Marlborough Gallery, London, 1985. These questions are also quoted by Steyn.
9 Steyn and Deepwell, op. cit., p. 9.
10 E. Jabès, 'There is such a thing as Jewish writing . . .', in E. Gould (ed.) *The Sin of the Book: Edmond Jabès* (University of Nebraska Press, Nebraska, 1985), p. 26. I have tried to develop the thematics for a reading of Jabès in 'La question du livre', *Digraphe*, no. 25, 1981.
11 It would serve, for example, to read *The Merchant of Venice* not as a play concerned with Judaism and Jewish identity but rather as involving the consequences of the interplay of the Christian conception of identity with

a law that sanctions this identity but only because it can deny it. It is Shylock's equality before the law that makes him the legal subject of Portia's argument and Antonio's demand that he give up his Jewish identity in order to remain equal before the law. Equality must itself be thought within a conception of pluralism and the cosmopolitan in order to avoid the trap of the liberal conception of justice.

12 M. Livingstone, *R. B. Kitaj* (Oxford, 1985), p. 36.
13 G. Scholem, *The Messianic Idea in Judaism* (Schocken Books, New York, 1971), p. 336.
14 It is of course at precisely this point that Portia's invocation of the law must be brought into play.

6

MALEVICH AND THE
AVANT-GARDE

The avant-garde implies movement.[1] The movement within it questions the possibility of art itself. The interplay of movement and possibility is signalled by Malevich in his autobiography: 'in what form, liberated from the contours of an object, is painting to be embodied, and can such a form be found?'[2] Here in the form of a question lies Malevich's understanding of the possibility of the avant-garde. It resides within the question and is captured by the postulated 'liberation'. Before taking up the stakes of this 'liberation' it is essential to stay with the question; the form of the question.

The question gestures towards a future. In the demand for an answer the question opens into a space (and therefore also within a time) that cannot be reduced to the present. This non-reduction means that the relationship between the present and the future needs to be given careful consideration. At the very least what is at play is the necessity of deciding between two specific determinations. The first demands that within the question either the answer itself or the range of possible answers has already been determined in advance. The second is that it is precisely the answer understood as the *as-yet-to-be-determined* entity, that the question – articulated within both philosophical and artistic experimentation – is seeking either to identify or establish. The question therefore opens within the impossibility of prediction. The importance of prediction lies in its link to teleology, and in particular to the conception of temporality that is proper to teleology. There is however a complicating factor: what is at play here is not a simple either/or; a simple choice between a question whose answer is, in some sense, inscribed within the possibility of its own initial formulation, and a question for which there is no pre-given answer. The complication emerges because even in the second case there must remain a link. In other words the future can never be the absolutely other. It is this link, and hence the complication, that will be explored, albeit briefly, in relation to the writings and paintings (the Suprematist paintings) of Malevich. It is still the case that the 'liberation' announced in his autobiography remains of central importance.

The autobiographical question pertains to the possibility of art after its having been 'liberated from the controls of an object'. What are these controls? How does the object figure as that which controls? Searching the writings for answers to these questions can be a complex, if not contradictory, undertaking. None the less there is a fundamental aspect of control that is consistently presented. It can, of course, be given a polemical and therefore misleading presentation. In one of his most important essays Malevich asserts that: 'The artist can be a creator only when the forms in his pictures have nothing in common with nature.'[3] It is on the surface possible to see the force of this claim within the Suprematist paintings. From the *Black Square* onwards the forms do not represent. And yet this is not sufficient. How is the claim 'nothing in common with nature' to be understood? Is this simply an argument for non-representational art? That it is not will be clear from the answer to the first question. The reason why this question is important is that Malevich's claim looks as though it is doing no more than opposing the representational to the non-representational. It is in fact far more difficult. Nature is for Malevich that which sanctions imitation. It is the home for imitative art and of imitation. The expression 'nothing in common with nature' therefore refers to the possibility of an art and indeed of an aesthetic (understood as involving both philosophical considerations as well as experience) that is no longer articulated within mimesis. If this path is pursued then interpretation, as will be noted, can no longer take place in terms of the metaphysical oppositions maintaining mimesis.

For Malevich mimesis is given its full force both in terms of simple imitation and in relation to the ontology of the object. Mimesis demands an ontology of stasis. Without such an ontology the retention of the metaphysical opposition between the inside and the outside which is fundamental to mimesis could no longer function. The recognition of what have been described as ontological consider-ations is signalled by Malevich in *The World as Non-Objectivity:*

> Imitative art attempts to halt the changing pattern, to fix the
> fact in an immutable pose, to lead it into the artistic condition,

the condition outside of time, such a relationship is the essence of imitative art, but in reality the artist understands this essence in a different way and it is assumed to be a method of painting reality, of depicting a phenomenon on canvas. But this attempt is vain, there is no reality.[4]

This passage warrants detailed investigation. The conclusion that there is no reality is argued for elsewhere in his writings in terms of a type of perspectivism which yields the impossibility of the fixed object. This mode of argument is also present in this passage in the claim that imitation will still 'the changing pattern'; to which needs to be added that the nature of things is this 'changing pattern' and that therefore the presentation of an object within mimetic terms cannot present things as they actually are even though imitative art purports to accomplish this task. However, once again, Malevich should not be read as offering no more than the suggestion that mimesis fails with its own terms or that it transgresses another reality which it cannot hope to present. This would be only to shift the emphasis within a broader conception of mimesis, (one having, in addition, a negative and positive pole). It is rather that the perspectivism – the object continually changing – works to move the emphasis away from the object and towards the possibility of that change itself. Objects give way to that which forms and allows for the relations between objects, namely space. Furthermore, time as marking the process of a continual becoming – of a movement that takes place independently of either a posited *arché* or *telos* – is thereby reintroduced into artistic production. They both allow for what Zhadova has called, in relation to the contrast of black and white, 'the effect of spatial infinity'.[5] She goes on to reiterate the importance of space within Suprematist paintings: 'Space, one of the means of representation in painting achieves in Suprematism the independent status of a subject and in fact becomes a central concept in its own right.'[6] The movement within the realm of painting does not posit the importance of representational as opposed to non-representational art. It is rather that the artistic enterprise – and hence the task of the artist – is reorientated towards the expression of exactly those elements which yield objects and the relations between objects, namely space and time. Fundamental to this task will be form and colour.

The importance of colour is suggested by Malevich in the following way: 'The gallop of a horse can be depicted with a pencil of one colour.

But it is impossible to depict the movement of red, green or blue masses with a pencil. Painters should abandon subject and object if they wish to be pure painters.'[7] This comment also, once again, underscores the way in which the centrality of mimesis (in terms of either its success or failure; the positive and negative pole) has been displaced. In other words this passage can be read as advocating that what is at stake is not whether or not a horse can be depicted, or even the gallop of a horse depicted, but rather that the artistic task should be reorientated towards that which, for Malevich, makes the gallop itself possible. Here it involves the relationship between positions within space.

Space and spatiality do not involve simply the non-representational. Such a designation would reduce them to a negativity; to being no more than a 'failure' within mimetic terms. Focusing on the non-representational does no more therefore than repeat a metaphysical opposition; thereby involving a repetition of and within the Same. Operating within the poles of such an opposition is the activity Nietzsche quite correctly described as nihilism. Furthermore such a repetition repeats the domination of tradition by repeating the dominant tradition. The Same will always be the *determination in advance*. It is only by linking space and the advocacy of spatiality as that which determines the artist's task that it becomes possible to see in what way Suprematism can be understood as involving affirmation. Zhadova traces this move from negativity to positivity and hence to affirmation: 'Non-objectivity in his sense is the perception of the absence of an object, in other words the non-objective perception of the environment, the perception of its pure spaciousness.'[8] The one clarification that needs to be introduced here is that what she describes as 'the absence of an object' must be viewed at the same time as both the presentation of that which makes objects possible and as freeing artistic activity (be it creation or interpretation) from its potential oscillation between the positive and negative poles of mimesis. A further reason for moving away from non-objectivity understood in terms of 'absence' is in fact presented by Malevich in his own terms. The move from that which is at hand to the new is given an affirmative dimension: 'I am only free when my will, on a critical and philosophical basis, can bring from what already exists the basis for new phenomena.'[9] It is the movement inherent in this passage that will allow for a re-introduction of the already mentioned 'liberation' and hence of the question: the question of the question.

The movement here introduces departure – a moving away – and hence the possibility of the new, where, of course, *new* does not designate novelty but the presence of an artistic endeavour which can no longer be understood or explicated in terms of the categories and concepts handed down by tradition for such a task. (It goes without saying that the handing down is the repetition of tradition itself.) Malevich's own interpretation of Cubism focuses on movement: 'it [Cubism] marks the artist's emancipation from slavish imitation of the object, and the beginning of his search for direct discovery of creativity.'[10] 'Emancipation' and 'liberation' derive their force from the impossibility of mimesis to govern artistic production and thereby to generate the creative activity taking place in the movement away. The Suprematist paintings therefore are not instances of a more general subversion of mimesis nor, as has already been mentioned, are they simply non-representational. Rather they eschew exemplarity and negativity since the move away from mimesis involves a departure from the domination of homology and thus opens up the possibility of plural and hence heterological artistic practices. There will never be one avant-garde and the avant-garde will never be one, in that due to the manner of its own effectuation – its coming to be – it precludes the self-referentiality demanded by homology and mimesis.[11] Indeed if there is a limit to Malevich's writings on art it resides at exactly this point. The movement that he traces from Cubism via Futurism to Suprematism does not deny the possibility of art *per se*; rather it restricts the range of experimentation and therefore imposes a limit on experimentation and as such on the avant-garde.

The importance of this limit cannot be denied or overlooked; however it needs to be read in relation to the claims that Malevich makes about the reception and interpretation of paintings. He orchestrates a subtle though decisive move that flows from the more general attempt to restrict the range of mimesis. It should not be forgotten that mimesis sanctions a specific form of aesthetics. In a discussion of colour he makes the following point:

> The colour spots here [i.e. in Suprematist works] appear as colour contrasts, and therefore in this case, colour and what we call form have no significance that would give us the right to classify them as colour and form. Accordingly we should not examine Suprematism, but merely *sense* [my emphasis] the contrasts that are created in it [dynamics, contrasts, space].[12]

The move from the conceptual to 'sense' is not as such the denial of the discursive in favour of the intuitive. It involves the recognition that the examination of Suprematism will take place in terms of the concepts and categories proper to mimesis. What this passage moves towards is the need – a generalized need – for a philosophical rethinking of sense and feeling so that they are freed from their position as the understanding's opposite and thus can come to function within the development of the concept of the avant-garde.

Finally, therefore, the question – Malevich's autobiographical question – comes to be answered beyond his own concerns. The possibility of 'liberation' – of 'emancipation' – unfolds within the experimentations that mark artistic activity. They are governed neither by teleology nor mimesis. The work of art is demanding. It is always one step in advance of philosophy.

NOTES

1 By the expression 'avant-garde' I am not referring either to a genre or a specific historical location. What is at stake here is the possibility and hence the actuality of a philosophical conception of the avant-garde. The avant-garde will become affirmation. Fundamental to what is at play within such a conception will be tradition. Tradition need not be interpreted in its own terms, but is deployed here and elsewhere as the concept in terms of which history figures within philosophy. In other words it provides a way within philosophy of taking history – and especially, though not exclusively, the history of philosophy – into consideration.

2 K. Malevich, 'Chapters from an artist's autobiography', *October*, Fall 1985, p. 43.

3 K. Malevich, 'From Cubism and Futurism to Suprematism. The new realism in painting', in *Essays on Art*, vol. 1, trans. X. Glowacki-Pros and A. McMillin (Rapp & Whiting, London, 1969), p. 24.

4 K. Malevich, *The World as Non-Objectivity*, trans. X. Glowacki-Pros and E. T. Little (Burgen, Copenhagen, 1976), p. 49.

5 L. A. Zhadova, *Malevich, Suprematism and Revolution in Russian Art, 1910-1930*, trans. A. Lieren (Thames & Hudson, London, 1982), p. 45.

6 ibid., p. 51.

7 K. Malevich, 'From Cubism . . .' op. cit., p. 340.

8 Zhadova, op. cit., pp. 49–50.

9 K. Malevich, 'Non-objective creation and Suprematism', in *Essays on Art*, vol. 1, p. 122. Even though it cannot be pursued here it is essential to note the importance of the will within Malevich's writings.

10 K. Malevich, 'On new systems in art', in *Essays on Art*, vol. 1, p. 101. The

same argument, though interestingly linked to the will, can be found in 'From Cubism . . .', op. cit., p. 33.
11 I have discussed the interrelationship between homology, mimesis and heterology in Chapters 1 and 4 above.
12 K. Malevich, 'An attempt to determine the relations between colour and form in painting', in *Essays on Art*, vol. 11, p. 138.

7

EISENMAN AND THE
HOUSING OF TRADITION

J'ai sans doute mal lu l'oeuvre de Derrida, mais mal lire c'est
finalement une façon de créer, et c'est en lisant mal que j'arrive à
vivre dans la réalité et que je pourrais travailler avec lui.

Peter Eisenman

Locating architecture would seem to be unproblematic. Architecture
houses. It is at home in – and provides a home for – philosophy,
aesthetics and those discourses which are thought to describe it. And
yet it is precisely the generality as well as the singularity of these
claims that makes such a description or location problematic. In each
instance something remains unquestioned. The assertion – even the
argument – that architecture houses, fails in a concrete, philosophical
and political sense to address housing. Equally the interplay between
architecture and the home in which philosophy, aesthetics and
discourse may be located, works with the assumption that the nature
of what is housed is such that the act of housing it will not call into
question the specificity of the act itself. In other words the unified
nature of philosophy is assumed and thus is thought to have been
provided either by the unity of tradition or the singularity of its
object. What needs to be examined therefore are some of the elements
at work within these assumptions; their premises and therefore that
on which they are built. Philosophy can never be free of architecture.
The impossibility of pure freedom, of pure positivity and thus of a
radical and absolute break entails that what is at stake here is, as a
consequence, precisely philosophy and architecture themselves. Of
the many locations that can be given to Eisenman's work one is to
situate it within the act of rethinking both architecture and philosophy. A way towards an understanding of the impossibility of an
absolute break and therefore of this location of Eisenman's work may

stem from a consideration of Descartes' use of an architectural metaphor in the *Discours de la méthode*. Descartes' attempt to re-found philosophy in the wake of a complete break with the past is presented within architectural terms. What must be traced is the founding of this attempt.[1]

DESCARTES' ARCHITECTURE

For philosophy what is at stake in the question of the relationship between architecture and tradition is the possibility of a rethinking of architectural thought. Tradition emerges as the site that occasions both an understanding of dominance – the categories and concepts which are handed down and which thus determine thinking within and as tradition – and the possibility of a thinking which, while it maintains (houses) the dominant, is neither reducible to nor explic-able in terms of it. In sum, tradition allows for history to be thought within philosophy. In addition the tension that marks the correspond-ing non-correspondence of a thinking (be it architectural or philoso-phical) that is situated within tradition, and a thinking that cannot be thus situated, provides a way to renew the concept of the avant-garde as well as providing access to an understanding of the accompanying mode of experience (that is sensibility) proper to the avant-garde.

Descartes' architectural 'metaphor' is a familiar point of entry. It goes without saying that within Descartes' architecture there is an explicit confrontation with tradition. The location of this 'metaphor' is the Second Part of the *Discours de la méthode*. The context concerns the possibility of philosophy, of a new philosophical thinking, and thus whether tradition can be refurbished – what has been handed down by and as tradition – or, on the contrary, whether philosophy is constrained to start again. It is not difficult to see in the very formulation of the problem that Descartes thinks that tradition may be, in fact, left behind. In other words that an absolute break with the past can be established. Consequently, in discussing Descartes it will be essential to analyse the unfolding of the metaphor as well as to examine or assess the possibility of this purported complete depar-ture. Descartes' metaphor is an 'example' of the general problem of how change occurs and, of course, who should bring it about. (It is thus not *just* a metaphor.) He notes that

there is not usually so much perfection in works composed of several parts and produced by various different craftsmen as in the works of one man. Thus we see that buildings undertaken and completed by a single architect are usually more attractive and better planned than those which several have tried to patch up by adapting old walls built for different purposes. Again, ancient towns which have gradually grown from mere villages into large towns are usually ill-proportioned, compared with those ordinary towns that planners lay out as the fancy [*fantaisie*] on level ground. Looking at the buildings of the former individually, you will often find as much art in them, if not more, than in those of the latter; but in view of their arrangement – a tall one here, a small one there – and the way they make the streets crooked and irregular, you would say it is chance [*fortune*] rather than the will of men using reason [*raison*] that placed them so. And when you consider that there have always been certain officials whose job is to see that private buildings embellish public places, you will understand how difficult it is to make something perfect by working only on what others have produced [*les ouvrages d'autrui*].[2]

This passage warrants careful analysis. It is not an isolated instance within Descartes' writings. It should be remembered, for example, that the actuality of starting again is articulated within architectural terms in the First Meditation, where he describes his task in the following way:

> to start once again from the foundations (*commencer tout de nouveau dès les fondements*).[3]

It is the possibility of this 'new' beginning that defines the relation to as well as the conception of tradition at work in both the *Meditations* and the *Discours de la méthode*. Now, returning to the passage from the *Discours de la méthode*, it is essential to note both the presentation of tradition, its interarticulation within the language of architecture, and thus its putting into play as well as demanding a specific conception of experience and thereby of the aesthetic.

Rather than working on, 'les ouvrages d'autrui' the implicit suggestion is that the philosopher like the architect (the philosopher as architect) should 'begin again'. The 'autrui' of this passage can be interpreted as standing for tradition. Inscribed therefore within the more general architectural metaphor is an additional trope. The relationship between self and other has become mapped onto the possibility of a departure from tradition. Tradition here, within this framework, is presented as the other. The other is the already present. The other here is history. The self becomes that possibility that emerges within the break from that conception of the self/other relation that views both parts as inextricably linked. The self must emerge as new – in a perpetual state of renewal – from this linkage. It is precisely in this sense that Descartes' juxtaposition of the solitary individual working alone and a team – the *'divers maîtres'* – needs to be understood.

Descartes' refusal of tradition is connected therefore to the emergence of the individual subject. It is thus that Cartesian thought establishes the centrality, both within architecture and philosophy, of the subject, and thus of subjectivism. Cartesianism is the emergence of the centrality of the subject; the subject of epistemology as well as the subject of sentiment. Rather than pursuing this particular path, however, it is essential to move to a more detailed analysis of what is at play in the rejection of tradition. Fundamental to the possibility of this rejection will be a specific construal of repetition. This has to be the case since Descartes believes that the break with the work of others (a break or rupture within repetition and therefore occasioning the cessation of repetition) establishes, and defines, the new. There can be no sense, within the terms of his own argument, that repetition can operate if repetition is understood as the repetition of a tradition. It will be seen however that there is another sense in which Descartes cannot escape another repetition. It is this sense that, it will be suggested, checks his claim concerning that which has already been described in terms of the possibility of an absolutely new beginning. The detour into repetition will take us to the centre of the problem of tradition, explanation, interpretation and therefore of a more generalized aesthetic – general in the sense that its stakes are not reducible simply to architecture.

Descartes understands tradition's repetition not necessarily in terms of the repetition of an unchanging and identical content, but rather as a continuity of content; one determined and structured by the precepts of medieval Aristotelianism, that is, Scholasticism. The break would be the refusal both to occasion and to sanction the repetition of these precepts; to take them over and hand them on. The resistance is to their continuity. Two questions arise here. First, if there is a radical break – one in which it is possible to *begin again* – how is the break to be maintained, housed, within Descartes' own philosophical adventure? Second, how does the break figure within the implicit conception of tradition at work in the departure itself? Before it is possible to answer these questions it is vital to try and understand repetition beyond the confines of Cartesianism. What is at stake now, therefore, is to move from the relationship between repetition and tradition within Descartes to a more generalized conception – remembering, of course, that for Descartes it is possible to call a halt to continuity. Indeed it is possible to interpret the doubt of the First Meditation as the break, and the subsequent overcoming of doubt as the recommencement.

There is a sense in which Descartes is correct. Tradition in general terms can be understood as the *determination in advance*. The way tradition operates is invariably in terms of teleology. There is a *telos* established within and as tradition. In the case of architecture, the *telos* refers to function and thus to housing. Architecture must house. Its being as architecture is, within the terms set by the dominant tradition, to be determined if not evaluated by the success of any architectural instance – any building – to fulfil such a criterion. It is, of course, a criterion determined in advance. The incorporation of teleology into tradition and into architecture does not preclude the possibility of excess. Indeed excess has to be understood not as a subversive element within a more general economy but as a designation that flows from the centrality of function. It is therefore essential to distinguish between excess and transgression. Excess is always going to be the addition that sustains the law or rule. Transgression is that which robs them of their power, while maintaining that power as a remnant. It endures but no longer as itself. Within the purview of teleology, however, the history of architecture, in fact the philosophy of architecture, have become as a result the history and philosophy of a specific process: one marked by an origin, a goal and a creator. This however is not the only way in which teleology figures within architecture.

The important additional dimension concerns the effect that specific elements within a building or house are supposed to have. The effect is continually thought to have been predictable. Whether or not the prediction is valid, what is at work within such an architectural practice is a thinking that involves the inclusion within itself and within the 'house' of either a repetitive monotony or a decorative excess that enacts no more than the attempt to mask the specific effect; the effect as the effect of function. The necessity, both within architecture and philosophy of rethinking repetition – of moving on from the domination of the Same – cannot be over-emphasized. Now it could be argued that the attempt to subvert the dominance of the Same is precisely what Descartes is doing. The problem here is to identify on exactly what level the Same is to be located.

In regards to architecture the Same is explicable, for the most part, in terms of teleology and thus in terms of function. The instance becomes, as was mentioned, either a particular instantiation of the general designation in the sense that the particular is coextensive with the general, or the particular is viewed in terms of its excess; that is that state of affairs where the general functional designation defines the excess. The repetition of the Same therefore is the repetition of function. Now the question here is, what would an architectural thinking be that was no longer dominated by the *telos* given by tradition to architecture? It is by returning to Descartes that an answer to this question can be given.

Within Descartes' attempt to establish the completely new – absolute originality – a certain philosophical strategy was deployed. Of the many philosophical oppositions within which Descartes' architectural 'metaphor' is positioned (thereby positioning itself and the oppositions) the two which were the most central were reason and chance and the one and the many. It is clear that they are related. Within the Cartesian texts the oppositions are advanced in terms, for example, of the distinction between the understanding and the imagination. In addition it is a retention and repetition of these terms, amongst others, that defines – defines in the sense of reorientates – the philosophical task. Furthermore it is the presentation of the opposition between reason and chance and the one and the many that sustains, supports, perhaps even provides the architectural meta-phor's foundation. In other words it is the repetition of these oppositions that provides the conditions of possibility for Descartes' arguments within the 'metaphor'. The city of reason as opposed to the city of chance is one that has been constructed without any retention of that which preceded it. It needs to be the work of one mind – the subject of epistemological certainty – as opposed to the joint operation of diverse minds. The consequence of this is that the possibility of breaking with tradition, in the Cartesian sense, that is of ending repetition, can itself only take place if the oppositions that sustain this possibility are themselves repeated. The Cartesian break with tradition ends up reinscribing tradition as that which allows for the possibility of the break. It is only if the oppositions that characterize the history of philosophy are allowed to be repeated that Descartes' desire to 'begin again' is in fact possible. Now there are two important conclusions that can be drawn from this reinscription of tradition.

The first is that it makes clear in what sense the Cartesian conception of tradition is to be understood. The second is that it allows for a critical understanding of what is at stake in the claim that an absolute break with tradition is impossible. It now emerges that a refusal of dominance still has to house what had hitherto dominated. The architectural question, even within philosophy, can never be ignored. In addition it can now be understood that the question of tradition involves a repetition in which concepts and categories are handed down. Moreover repetition is not neutral but involves dominance and therefore power. The resistance to, or refusal of, tradition must take place in relation to the conceptual and categorial. (The way in which dominance and power figure here gives rise to another philosophical task.) They need to be housed while their domination is resisted. This interplay of resistance and inclusion marks the tension within the domain of contemporary interpretation. It goes without saying that there are many works of philosophy or architecture that involve a simple repetition of tradition. Descartes conceived of his philosophical task as avoiding nihilistic repetition. The task failed as it was premised on the reinscription of another repetition.

Understood ontologically, therefore, the repetition within Cartesianism becomes the repetition of the same within the Same. This repetition is linked to the particular conception of the object within Cartesianism. In the *Discours de la méthode* Descartes describes the connection between truth and the object: 'there being only one truth about each thing whosoever finds it knows as much about that thing as can be known.'[4] The object of knowledge like the subject of knowledge must be a unity. Subject and object must be homological in themselves as well as constructing a homological relation within the act of knowing. Ontologically therefore they must be the same. The origin must be unified if knowledge is to be possible. Repetition is the repetition of Sameness. What Cartesian repetition cannot include is a conception of repetition that is not articulated within and therefore as the Same. This takes place in the positive sense in terms of a repetition of and within the Same and in the negative in terms of the postulated complete rejection of repetition. If repetition is to be rethought then what has to emerge as central is the ontology that sanctions a repetition in which what comes to be repeated is at the same time same and different. (The time of this simultaneity is complex.)

These tentative deliberations concerning ontology can be taken a step further. One way of interpreting Descartes' reinscription of a repetition within the attempt to break down the repetition of tradition is that the work – Descartes' own text – as an object of interpretation thereby becomes a site that is no longer reconciled with itself. Its desire for original unity was rendered impossible by that which intended to establish it as a unity; as unified. The aspiration (understood as intentional logic) for an initial and original unity gives way, within the recognition of its impossibility (an impossible possibility), to an original heterogeneity; that is to anoriginal heterogeneity. The origin has become redescribed. The foundations are renewed within repetition such that they are then repeated for the first time. The consequence of this means that if there is to be a refusal to take over and carry on that which tradition hands down then there has to be another way in which this task can be understood. It is precisely in these terms that it will be necessary to rethink the force of the claim that 'architecture houses'.

THE HOUSING OF ARCHITECTURES

The limit already emerging within the architectural constraints determined by teleology are also at work within philosophy. There are two aspects that are of strategic importance here. The first is the envisaged relationship between philosophy and its object, and the second emerges from the consideration of what is to be understood by philosophy both within the terms set by tradition and, in addition, in the resistance to the dominance and domination of tradition. Clearly the second of these provides the place to start. In a sense however it opens up much larger problems concerning, history, naming, interpretation, the political, etc., all of which are central to any understanding of Eisenman's work.

What is at stake in asking the question 'what is philosophy?' arises not from the specificity of a particular response but from the recognition that an answer has already been determined in advance of the question; this determination in advance is tradition.[5] The tradition within which philosophy is enacted – and hence which it enacts – has decreed what is going to count as philosophical and therefore what will fall beyond the borders it constructs. The repetition of philosophy within, by, and as tradition reduces it to the repetition of an ideal essence. It must not be assumed, of course, that that essence need be at hand. Indeed it is possible to present a conception of philosophy where its object and its nature are in some sense hidden, and thus what becomes fundamental to, if not descriptive of, the philosophical task is the revelation of that which is not at hand. Here repetition is the repetition of that which is essential though concealed.

Countering a conception of philosophy that defines its identity in terms of an ideal essence means allowing the question 'what is philosophy?' to be re-posed. The re-posing of this question unfolds within a repetition that changes the stakes of the question (recalling the ontology of the object with Cartesianism). The repetition of this question breaks with the control exercised by the Same. It sanctions a repetition in which the same is different. The reason for this being the case is explicable in terms of the different ontologico-temporal dimensions at work within, on the one hand, a repetition that resists the dominance of the Same, and, on the other, one that repeats it.

The repetition of an ideal essence, whether it be of philosophy or architecture, necessitates the repetition of that which cannot change. The essence of philosophy or architecture – an essence which shows itself within their *arché* and *telos* – has to endure. Its endurance must enact and take place within an ontology and temporality of stasis. The question of the essence therefore comes to be re-posed within that specific ontologico-temporal concatenation proper to stasis. The unstated premise at work here is that the name 'philosophy' – though this will be equally true of the name 'architecture' – names that essence. (This premise also operates in those cases where the essence is assumed even though it is yet to be revealed.) It is clear therefore that re-posing the question of philosophy or architecture – sanctioning a repetition beyond the Same – involves a reconsideration of naming as well as of time and existence. If the assumption, that the nature of philosophy and architecture is not determined by tradition (tradition as the determination in advance), is accepted then this gives rise to three important and difficult questions: How are the names philosophy and architecture to be understood? What do they name? and finally, How do they house tradition?

In a sense all these question are related in so far as they pivot around the problem of identity and hence of the ontology of identity. On the basis that the identity of philosophy, and equally of architecture, need not be reduced to the identity handed down by tradition and which is thus determined in advance, then this will mean that the repetition of an ideal essence is no longer under consideration as providing the means whereby the questions of identity and naming can be answered.[6] Furthermore it means that the borders established by tradition to fend off 'outside' claims to be philosophical or architectural, that were, by definition, not sanctioned by tradition, are no longer in place. Their displacement means that the question of identity is such that it can never be finally settled. It will remain open. The question 'what is philosophy?' will henceforth include within its range all those answers (answers which will be potentially or actually conflictual) that claim to be answers to the question. Philosophy, and by extension all such names, will name the continual attempt to provide an answer to the question of the identity, both named and demanded, within the question. The resistance to tradition here becomes the refusal to take over the answer to the question of identity. The taking over of what is handed down is the repetition of tradition; a repetition articulated within and by the Same. This will occasion the possibility of a rereading or rather a reworking of texts (that is objects of interpretation, books, paintings, sculptures, buildings, etc.) that comprise the history – the past – of the specific name in question. The temporality of this reworking is extremely complex since it involves a doubling of the object of interpretation within the act of interpretation. A way of understanding this particular interplay between time and interpretation is provided by the Freudian conception of *Nachträglichkeit*.

Rethinking naming, both the name and what is named, cannot be adequately undertaken without reference to the ontologico-temporal dimension within which it is situated. It has already been argued that what marked the repetition of the Same was an ideal essence articulated within an ontology and temporality of stasis; in other words within the premises of a philosophy of Being. The conception of naming alluded to above demands a different understanding of the relationship between time and existence. It follows from the claim that the question of identity remains an open question, that it is, by definition, impossible to understand within those categories which demand either an ideal essence or a unique and singular referent.

116

(This point can, of course, be extended to include teleology within it.) Furthermore if the answer to the question 'what is . . .?' necessitates an initial acceptance of that plurality of answers that are answers to the question in so far as they intend to be answers, then their clash will provide precisely what the name within the 'what is . . .?' question actually names. In sum therefore identity will henceforth be understood as the continual struggle to establish identity. It is at the very least because of the emphasis on the continuity of struggle (Heraclitean 'strife') and the plurality of possible answers (a plurality that is of necessity differential) that this particular understanding of identity and naming cannot be incorporated into a philosophy of Being; here, therefore, becoming triumphs over being. It is not surprising that Eisenman situates his own work within this triumph.

> architecture cannot be except as it continuously distances itself
> from its own boundaries; it is always in the process of becoming,
> of changing, while it is also establishing, institutionalising.[7]

It must be added that, in addition, the absence and impossibility of an ideal essence needs to be understood as resisting tradition. It also means that the ways in which tradition can be resisted are themselves plural and do not have an ideal essence. Were they to be single in nature then this would construct – if only because it necessitated – an ontological homology between each answer and the tradition. However there is more at play here than mere refusal.

The plurality and affirmation of heterogeneity that marks the refusal of tradition cannot be reduced to a simple negativity. Negativity is incorporated, located – houses still have to shelter – in what is at play here, but the experimentations and developments within art, architecture and philosophy that signal the affirmative within the present are themselves not explicable in terms of that negativity.[8] They are not the simple negation of dominance. This is because there is a necessary discontinuity between the interpretive apparatus handed down by tradition and experimentation. The avant-garde demands experimentation within philosophy, interpretation, etc., as well as in works of art, architecture and literature. Works situated within this discontinuity – the site of tension – are affirmative. They mark what could be described as the co-presence of negation and creativity. It goes without saying that this is the site of Eisenman's work. Its relation to tradition, to teleology, to there being an ideal essence of architecture, all enact this interpretive, conceptual and philosophical tension. Indeed it is precisely in these terms that it is possible to understand the developments within Eisenman's work. 'Scaling', 'decomposition' and 'dislocation', are all means whereby resistance and affirmation take place.

Eisenman's development as an architect is to be understood as the continual search for the means – both material and philosophical – to overcome the 'complacency' of tradition. He writes of House VI in the following terms;

> The design process of this house, as with all the architectural work in this book, intended to move the act of architecture from its complacent relationship with the metaphysic of architecture by reactivating its capacity to dislocate; thereby extending the search into the possibilities of occupiable form.[9]

In a recent interview he links the practice of dislocation to that of location thereby indicating how the question of the housing of tradition is to be understood. It is an answer that highlights the specificity of architecture though at the same time allowing it to be extended beyond the range of material habitation.

> architecture faces a difficult task: to dislocate that which it locates. This is the paradox of architecture. Because of the imperative of presence, the importance of the architectural object to the experience of the here and now, architecture faces this paradox as does no other discipline.[10]

While the importance of this particular paradox within architecture cannot be denied, it is also present within other areas of study, research and artistic practice. Location within architecture is repeated elsewhere in terms of the imperative of sense. No matter how disruptive or subversive a text or work of art may be the possibility of meaning must none the less inhere. The recognition of the necessary interplay between location and dislocation and the grounds for arguing for its extension are outlined by Eisenman in terms of function; that is in teleological terms.

> while a house today must still shelter, it does not need to symbolise or romanticise its sheltering function, to the contrary such symbols are today meaningless and merely nostalgic.[11]

It is precisely in these terms that it is possible to speak of the housing of tradition; that is a form of housing that contains within it the tradition of housing and yet is neither reducible to nor explicable in the terms set by that tradition. This is the paradox referred to earlier and which is marked by the interplay between dislocation and location.

Before trying to trace the consequences of this relationship beyond the borders of architecture it is essential to describe this paradox in greater detail. In fact it is only a paradox in the most conventional sense. What is at play here – and this is also true of all Eisenman's architectural strategies – is, to use his own formulation, an attempt 'to question the accumulated tradition of the institution of dwelling'. It is a questioning, however, that is neither theoretical nor abstract but which is enacted in the buildings themselves. It does not take place outside, as though there were an outside. Not only does this check the assumed and often unquestioned viability of the distinction between theory and practice, it brings to the fore the twofold need for a new aesthetics and, perhaps more importantly, a new conception of sensibility; understood, of course as part of a re-expression of experience.

Eisenman's plans for the Bio-Centrum at the University of Frankfurt provide a more concrete way of extending these pre- liminary comments. The Centre is being constructed for advance work in biological research. It is this 'use' that in the first instance determines the elements that are involved. They enact – architectur- ally – the codes used by the biologists in their own scientific work. Mark Wigley has, with great accuracy and care, described the consequences of the interplay between the code and the basic forms of the 'modernist blocks':

these intersections of modernist abstraction and an arbitrary figurative code, which act as the basic form, are then pro- gressively distorted to provide the functionally specific social and technical spaces. This distortion is effected by systemati- cally adding further shapes in a way that clashes – new shapes that come out of the same system of four basic shapes that they distort.[12]

This description both highlights the difficulty of Eisenman's recent work and indicates how the site – the project – is itself enacted in terms of an initial heterogeneity which is, by definition, incapable of synthesis. 'Distortion' is creative. The addition of new elements brought about a change in the aesthetic reception or response to the

119

earlier ones. The complexity of the interrelationship between the elements of the project means, as Wigley has argued, that the elements combine in a complex and unending 'dialogue'. There is therefore an original and multiple babble whose end is the absence of ends. The function rather than functionality has determined the initial structure. At the same time it not only sanctions but also determines its own distortion. This unpredictable and creative interconnection means that it is impossible to privilege any particular part of the 'project'. Indeed the criteria in terms of which evaluation, response, etc., would take place are themselves no longer straightforward. This decentring function is at the same time the subversion of the centrality and dominance of aesthetic and evaluative universality. While the project as an object of interpretation appears to be self-referential, located within that self-referentiality is the tradition, though now displaced and disseminated. It can no longer be thematized. It is no longer itself. It is repeated though it is no longer the same as itself. Homology has become heterology: not after the event but in its being reworked. This is precisely what is at stake in dislocation. Eisenman's own description of the strategy of allowing the interplay of a rethinking of biology and architecture attests to the creative potential of this location of dislocation; perhaps even a relocation that dislocates.

> As biology today dislocates the traditions of science, so the architecture of our Bio-Centrum project dislocates the traditions of architecture. While architecture's role is traditionally seen to be that of accommodating and representing function, this project does not simply accommodate the methods by which research into biological process is carried out, rather it articulates those processes themselves. Indeed it could be said its architecture is produced by those very processes.[13]

The inapplicability of function opens up a space that can no longer be filled by prediction. Prediction is the determination inscribed within the building that is generated by, and hence which also sustains, the dominance of use. The space, in opening the building, of robbing prediction of its predictive power, once again constructs the building as an object – an object of interpretation – which can never be self-referential. There is always the space that cannot be filled. The temporality of past, present and future understood within sequential continuity is no longer, even in this instance, viable. This state of affairs has already been noted when Eisenman writes of a design that extends 'the search into the possibilities of occupiable form'. The search opens out. The end cannot be predicted; though it can always, in the end, be located. Opening limits self-referentiality.

The question of self-referentiality is in addition linked to the paradox mentioned above. In Eisenman's House VI the presence of columns in the dining room that neither aid (in terms of function or decoration) nor hinder the intended activity, 'have according to the occupants of the house changed the dining experience in a real and more importantly unpredictable sense'.[14] The experience of dislocating, expressed in a light, almost glancing way in the above, opens up two related paths of investigation, if not of experimentation. The first concerns the question of experience, while the second concerns how the connection (if indeed connection is the right term) between homogeneity and heterogeneity is to be understood, since they neither involve nor take place within either an either/or, or a binary opposition. Understanding this 'connection', beyond the purview of these oppositions, involves rethinking the relationship between time and interpretation. (Because of the complexity of this problem all that will be presented here is a brief sketch of some of the issues involved.)

The ascription of heterogeneity and homogeneity within the object of interpretation take place within tradition. In other words the assumed homogeneity of the object of interpretation – and indeed of the philosophical enterprise itself – is both an assumption and a consequence of tradition understood as the determination in advance. This means that within the frame designated by tradition the homogeneous is original. Now, it is not the case that Eisenman's work enacts, or is to be understood in terms of its enacting, a countering move, that is one where the purported initial homogeneity is contrasted with or opposed by an initial heterogeneity. In either sense that would be to repeat the either/or. There is, in fact, an additional premise at work here.

The tradition, in its attempt to make the heterogeneous (for example the figurative) a secondary event that presupposed a homogeneous original event (for example the literal), always privileged the Same over diversity. The temporality here is straightforward; one precedes the other. Unity, identity, the Same, in other words any conception of the homogeneous or the self-identical, is positioned as being prior and thereby as having priority. However this priority, that which was prior, is, in Nietzsche's sense of the term, a 'fiction'. It is an attempt both to still becoming and to naturalize that which was always a secondary event. Naturalization here means that an event becomes redescribed (for the 'first' time). It appears to be original because the act and effect of this first 'redescription' has been forgotten. The forgetting therefore is fundamental both to the positioning of unity, the homogeneous, the Same, etc., as original, as well as accounting for how this particular designation is repeated in and as tradition. Overcoming forgetting is, here, the recognition of forgetting. It is thus that the object/event is reworked, giving rise to a mode of interpretation.

The result of accepting this description is that not only does the 'original' event become the site of heterogeneity, thereby calling into question any straightforward opposition between heterogeneity and homogeneity; the 'literal' becomes a trope, thereby undermining the distinction between the literal and the figural. Works, objects of interpretation have to be reworked and thereby reread and reinterpreted. The initial object/event/site of interpretation will no longer be the same as itself. Self-identity will have become fractured. The work will have been repeated. But now the repetition will no longer take place under the reign of the Same. Here, in the reworking the work will become repeated and therefore re-presented for the first time.

The obvious consequence of locating the heterogeneous as prior is that it provides a way of interpreting works in terms of the attempt to suppress (to forget) that original heterogeneity. (The philosophical enterprise associated with Derrida can, in part, be situated here.)[15] The suppression is demanded by tradition and yet it is precisely the activity of suppression that marks the unfolding, if not the very possibility, of the strategy enacted by the text/work/object of interpretation. There are, of course, those works which, rather than assuming an initial homogeneity and therefore necessitating that form of interpretation whereby that initial assumption is shown to be impossible, attempt to present, within the plurality of ways it is possible, the reality of an initial heterogeneity. Such works are affirmative. The works, writings, buildings of Peter Eisenman are in this sense affirmative.[16] This does, in a sense, mark their importance. They count as developments within architecture. They mark either a break or refusal of nihilistic repetition. It also opens up the problem of sensibility; of the experience of that which can no longer be assimilated nor understood in terms of the categories and concepts handed down as the unfolding of tradition. In sum this could be described as the problem of avant-garde experience.

BUILDING EXPERIENCE

The problem of experience must continually traverse any attempt to dwell on or to present either modernism or the present. For Walter Benjamin modernity was both marked and structured by a cleavage in experience. An irreconcilable split between *Erfahrung* and *Erlebnis*. The present therefore is, for Benjamin, marked by loss. The reality of tradition – of *Erfahrung* – is no longer at hand. What can no longer be experienced is the continuity of tradition. Fragmentation, the collapse of what Benjamin describes elsewhere as 'the community of listeners', divides the present. Within this conception of modernity fragmentation and loss are a result; a consequence. They take place after – in the wake of – an initial unity or community.[17] The present here repeats the 'fiction' that positions unity as preceding plurality.

The conception of experience that is linked to an interplay between presence and loss cannot adequately come to terms with what was called avant-garde experience. Here what is at stake is precisely the experience of that which cannot be incorporated within tradition. It is the experience of that which refuses to take over and hand on tradition but whose *façon d'être* cannot be reduced to this simple negativity. The other dimension is the affirmative. The experience of both negativity and affirmation is the experience of shock. It is not, however, the *Chockerlebnis* that Benjamin identifies in Baudelaire. It is not a shock that returns and which gestures at the no longer at hand. The shock here is that moment prior to the attempt to name, to describe, to situate. The temporal divide of silence and shock, a divide that both calls for philosophy and in which philosophy moves, is the demand created by an experience that is always as yet to be assimilated. The moment of silence, the shock, the 'as yet', is the avant-garde experience captured and presented, in outline, within the Burkean sublime.

In order to take these deliberations a step forward it is essential to take up – perhaps even to redeem – elements of Burke's aesthetics. The value of Burke lies in the importance that is attributed to experience. It is an emphasis that springs from the almost physiological foundation he gives to the aesthetic. None the less within Burke's body – the body as place – lies the possibility of drawing, withdrawing, specific elements that will be a fundamental to a conception of avant-garde experience.

These elements emerge with greatest clarity when Burke is attempting to distinguish between terror and delight as part of a general clarification of the sublime.

> When danger or pain press too nearly, they are incapable of giving any delight, and are simply terrible, but at *a certain distance*, and with *slight modification*, they may be and are delightful, as we every day experience.[18]   (My emphasis)

This particular passage is of central importance. It introduces time into experience. There is a more or less straightforward sense in which 'distance' can be seen to involve time. It would seem, on the surface at least, to be the temporality at work in Turner's painting *The Morning after the Storm*. Here the storm is over and its absence marked by the choppy water, the heavy condensation. Distance, however, does not mean simply 'after' or 'over'. Were it to be the case, then the temporality signalled in the passage from Burke, as well as in Turner's painting, would involve a backward and forward movement structured by the temporality of sequential continuity (with its related ontological considerations). That Burke can be read otherwise, and thus that Turner's painting demands more sophisticated and complex temporal and ontological considerations, provides a way forward. It is only in the wake of this adventure, perhaps only in its calmer waters, that it will be possible to take up the problem of avant-garde experience.

There is another problem that is at stake within the interpretation of architecture. It concerns the relationship between an architect's writings and the buildings themselves. Clearly both are objects of interpretation. The problem concerns their identity *qua* objects of interpretation and their difference within that designation. Experience will provide, in the case of Eisenman, a way of approaching this problem. It is perhaps not surprising that Eisenman's own writings nearly always refer to the experience of buildings. In so doing the event of experience and the experience of the event come to be rethought in their being reworked. Prior to taking up the interpretive possibilities implicit in Burke's conception of the sublime – possibilities stemming for the most part from the conception of temporality proper to the sublime – it is essential to note, once again, the centrality attributed by Eisenman to experience.

Writing about the work undertaken on a loft in New York he notes that:

> The structure of the loft space is understood piece by piece as one glimpses fragments of the integrating text. The entire space has the effect of being a rare, isolated glimpse of some larger, usually invisible context of vectors, currents and coded messages.[19]

This description needs to be read in relation to the already cited passage detailing the consequences of dining in House VI. There is, however, an additional important element that is introduced here and while it cannot be pursued it must, at least, be noted. It concerns the relationship between the visible and the invisible. The question that must be asked is what type of totality is the 'context' invoked by Eisenman. (A way towards understanding the complexity of this question may be provided by Burke's description of succession as conveying the artificial sublime.) The problem of the precise nature of the totality is also linked to the openness marking the overcoming of prediction.

The centrality of experience within Eisenman's writings does not mean that experience needs to be taken at face value. There are no experiences as such. Experience, as will be suggested, involves a complex doubling. The question within which a start can be made, is why it is that, when in Burke's terms, 'danger and pain press too nearly, they are incapable of giving any delight, and are more simply terrible'. The experience of 'danger and pain' is such that they are not within the actuality of their presence also objects of experience. There is therefore no sense in which there is a split such that it would then be possible to posit the reality of a recognition of experience that is coterminous with the experience itself. The body, fear and terror are present as one. The possibility of delight and hence of the sublime occurs only after 'a certain distance' and with 'certain modifications'. The terms 'distance' and 'modification' refer to a complex state of affairs.

The first element that must be noted is the causal relationship between the source of terror and the state of terror. Neither, however, can be said to exist as an object of experience in which there is any sense of reflexivity. The unity of body, fear, and terror predominates. The instant, as a consequence, must be understood as excluding objectivity. Now the distance that emerges is the breakdown of this unity in which the causal relation itself becomes an object of experience. Its becoming an object is founded on the emergence within it of alterity.

The same movement also occurs in the passage quoted (in fact misquoted) from Pope earlier in the *Enquiry*. The passage as cited by Burke reads:

> As when a wretch, who conscious of his crime
> Pursued for murder from his native clime,
> Just gains sure frontier, breathless pale amaz'd
> All gaze, all wonder.[20]

After which Burke adds:

> when we have suffered from some violent emotion, the mind
> naturally continues in something like the same conditions after
> the cause which first produced it ceases to function.[21]

While the argument Burke advances concerns the relationship between pleasure and pain in terms of which it will be possible to distinguish between delight and pleasure, it is the internal operation of these passages that is important here. They rehearse the movement that has already been noted. In the lines from Pope the sublime effect emerges only when the terror no longer dominates and is itself therefore taken as an object. The amazement marks the emergence of the object and therefore of the causal relation also as an object.

In both passages distance creates the conditions in which objectivity becomes possible. This distance, however, is not simple distance. It involves doubling. With terror, within the all-encompassing power of a 'violent emotion', there is no split between cause and effect such that the cause and the effect are themselves possible objects of experience. This possibility becomes real with – and within – the split itself. The split creates the distance within which the object becomes reworked and repeated such that it presents itself – *qua* object of experience – for the first time. For Burke, therefore, the sublime experience involves objects that are both the same and different. Amazement is the re-recognition that is original. Distance involves a repetition in which the object is reworked; hence the use of the term 'modification'. The distance is not one of simple chronology in that the object is not re-presented; it is never just given again within an atemporal sequence governed by similitude.[22] Hence the analogy with the Freudian conception of *Nachträglichkeit*.[23] The action engendering the sublime is deferred.

126

The doubling of the object within repetition in which it is presented again for the first time is not sublime. It is rather that the Burkean conception of the sublime allows for such a conception of the object to be understood. The use of Burke is not intended to establish an analogy between avant-garde experience and the sublime, but rather to provide the temporality proper to this particular form of experience. The analogy, if there is one, is between the experience of an object that resists understanding and explanation in the terms provided by tradition (understood as the determination in advance), and 'terror' or 'violent emotion'. It is only with distance in which the experience itself becomes an object of experience that it is possible to break through shock and overcome silence. (The work of art remains a step ahead.)

The way therefore that tradition comes to be known emerges out of the work – both the work as object and the work as the process of objectification within interpretation. The truth of the object of avant-garde experience will be to mark the distance it constructs between sensibility and understanding. The understanding here is not the one equipped with regulative ideas. Understanding is the process that emerges out of sensibility. It is the understanding that is involved in the recognition of 'terror' and 'violent emotions' as objects of experience. Understanding will contain sensibility since it occasions delight. The postulated existence of regulative ideas is, when removed from the realm of the cognitive, the analogue of tradition. It is the resistance to them, transgression, felt within avant-garde experience, that comes to be grasped by the understanding, in its having found objectivity. The grasp is never complete.

It is within the domain of the avant-garde that the heterological will be affirmative. The re-reading of the tradition in which an-original heterogeneity is rediscovered for the first time will involve a particular conception of philosophical activity; the task of affirmation. It is clear that such a conception of interpretation bears the same relation to tradition as Eisenman's 'buildings' do to the tradition of architecture.

WORKS WITH OPEN DOORS

Eisenman's work, the experience of that work, the philosophy demanded by it, opens up the need to think philosophically beyond the recuperative and nihilistic unfolding of tradition. Tradition is

127

housed – since there is no pure beyond – but the housing of tradition takes place within a plurality of possibilities that can no longer be foreclosed by function, by teleology or by the aesthetics of form. Works with open doors must be what is henceforth demanded by philosophy and architecture.

NOTES

1 I have discussed Descartes' architectural 'metaphor' in relation to Derrida's writings on architecture in 'Derrida, architecture and philosophy', *Architectural Design*, vol. 58, no. 3/4, 1988.

2 R. Descartes, *Discours de la méthode* (Edition Vrin, Paris 1979, pp. 59–60).

3 R. Descartes, 'Meditations', in *Oeuvres Philosophiques*, ed. F. Alquié (Garnier, Paris, 1963).

4 R. Descartes, *Discours de la méthode*, p. 74.

5 The question 'what is philosophy?' takes the place of all questions of the 'what is . . .?' form. It is a question that seeks the identity of that which is named within the question. Consequently architecture, painting, sculpture, and even interpretation and aesthetics, could all come to be posed within this form of questioning. This point is outlined in slightly greater detail further on.

6 It is of course not just the essence which is in question here. The point could equally be made in relation to a singular and unique referent that was not expressed in terms of having an essence. This possibility means that what is, in fact, at stake is the necessity that what the name names is at the same time homogeneous and excludes the possibility of an initial heterogeneity. It is precisely this twofold necessity that contemporary philosophical writing, especially that associated with Derrida, has shown to be impossible.

7 P. Eisenman, *Houses of Cards* (Oxford University Press, New York, 1987), pp. 182–3.

8 The affirmative – a term 'borrowed' from Nietzsche and Derrida – has been redeployed here in order to describe/locate those experimentations within the present that demand forms of philosophical, aesthetic, political, physical responses that have not been handed down by tradition. In this sense the affirmative becomes a way of redeeming the avant-garde.

9 Eisenman, op. cit., p. 169.

10 P. Eisenman, 'The Blue Line Text', in *Architectural Design*, vol. 58, no. 7/8, August 1988.

11 ibid., p. 172.

12 P. Johnson and M. Wigley, *Deconstructive Architecture* (Museum of Modern Art, New York, 1988), p. 56.

13 P. Eisenman, 'Bio-Centrum Frankfurt', in *Architectural Design*, vol. 59, no. 1/2, 1989.

14 Eisenman, *Houses of Cards*, p. 181.

15 I have attempted to sketch this interconnection in 'Deconstruction and art/the art of deconstruction', in C. Norris and A. Benjamin, *What is Deconstruction?* (Academy Editions, London, 1988).

16 While he does not use the term 'affirmative', Alain Pélissier provides an excellent analysis of Eisenman's work, and especially of *House El Even Odd*, that attempts to identify what has been designated by it. See 'Microcosmos', in *Cahiers du CCI*, no. 1, *Architecture: récits, figures, fictions* (AA, Paris, 1986).

17 For a more detailed discussion of this point and of Benjamin's work in general see chapters 9 and 10.

18 E. Burke, *A Philosophical Enquiry into the Origin of our Ideas of the Sublime and the Beautiful*, ed. J. T. Boulton (University of Notre Dame Press, Notre Dame, 1968), p. 40.

19 P. Eisenman and F. Yorgancioglu, 'Tom's loft, New York,' in *Architectural Design*, vol. 58, no. 7/8, 1988, p. 35.

20 Burke, op. cit., p. 34.

21 ibid., p. 35.

22 The problem of the relationship between writings and buildings can be, at least in part, resolved by the recognition that Eisenman in his writings is writing after and before the experience. The writings cannot set the conditions of possibility for experience. The writings do not come to be experienced as buildings. The writings mark the object. One can never be the other. And yet, of course, they are mutually informing. They both demand a different understanding of experience and of the act of interpretation. Their relationship will always be marked by the heterological.

23 I have dealt with the relationship between *Nachträglichkeit* and interpretation in considerable detail in 'Translating Origins: Philosophy and Psychoanalysis' in L. Venuti (ed.), *Rethinking Translation: Discourse, Subjectivity and Ideology* (Routledge, London, 1992).

8
PLURALISM, THE COSMOPOLITAN AND THE AVANT-GARDE

At present one of the major philosophical questions to be answered concerns the nature of the present. It is precisely in terms of this question that it becomes possible to situate the plurality of contemporary artistic production. It takes place at the present. Even here a distinction needs to be drawn between what is produced at the present and the totality of what is offered for interpretation. Pluralism invades if not defines both spheres. However the possibility of pluralism was always a *risk*. The history of philosophy can be understood as an attempt to rid itself of that risk; to quell its disruptive force. However there is more at play here than just philosophy. In addition it would be fair to describe the majority of the human sciences as incorporating the same desire and therefore as being driven in part by an attempt to exclude that type of difference that threatens totality. This attempt can be enacted either by simple exclusion, or in terms of the more sophisticated reduction of the different to a variant of the same, which has the obvious consequence of effacing the specificity of difference.[1] These are complex issues and care is needed.

Any attempt to delimit or define the nature of the present is constrained to provide, either implicitly or explicitly, the criteria whereby such acts can be justified. Description and definition seem to demand legitimation. The problem that marks this present is the crisis of legitimation. Julia Kristeva in giving her answer to the question of what is post-modernism describes the present – the time of writing – in the following terms;

Never before in the history of humanity has this exploration of the limits of meaning taken place in such an unprotected manner, and by this I mean without religious, mystical, or any other justification.

There seem to be predominantly two ways in which it is possible to respond to this present. One is to search for new forms of legitimation.[2] Within the world of art this often takes the form of a recourse to tradition; to nationalism and, perhaps perversely, via appeals to universality. In opposition to this nostalgia there is the possibility of an affirmation of the present. In the place of tradition would stand a thinking of the avant-garde; in the place of nationalism there would be the cosmopolitan, and finally the place of universality would cede to pluralism. In privileging conflict, and therefore in allowing the dissensus at work in these oppositions to take precedence over any possible consensus (even were that to be possible), a stand is being taken that further delimits and defines the present – this present – the time of this writing. Not only must dissensus be described, there must also be the gradual attempt to redeploy the terms community, cosmopolitan, difference, within the ambit opened by the absence of a transcendent truth. Truth has not been negated. It is rather that its capacity to police and control has been displaced. Absence and displacement need to be thought beyond Hegelianism. The Hegelianism in question here is not the one uncovered by a reading that concentrates on difference, thereby reading Hegel against himself, but the one that announces the actuality of the Absolute and hence the potential overcoming of conflict, dissensus and difference. Since difference within the Absolute is only possible if it is construed as a variant and therefore could never exist so that difference could of itself involve a necessary and inherent differentiality. Difference as anoriginal presence and as differential is unthinkable within the Hegelian philosophy of the absolute.

TRADITION – AVANT-GARDE

The initial difficulty in positing this distinction resides in determining a specific semantic range for the term 'tradition'. In her recent study, *Has Modernism Failed?*, Suzi Gablik argues that the force of the question posed by the book's title 'turns, finally, on the question of whether it is appropriate to reject tradition'.[3] What is this tradition that may or may not be rejected? For Gablik, as she suggests elsewhere in the book, it is what gives 'us our values'. The intriguing and significant element in this formulation is the use of the pronouns 'us' and 'our'. Before returning to them it is essential to dwell on tradition, for what is already clear is that tradition, in order for it to have the function that she attaches to it, must exclude any internal conflict that would work to undermine its posited unity and thereby its repetition. The recourse to tradition therefore becomes a recourse to aesthetic values which in being handed down come to be handed on. It is therefore an aesthetic in which the values are universal, 'absolute' and to that extent ahistorical. (Indeed their universality has to be assumed to be necessary.) Clearly they are handed down within history but they fail to be determined by that history because they function to legitimize claims concerning 'excellence' etcetera made within that historical period; within a specific historical present. The problem addressed by Gablik is that 'our' present has refused to take over what tradition has tried to hand on. She provides a precise formulation of this state of affairs:

> Our present situation is one in which art, having abdicated any connection with a transcendent realm of being, has lost its charter as a world view – as a way of interpreting either nature or history.[4]

Her argument is that pluralism has undermined the possibility of distinguishing from within the range of works of art what she calls the 'acceptable' from the 'unacceptable'. The growing impossibility of legitimizing selection is compounded by what for her could be described as the actuality of the secularization of art.

Gablik's response modernity is not new. It is possible to argue that within certain elements of Walter Benjamin's work the present was understood as a locus of loss. It was the site where tradition could no longer be handed on.[5] Furthermore when Heidegger describes the present as 'indifferent to Being',[6] he, too, construes the present as the site of an absence; here present as the locus of a lack. For Gablik, overcoming loss involves recourse to tradition. In other words inaugurating the end of 'our present situation' via a rearticulation of tradition. The real problem with this position is that it is still unclear what tradition is. That it is a unity that is repeated and whose function is to legitimize follows from the general argument. And yet it cannot be just the rules that exist at any one time, for this would preclude posing the preliminary question of how those rules came to exist. Furthermore it also fails to deal with the larger problem of what a tradition 'embodies'.

Gablik does not adequately address the problem of tradition's content since she is only ever really concerned with the consequence stemming from the absence of its legitimizing force. In opposition to the approach to the treatment of tradition that her book offers, it could be suggested that what a tradition embodies is precisely that conflict that allows for a particular set of rules to be dominant. These rules, however, do not determine in any absolute or universal sense either the nature of art or what would count within a given historical period as either acceptable or unacceptable art. This distinction therefore would always involve shifting ground. Tradition, rather than being either a positive term delimiting history or a negative term describing that against which innovation or experimentation is to be judged, becomes the site of a conflict whose aim is the search for legitimation. The impossibility of unity would thereby be accepted. In other words pluralism would always be a *risk*. It is the *risk* of difference that is always already inscribed within universality. It is of course in terms of the attempt to shore up universality that Gablik's pronouns can be situated. Both 'us' and 'our' function as universal, collective terms. If it is tradition that gives 'us our values' then in a very straightforward sense the 'us' is constituted as a unity by the taking over of tradition. Furthermore if tradition gives us 'our' values then the tradition must be non-conflictual – that is articulated in terms of a projected consensus – in order that the universality and collective singularity of the 'our' be both established and maintained.

The work of Jean-François Lyotard has provided a different way of describing the present. It is one that calls into question what could be described as the interplay of interdependence between the unity of tradition, consensus and universality. Post-modernism, however, while involving pluralism, does not give rise to the inability to judge. It rather re-poses the question of what judgement, in this instance, within aesthetics actually is. This is a question that must in the end lead to an attempt to reformulate pluralism. Moreover the advent of post-modernism allows for a distinction to be drawn – within interpretation – between artistic practices that aim at repeating that 'interplay of interdependence', and ones that via experimentation can no longer be accounted for within the terms set by tradition. It is in the movement beyond a mere negative response to tradition that the avant-garde can be situated. While recognizing that the term post-modern has become problematic,[7] it can still be said to allude to the reality of the present. This 'reality' is gestured at in Lyotard's question:

> can we continue today to organise the multitude of events that come to us from the world, both human and non-human, by subsuming them under the idea of a universal history of mankind?[8]

While the precise object of Lyotard's question is history, it can none the less be generalized to cover any specific totality. If multiplicity cannot be understood or interpreted in terms of a single determination, where does that leave the practice of an art criticism that can no longer depend upon universal values? Is there an artistic practice and an art criticism whose temporality is not reducible to the temporality of tradition? Dwelling on what is involved in answering these questions must wait. None the less it is already clear that the conflict that marks the debate concerning the presence or absence of what Kristeva called 'transcendent truth', or what Lyotard calls 'grand narratives', can only be understood and accounted for in terms of a theory of dissensus; one which recognized the absence of a final resolution. In other words justice can only be done to dissensus within pluralism.

NATIONALISM – THE COSMOPOLITAN

Perhaps one of the most important and, it must be added, inherently disturbing responses to the reality of pluralism or post-modernism has been the attempt to define value within a framework established by national identity. This would mean that tradition then became articulated in terms of the interconnection between the universal and the national. What would become important therefore would be the ability of a particular artist either to repeat and develop the themes that made up the national heritage or to give expression to a particular aspect – be it geographical or transcendental – of national character. The linking of tradition and nation would provide the grounds for a critical exclusion or inclusion; one sanctioning the promulgation of a canon of national artists. Admission to the canon would reside in the work's capacity to further artistic national identity.

One of the most dramatic attempts to join nation and art is found in Nietzsche's *The Birth of Tragedy*. The first element to note in this, one of Nietzsche's earliest works, was his sense of the present as a locus of loss. What Nietzsche hoped for from the rebirth of German music was 'the rebirth of German myth'. This rebirth was to be occasioned by art. A rediscovery of the essentially German would lead to an elimination of the foreign. Nietzsche's early work involves an argument for the national against the international; for the nation as unity and against the nation as itself plural and therefore cosmopolitan. It is vital to reiterate the fact that the conception of nation involved here is one whose tradition is unified and therefore it is one that has an essential unity of its own.

> We think so highly of the pure and vigorous core of the German character that we dare expect of it above all others this elimination of the forcibly implanted foreign elements and consider it possible that the German spirit will return to itself.[9]

In Nietzsche's case the interconnection was slightly complicated by the necessity of the mediating 'Dionysian bird'. Indeed it is fortunate that in his later writings the reworking of the Dionysian allowed him to drop all positive references to national identity, where the nation and hence the identity were understood in terms of an essential unity. In fact as his philosophical work developed, the nation and in particular the German nation became figures. They were shown to be constructs, part of the ruse which, when taken as natural, seemed to form the bedrock of western philosophy and history. Breaking this bedrock allowed art to escape the restricting force of the unity and hence 'falsity' of national identity. One consequence of this is that it allowed Nietzsche to present a philosophical analysis of his break with Wagner. In addition his recognition of the impossibility of a 'rebirth' and therefore of a recovery of the past gave rise to what became called 'genealogy'. In sum it was the possibility of breaking the link between art and nation that was instrumental to the development of his most important and original philosophical work.

The significance of the break emerges with perhaps its greatest clarity from the now famous section 377 of *The Gay Science*. The opposition established by Nietzsche is between the nationalist and the modern. It is expressed with Nietzsche's usual force:

> We who are homeless [*Wir Heimatlosen*] are too manifold and mixed racially in our descent, being 'modern men' [*moderne Menschen*] and consequently do not feel tempted to participate in the mendacious racial self-admiration and racial indecency

136

that parades in Germany today as a sign of German thinking and that is doubly false and obscene among the people of the historical sense.[10]

The object of Nietzsche's vehemence is the Germany of 1882. However the significance of the term 'Heimatlosen' should not be overlooked. It is not just descriptive of the homeless, it is also a term of abuse for oppositional figures who were thought to have no sense of the nation. The self-description 'Wir Heimatlosen' marks the refusal of the refuge of both home and nation – a refusal that creates the frame for an understanding of his description of the modern.

Now even though it is of 'man' – 'modern man' – it can be extended in order to develop an understanding of the present. At home in Nietzsche's modernity is a concept of unity that refuses essentialism. It is for this reason that it provides the possibility of thinking a social present which, while a totality, now has no essential cultural unity. The present is to use Nietzsche's terms 'mixed racially' – and of course culturally.

Part of the process as well as the result of this mixing is the inadequacy of national boundaries to delimit the specificity of either the object of interpretation or the nature of interpretation itself. They have become cosmopolitan. The cosmopolitan is of course another way of talking about pluralism. It is always important to be able to rewrite pluralism in terms of the cosmopolitan. For it allows for the recognition that the present is one in which there is always already a play of the multiplicity of racial and cultural voices, where the national and international exchange and interchange.[11] A strife named as harmony.

A return to the singularity of the nation is an attempt to universalize and thereby to deny this play of difference. It is precisely within this locus that some of Peter Fuller's recent work can be situated, and thereby understood for what it is. He writes, for example, that John Piper's painting

affirms that though life in the twentieth century necessarily involves a changed vision, and changed values, it need not, or perhaps *ought* not, to involve some absolute, philistine rupture with the achievement of *our cultural past*, nor yet with art's capacity to give pleasure through decoration.[12] (My emphasis)

The culture in question is 'English culture'. What is established here is the link between national identity and art in terms of the link between

English culture and what Fuller calls 'decoration'. Opposed to this is Nietzsche's European for whom there is no desire for any return. There is a plural present to be affirmed. The problem with the expression 'our cultural past' is that what is referred to by the 'our' in the past no longer makes up the totality of the present. The plurality of the present does not have a past in any straightforward or obvious sense. A further consequence of this is that the plurality of the present renders impossible any recourse to Fuller's 'Englishness'; except of course the recourse that springs from the actuality of political nationalism.

UNIVERSALITY – PLURALISM

Is the distinction between universality and pluralism a simple either/or? Pluralism is not liberalism. Moreover it is not the confused and contradictory claim that asserts the impossibility of judgement and is therefore committed to the equal acceptability and viability of all ethical, political and aesthetic positions. Pluralism involves the recognition that judgement has to take place despite the absence of universal criteria for judgement. (The contemporary problem of judgement is announced within this paradox. Any attempt to resolve it will necessitate recourse to an ontology that can sustain paradox.) The two fundamental elements of universality at work here are unity and the essence. Pluralism does not deny the existence of unities. It is rather that it calls into question the possibility of grounding unity in terms of an essence. A unity – be it a nation or an object of interpretation – becomes the site of the belonging together of differences. In the case of the nation this means accepting the reality of the multicultural and the multiracial in conjunction with the internationalization of the nation. References to the nation, to the boundary, become interventions, pragmatic moves within a game that posits unity. Here the nation has become gestural. It is not that the nation as an inclusive (and hence exclusive) unity is ever posited in itself. The nation names the differences that constitute it. This gives rise to the necessity of developing a theory of naming that allows for the referent to be the site of what can be called semantic differential plurality;[13] in other words, the site of different and perhaps even conflictual meanings. Within any situation one meaning is always taken up – it becomes determinant – but the semantic potential of differential plurality can never be excluded.

In the case of the object of interpretation this means accepting the object as that which sustains the possibility – be it actual or potential – of conflicts of interpretation. Within such conflicts a great deal can be at stake. This can only be investigated by bringing out and analysing the presuppositions at play within any one specific interpretation. The object of interpretation can never be redeemed and hence unified within the domain of one exclusive interpretive pronouncement. There can be no truth about the object because the object contains no single truth about itself. The consequence of this is that it is only by removing truth from its position of conceptual dominance and bringing the practice of interpretation to the fore that a progressive, plural art criticism will become possible. It is precisely in terms of this possibility that the political dimension within such criticism is to be identified. Pluralism accepts the reality of the many and in so doing is concerned to establish criteria of judgement that do justice to the many. The future of judgement takes place without the One.

There is no simple choice between universality and pluralism; it is not an either/or. The plural must be understood as differential. Universality on the other hand is constrained to exclude difference. It refuses to think the possibility of difference; except as an unwelcome deviation from the Same. Universality cannot think the plural, and thus cannot account for the experimentations and innovations that mark the present. It is only by focusing on the interrelationships between difference, post-modernism and pluralism that it is possible to differentiate pluralism from liberalism. The liberal dilemma concerns conflicting truth claims, where each claim tends toward universality. Liberalism becomes the attempt to do justice to the irreconcilable. Pluralism on the other hand involves the recognition that justice concerns the relationship between the irreconcilable. It demands therefore, a reconciliation to the irreconcilable. (In terms of the societal implications of this philosophical position, what would emerge is a conception of civil society as the site in which reconciliation to the irreconcilable took place with the state as that which facilitated it. Difference and conflict would be taken as a 'norm'. This would involve a further distinction between different types of conflict; those which subordinated and those which did not. Clearly this formulation is too simplistic and perhaps too trenchant. None the less it does at least delimit a further philosophical task.)

Finally, the refusal of pluralism that has been located in the work of Gablik and Fuller initially looks as though it involves a confusion between liberalism and pluralism. This apparent confusion, however, is an attempt to reduce pluralism to liberalism. The consequence of this is that it serves to preclude the possibility of a conception of the plural in which difference is differential. In other words, the reduction of pluralism to liberalism equates the plural with pure difference and hence with having a content in which each element would be the same, in the sense of being of the same value. Difference would have been synthesized. It is only by resisting this reduction that it is possible to understand difference as differential. It is precisely this aspect of pluralism, which, as has already been argued, 'grounds' justice, allows for criticism and occasions the possibility of a revaluation of value in terms of the distinction between affirmation and repetition[14] – a distinction which is itself a repetition of that noted earlier between experimentation and tradition. Pluralism takes place in relation to but beyond the interplay of unity and the essence. It facilitates and allows the multitude of voices that announce their presence as the present.

NOTES

1 It is precisely the relationship between exclusion and inclusion that should figure within any attempt, today, to interpret the Enlightenment heritage. A step along this path may be provided from the consequences of having tried to establish a dialogue between Kant's writings on history and politics and Hannah Arendt's rarely studied though fundamental paper 'Aufklärung and Judenfrage', in *Die verborgene Tradition* (Suhrkamp, Frankfurt, 1976).

2 For another response to the growing conservative opposition to pluralism and post-modernism see Jean-François Lyotard and Jacob Rogozinski, 'La Police de la Pensée', in *L'Autre Journal*, December 1985.

3 S. Gablik, *Has Modernism Failed?* (Thames & Hudson, London, 1984), p. 118.

4 ibid., p. 80.

5 I have tried to analyse Benjamin's conception of tradition in Chapter 10, Tradition and experience: Walter Benjamin's 'On Some motifs in Baudelaire'.

6 This description should be pursued through the second volume of Heidegger's Nietzsche study, *Nietzsche, Zweiter Band*, (Neske, Pfullingen, 1961).

7 For a discussion of what are some of the things at stake in any description of post-modernism see Jean-François Lyotard, *Le Postmoderne expliqué aux enfants* (Galilée, Paris, 1984). Indeed post-modernism here has been used in Lyotard's sense.

8 Jean-François Lyotard, 'Histoire universelle et différences culturelles', in *Critique*, May 1985, p. 559.

9 F. Nietzsche, *The Birth of Tragedy*, trans. W. Kaufman (Vintage Books, New York, 1967), p. 138.

10 F. Nietzsche, *The Gay Science*, trans. W. Kaufman (Vintage Books, New York, 1974), p. 338. (*Die fröhliche Wissenschaft*, in *Friedrich Nietzsche Werke 11*, ed. K. Schlechta (Verlag Ullstein, Frankfurt, 1976), p. 251.

11 John Rajchman has discussed the international dimension of post-modernism in 'Postmodernism in a nominalist frame', *Flash Art*, no. 137, November–December 1987.

12 P. Fuller, *Images of God* (Hogarth Press, London, 1985), p. 96. My critical comments are directed at Fuller and not at Piper.

13 I have attempted this task in *Translation and the Nature of Philosophy: A New Theory of Words* (Routledge, London, 1989).

14 Derrida uses this distinction to discuss the architectural practice of Bernard Tschumi. See J. Derrida, 'Point de Folie', trans. Kate Linker, *AA Files*, no. 12, 1988. I have written an introductory overview of Derrida's work on architecture, 'Derrida, architecture and philosophy', *Architectural Design*, vol. 58. no. 3/4, 1988.

9
THE DECLINE OF ART:
BENJAMIN'S AURA

The difficulty with Benjamin's oeuvre is division. A division that takes place within the oeuvre itself. However there is nothing remarkable in the capacity to trace the marks of differences that divide a complete works, thereby establishing a war of interpretive worlds. Nor is the presence of difference in itself the only significant moment marking the text. For all intents and purposes the Benjamin who wrote about Karl Krauss, Eduard Fuchs, and who wrote 'A Small History of Photography', need not be the same Benjamin who wrote 'On some motifs in Baudelaire', 'The storyteller' and 'On the concept of history'. Indeed the difference gives rise to choice and selection. Scholem,[1] Roberts[2] and Eagleton[3] expressed their choice. Other and at times more sophisticated, commentators[4] have attempted to establish thematic and structural connections within the works as a whole. The history of choice and the choices made remain to be told.

Any attempt to establish a unity from a series of texts as clearly diverse as Benjamin's will always be thwarted from the start. Benjamin will never be canonical but has rather emerged as the site of different canons. Canons like cannons, wage war. One is condemned to choose and hence to stand by a particular canon. The complete works are the site of an irretrievable difference. The proper name is merely the object of different appropriations. It is only by the side of one cannon with the other in its sights that Benjamin's name may stand aloft and be deployed in war. Benjamin's name – though this is true for all proper names – is the site of war. He is neither father nor son. He has no one legitimate heir and is heir to no one tradition. The name has become the recitation of war and thus the site of an impossible unity. And if the proper name and its unifying, if not recuperative, power is the meta-narrative *par excellence*, then the proper name 'Benjamin' has become the exemplar of the predicament in which both contemporary philosophy and criticism find themselves. The concern of this chapter is with the interplay between this predicament and Walter Benjamin. Another way of expressing this concern would be to determine what is living and what is dead in Benjamin's thought, where life and death are linked not just to survival and the capacity to live on but also to the conception of time within which they are articulated. Endurance and what endures do not simply take place within time, but rather there is a temporality proper to endurance itself. The relationship between time and interpretation is one of the most important problems facing criticism and philosophy.

The image of the photograph and the philosophical and interpretive problems that it raises will provide a way into this concern. However, close as we may be to Benjamin's name, we are still some distance from his actual texts. I want to start a trek back to them via a way opened by Roland Barthes', important paper on photography, 'Le Troisième Sens.'[5] It should be noted that this particular text has a subtitle that marks the specificity given to the text. However it is a specificity that in being isolated is automatically transgressed. The subtitle is 'Notes de recherche sur quelques photogrammes de S. M. Eisenstein'. The transgression could almost be described as an obvious consequence of the text's strategy in so far as *le troisième sens* both as a text and a concept within a text cannot be limited by the contours of any particular research programme. Even though Barthes' paper is well known it is still worthwhile giving an outline of the three domains of meaning it proposes in order that the disturbing force of the third be grasped contextually.

The first level of meaning is one of pure information which, as Barthes states, is the level of communication and which can be analysed in terms of a 'semiotic of the message'. The second is a 'symbolic level'. At play on this level are the symbols and rituals unfolding in the photograph itself. The level and the method of analysis it demands are described by Barthes in the following terms:

> The second level, in its totality (*ensemble*) is one of significa-
> tion. Its mode of analysis will be a more elaborate semiotic than
> the first. A second or neo-semiotic open not only to the science
> of the message, but also to the sciences of the symbol (psycho-
> analysis, economics, dramatic art).[6]

The second level therefore may be included under and explained by those sciences concerned with symbolization. On this level, the object of analysis has a material existence whose materiality is purely contextual and thus whose temporality is inscribed within its contextual existence. Time and being are in this instance reducible to the place (the place and context of meaning) and hence involve a temporality and ontology of the instant, that is a temporality and ontology of delimited and finite existence.

Having proposed these two 'obvious' levels of meaning and the mode of analysis proper to them Barthes poses the straightforward though provocative question, 'Is that all?' to which he gives the immediate reply, 'no, for I cannot detach myself from the image.' He remains confronting – or in confrontation with – the work of art. Implicit in Barthes' text is the possibility of moving from the photograph to the work of art because the presence of '*le troisième sens*' can be understood as the *sine qua non* of a work of art being a work of art. This implicit possibility is what facilitates the transgression of the limit proposed by the text's subtitle.

The third meaning, the 'that' to which Barthes remains attached, he calls, following Kristeva, 'signifiance'. Its disturbing nature is signalled in Barthes' claim that it opens the field of meaning to *'l'infini du langage'*. Further reasons why the third meaning or 'the obtuse meaning' (*'le sens obtus'*) has such disturbing consequences are stated by Barthes thus:

> In sum what the obtuse meaning troubles and sterilises is metalanguage (*critique*). Several reasons can be given why. First of all, the obtuse meaning is discontinuous, indifferent to history (*l'histoire*) and to the obvious meaning (as the signification of history); this dissociation has the effect of a counter-nature (*contre-nature*) or a least a distancing with respect to the referent (from the 'real' as a nature, instancy, reality).[7]

The third meaning is not present in the work of art in any obvious or manifest sense, nor is it reducible either to the presentation of the literal content or to the presentation of symbols. The immediate difficulty is to give a voice to the third meaning. Examples used by Barthes in his discussion of the Eisenstein stills always seem to concern an element that, while attracting the eye and demanding interpretation, none the less seems to resist an exhaustive explanation. The description of 'signifiance' will therefore involve dis-placing the possibility of attributing to the work of art a complete and determinant meaning. 'Signifiance' is a primordial presence occasioning, if not grounding, the possibility of the continuity of interpretation and hence of reinterpretation. Furthermore, it is a presence that can never be included within the temporality of the instant and therefore the ontology of place, both of which involve the conceptions of time and being proper to the context.

'Signifiance' is linked therefore to survival and the capacity of the object of interpretation to live on. The explanatory exhaustion made possible by the first two levels of meaning, and which are often demanded by the cultural historian, is made impossible by the continual presence of 'signifiance'. While the work is always a cultural commodity, and therefore always an object of exchange, its capacity for reinterpretation means that it also has a related though separate existence as an object of actual and potential interpretation. Even though these are two related levels of existence and, furthermore, even though one may inform the other, one is not reducible to the other. This irreducibility – and hence capacity for semantic survival – I would like to call the aura. I have adopted this term both to differentiate it for all the implications of Barthes' understanding of 'signifiance' (for in the long run there are a number of problems inherent in it) and to link it critically to Benjamin's conception of the aura. The ambivalence in Benjamin's understanding of the auratic, and the way he attempts to resolve it, both touch on the issues at play in what has been called semantic survival.

The difficulty with Benjamin's writings on the aura is a lack of consistency. There is no doubt that there is a continuity as regards the question of whether or not the aura has been lost; however there is an oscillation, as Buck-Morss has pointed, out between a negative and positive response to the loss.[8] H. W. Puppe, in his discussion of the negative response, sums it up in the following way:

> loss of aura, severing the links with which art is tied to cult and ritual, the end of the autonomy of art in the age of the mass production of images. The change of the role of art, its production and reception, are seen as a paradigm, a symptom of the larger changes in society as a whole, and these, in turn are manifested in new ways of perception and manners of thinking.[9]

The presentation of the positive response which appears in

146

Benjamin's important paper on art and technology is couched in terms of freedom and the democratic access to art that is afforded by, as well as being a consequence of, photography and film. In order to deliberate further on Benjamin's understanding of the aura one or two instances of his use of the term need to be identified. The importance of this contextualization of the concept stems from the fact that it gives rise to the possibility of tracing the analogies and examples of the auratic in his writings. The first example comes from 'The work of art in the age of mechanical reproduction' and the second from 'On some motifs in Baudelaire'.

> The concept of aura ... may be usefully illustrated with reference to the aura of natural objects. We define the aura of the latter as the unique phenomenon of distance, however close it may be. If while resting on a summer's afternoon, you follow with your eyes a mountain range on the horizon or a branch, you experience the aura of the mountain or of the branch. This image makes it easy to comprehend the social basis of the contemporary decay of the aura.[10]

The second broadens the conception of the aura and links it quite dramatically to the experience of the other, and thereby introduces both the intersubjective as well as the ethical into the conception of the aura:

> looking at someone carries the implicit expectation that our look will be returned by the object of our gaze. When this expectation is met (which, in the case of thought processes, can apply equally to the look of the eye of the mind as to a glance pure and simple), there is an experience of the aura to the fullest extent.[11]

This latter description of the aura takes us to the face of the other, and, as has already been suggested, introduces an ethical dimension (or at the very least the possibility of an ethical dimension) into what have hitherto been straightforward questions of aesthetics.

The decline of the aura is marked in the experience of the natural, of the produced and of the intersubjective realm of the face to face. Experience is in a state of decay. However, there is an intriguing problem concerning experience. To talk of a decline in the capacity to experience what there is can have at least two different meanings. The first is that there is a decline in the capacity to experience what there is and the second is that the object declines even within the plenitude of experience.

A decline in the capacity to experience is precisely the problem identified by Benjamin as the consequence of the commodification of art coupled to a general estrangement and alienation from an existence marked by authenticity. Connected, however, to this sense of decline is the second sense. For Benjamin, the object of experience, be it the face or the work of art, is losing its ability to look back. The two possible understandings of a decline in capacity to experience are linked, because they are both mediated by time. Raising the theme of time is not intended as an attempt to write of Benjamin's concern with Proust nor is it to investigate the more general question raised in his writings concerning the relationship between time and memory, rather it is intended to bring out the major problem in his conception of the aura. The problem raised by the aura is not as Benjamin conceived it, namely in terms of the aura's continued existence, but rather concerns the temporality proper to the aura itself. It goes without saying that these two points are related; none the less attempting to resolve the problem of temporality will indicate a way whereby the problem of the aura's continued existence can also be resolved.

The complexity of the problem of the relationship between time and aura stems from the fact that solving the problem necessitates making substantial claims about the way in which the relationship between time and being has been structured in the history of philosophy. Philosophy, it can be argued, is marked by a series of irreconcilable differences between varying conceptions of the relationship between time and being. Within this variety there are two major antagonistic positions. One of the major difficulties, however, is that this difference is often occluded due to the way in which the history of philosophy is understood. A final point needs to be noted in relation to the general problem of the relationship between time and being. The relationship informs both philosophy and theology and, as there is yet to be a systematic attempt to differentiate between them on any fundamental or structural level, any claim made about the identity of each must at this stage be viewed as provisional.

Perhaps the most acute expression of the different structures of time and being within philosophy can be found in the actative dimension which provides the difference between Heraclitus and

Plato. Heraclitus' most important cosmological statement links time and being in a specific way:

> The cosmos neither god nor man has made but it always was and is and will be.[12]

In this fragment, Heraclitus introduces into the history of philosophy the capacity or potential for philosophical as opposed to theological thinking. In its exhaustive use of the Greek verb 'to be' the fragment poses a distinction between the temporality proper to the cosmos and a conception of the actual in which its identity neither depends on teleology nor on the transcendental. The cosmos is primordially present within the actual; however one is not reducible to the other nor is the identity of the actual dependent upon the function of the primordial. Platonism, on the other hand, is marked by a distinction between the transcendental and the actual which is articulated in terms of two distinct (though functionally interrelated) ontological and temporal realms where the reality and nature of the actual (its being good, beautiful, pious, just, etc.) is dependent upon the transcendental having the function of giving and sustaining the identity of that which is actually present. The structure of Platonism, which becomes the structure of Christian-theological thought, is from its inception incommensurably divided from the potential for philosophical thought inherent in the Heraclitean conception of the relationship between time and being.

The distinction between the primordial and the actual will allow, if not occasion, an understanding of the actual which is neither subject to the charge of idealism nor of empiricism. The actual is neither the simply concrete (or contextual) nor is it the representation, image, manifestation, avatar, etc., of a transcendental category or form. The actual is a presence marked by the empirical and yet not reducible to the empirical. Actual presence – the actual's presence – presences the primordial which is itself neither an object nor a transcendental ground and yet belongs together with the object itself. The primordial is an otherness within presence which is part of presence itself.

Neither philosophy nor theology come to be, but rather they are articulated within different ontologico-temporal frameworks. It is not that being must be thought within the horizon of temporality but that the thinking of being is itself a temporal thinking. The framework of the theological is the interdependent duality of the transcendental and the actual. The actual within theology is the domain of the lived world as well as the domain of sin and estrangement. Here the work of art is only ever an imitation that hankers for the transcendental. Here, too, memory is a hankering, a loss, in which remembrance is underwritten by anamnesis. Memory becomes an act sanctioned by the demand for recovery and where failure gives rise either to a repetitive dwelling on failure, namely melancholia, or an attempted overcoming of failure, for example, Proust's distinction between involuntary and voluntary memory. Melancholy, loss and nostalgia are all an integral part of Christian theological thinking and are thereby implicated in, as well as generated by, the interplay between temporality and ontology proper to theology itself. Revolutionary nostalgia is the political strategy occasioned by the *Angelus Novus*.

The primordial as otherness and as the mark of a difference that is not implicated in the distinction between the for-itself and the in-itself is the dramatic possibility within Heraclitus' conception of cosmology. In Heraclitus, terms such as 'logos', 'cosmos', 'harmonia', etc., mark the primordial. In a general sense they allow the non-empirical and the other to be thought outside of teleology and the transcendental, and therefore to be thought beyond a preoccupation with loss. Conceiving of the present as marked by loss generates a conception of redemption as a future, whether open or enclosed, that is governed by a returning. The question of the experience of the primordial becomes the possibility of experiencing the actual within its belonging together with the primordial – the belonging together of life and potential after life within the actual. *Leben und fortleben.* While it is always possible to reduce this belonging together to simple life, to a context, the reduction will never be satisfactory, for there will always be something else. Consequently, while it is possible to efface the primordial in any particular experience (or in any interpretation) the primordial remains, delimiting the possibility of a future and thus of a potential transgression of the limits imposed by any one context, interpretation or experience. The aura is therefore anoriginal.

The aura must be understood in relation to the primordial. The experience of the aura is the experience of an expectation or a possibility. This is made very clear in the description of aura in 'On some motifs in Baudelaire'. The fulfilment of the expectation that the other will return 'our gaze' is the experience of the aura. The primordial is the potential inherent in the face of the other. The other's face is an open field; open to the possibility of a continual and unending face-to-face encounter. The open face is the continual possibility of the ethical, for the returned gaze implicates the actual within the primordially present relationship between self and other.

If the aura can be related to the primordial then the experience of aura needs to be understood beyond the melancholy interplay of nostalgia, loss and redemption. The gaze of the other is inexhaustible and it is this potential inexhaustibility that is primordially present in the actual presence of the other. The first example of the aura cited above concerned 'natural objects'. Many commentators have noted the implausibility of this passage. It lies, of course, in the suggested link between the natural and the produced. However, the important part of this passage does not lie there but rather in the duality of the distant and the close. 'We define the aura of the latter [natural objects] as the unique phenomenon of distance however close it may be.' No matter how close the mountain range and the branch may be, our experience involves an element to which, while inseparable from physical presence, actual presence cannot be reduced. Otherness within the actual, here as distance within presence, means that the aura endures as primordially present. It is, however, the moment after making this move that Benjamin denies the primordiality of the aura. When he adds that 'This image makes it easy to comprehend the social basis of the contemporary decay of aura', he reduces the aura, and by implication the work of art and the face of the other, to a mere contextual presence. However, this does not chart the limit of Benjamin's aesthetics, for elsewhere in his writings he allows for what has been called the primordial.

In 'The storyteller' Benjamin draws an important distinction between the story and information:

> The value of information does not survive the moment in which it was new. It lives only at the moment: it has to surrender to it completely and explain itself without losing any time. A story is different. It does not expend itself. It preserves and concentrates its strength and is capable of releasing it even after a long time.[13]

Information is exhaustible. In Barthes' terminology, it is simply communication. The story, however, lives on. The question is, of course, how is this survival to be understood? What is its strength? The strength is simply its inexhaustibility; its capacity to look back continually – a capacity that is primordially present in the story itself. A story, in Benjamin's sense, both lives in the moment of its actualization but it also lives on. Its reference to history and to its own *histoire*, is delimited by its capacity for survival.

In his text 'The task of the translator', Benjamin links history, life and survival:

> a translation comes later than the original, and since the important works of world literature never find their chosen translators at the time of their origin, their translation marks their stage of continued life. The idea of life and after life in works of art should be regarded with an entirely unmetaphorical objectivity.[14]

And later in the same section he adds:

> The concept of life is given its due only if everything that has a history of its own, and is not merely the setting for history, is credited with life. In the first analysis, the range of life must be determined by history rather than by nature. . . . The philosopher's task consists in comprehending all of natural life through the more encompassing life of history.[15]

Despite their complexity these passages have a certain fascination. The after-life of the work of art is not simply that it has been translated but rather that translation is an enacting of a capacity inherent in the work itself, that is its capacity to have an after life. The link between the capacity to be translated and the capacity for reinterpretation is obvious. In both instances they comprise an essential aspect of the work of art and whose presence can only be primordial. The consequence of this is that the primordial becomes a *sine qua non* for the work of art.

The first part of the passage cited above is relatively straightforward; it is the relationship between life and history that is more problematic. Benjamin describes the relationship between the original and the translation as a natural connection from which it could be concluded that life and nature stand opposed to history. This is not the case, of course, since 'the range of life' is historically determined. Nature must be written out and history written in. Indeed, it would be absurd to think of the possibility of the absence of history. Context remains indispensable and yet the context provided by history is not itself absolute.[16] What cannot be contextualized, and what exists in a temporal domain other than history, is the potential for after life, for reinterpretation, for continual translation, inherent in the work of art itself. Life therefore cannot eliminate the possibility of an after life.

The analogy is, of course, with the impossibility of removing from any one text that which makes translation possible, or indeed removing from the object of interpretation the potential for reinterpretation.

The value that emerges from the problem with Benjamin's conception of the aura and the way it can be resolved by looking at the distinction between information and the story and at elements of the theory of translation, is that it underlies the importance of recognizing both the interplay and the difference between the work of art as commodity and the work of art as object of interpretation. While it can never be denied that the work of art is a commodity and hence an object of exchange, to understand it as such would involve restricting its presence to an ontology and temporality of the instant. The work of art exists in a 'here and now' but always has the potential to exist beyond the restriction of any instant. While this point is occasionally given tacit recognition, what is invariably forgotten is that in order for this point to stand it involves a conception of temporality within which this potential endures and therefore which is also present within presence, though not reducible to presence.

Barthes' conception of 'signifiance' reworked as the aura, coupled to the reworking of Benjamin's conception of the aura, while not the same, do none the less both depend upon a specific construction of the relationship between time and being. Barthes provides a way of understanding that the interpretation of a text can never be reduced to the con-text of the text itself. In the case of Benjamin the distinction between information and the story, as well as translation, involve the conception of temporality at work implicitly, in 'signifiance', as well as exemplifying the interpretive potential at work within it. The conclusion that can be drawn from this is that if there is a truth content to the work of art, then the truth of art becomes its capacity to live, not to live on in truth, but to live on.

The Benjamin at play here is one who is wary of the claims of and desire for universality and universal history. A Benjamin who opposed the programme of art for art's sake but who recognizied that part of the potential of liberation and freedom lay in the experience of the aura. A Benjamin whose attraction lies in the future.

NOTES

1 Scholem's interpretation of Benjamin can be found in his two papers, 'Walter Benjamin and his angel' and 'Walter Benjamin', both of which are

reprinted in his collection *On Jews and Judaism in Crisis* (Schocken Books, New York, 1976). His biography of Benjamin should also be consulted: *Walter Benjamin - die Geschichte einer Freundschaft* (Suhrkamp, Frankfurt, 1975).

2 Julian Roberts, *Walter Benjamin* (Macmillan, London, 1982).

3 Terry Eagleton, *Walter Benjamin or Towards a Revolutionary Criticism* (Verso, London, 1981).

4 See in particular, Irving Wohlfarth, 'On the messianic structure of Walter Benjamin's last reflections', *Glyph*, 3, 1978.

5 This paper is reprinted in *L'Obvie et l'obtus* (Editions du Seuil, Paris, 1982).

6 ibid., p. 44.

7 ibid., p. 55. It should be noted that the French *'l'histoire'* can mean both history and story. This dual possibility is, of course, lost in translation.

8 Susan Buck-Morss, *The Origin of Negative Dialectics* (MIT Press, New York, 1977), pp. 160-1.

9 H. W. Puppe, 'Walter Benjamin on photography', *Colloquia Germania*, XII, 3, 1979, p. 274.

10 This paper is available in *Illuminations*, trans. Harry Zohn (Fontana, London, 1973), pp. 224-5.

11 This paper is found in *Charles Baudelaire: A Lyric Poet in the Era of High Capitalism* (Verso, London, 1983), p. 147.

12 This fragment is number XXXVII in Charles Kahn's edition, *The Art and Thought of Heraclitus* (Cambridge University Press, Cambridge, 1979).

13 *Illuminations*, p. 90.

14 ibid., p. 75.

15 idem.

16 The following interpretation has been greatly influenced by Derrida's paper, 'Signature événement contexte', in *Marges de la philosophie* (Editions de Minuit, Paris, 1972). I have tried to formulate the presentation within a generalised becoming in terms of the pragma.

10

TRADITION AND
EXPERIENCE: WALTER
BENJAMIN'S 'ON SOME
MOTIFS IN BAUDELAIRE'

Benjamin starts his discussion of Baudelaire by repeating, to some extent, Baudelaire's own beginning of *Les Fleurs du mal*. Baudelaire questions the possibility of comprehension. Benjamin is at the same time more dramatic and more reasonable. He is concerned to explain Baudelaire's own predicament. It is of course an explanation not simply of the predicament of Baudelaire, but the one in which Baudelaire finds himself. It is to that extent therefore Benjamin's own predicament, the secular. Benjamin's initial stated concern is to establish and explain the reason why the conditions no longer pertain for a 'positive reception of lyric poetry'. The reason Benjamin adduces is that it 'may be due to a change in the structure of experience (*Erfahrung*)'.[1] In order to construct a frame within which to trace the interplay of experience and tradition in Benjamin's '*On some motifs in Baudelaire*', I want to look, albeit briefly, at the way in which experience figures in his short study of the Russian writer Nikolai Leskov, 'The storyteller'.[2] Central to this particular study is the problem of experience, since Benjamin will explain the disappearance of the storyteller as contemporaneous with the 'atrophy' of experience.

In any analysis of texts as complex as Benjamin's there is always the risk that the issues at play in them and which emerge from them can get displaced by the task of exposition. Consequently it is worth noting in advance the central issues at stake in experience and tradition and which are under study here. It should be pointed out of course that fundamental components of any investigation of tradition and experience are the concepts of identity and difference in terms of which they are articulated. The central problems in this instance are the subject of experience and the temporality of experience; clearly of course they are related. It will be argued in the latter stages of this chapter that a critique of Benjamin's work provides the possibility of thinking anew the interplay of subjectivity, agency and time.

THE COMMUNITY OF LISTENERS DISAPPEARS

'The storyteller' opens with an important and intriguing reference to time. It is located in the claim that, despite the familiarity of the storyteller's name, in terms of his 'living effectivity' (*lebendige Wirksamkeit*) he is no longer present. The storyteller, in other words, is no longer at hand and therefore no longer part of the present. The time of the storyteller is past. The ending of the time of storytelling is described by Benjamin in terms of there no longer being 'the ability to exchange experiences' (*Erfahrungen auszutauschen*). The storyteller draws on experience and in narrating turns that experience into the experience of the listener. Narrating is lodged within and therefore comes to articulate 'the community of listeners'.

In the opening sections of the paper Benjamin contrasts information and the story. Even though the manner in which he distinguishes between the temporality of each (the temporality of the instant as opposed to the temporality of survival) is of great significance, the important point here is the link established between the story and memory. Developing an understanding of tradition necessitates unpicking Benjamin's different conceptions of memory, since it is memory as *Erinnerung* which he argues 'creates the chain of tradition'. The first important link between memory and experience occurs in section VIII. Here it is argued that a story is easily committed to memory (*Gedächtnis*) if it does not necessitate psychological analysis. If in other words its comprehension involves immediate integration into the experience of the listener. Benjamin argues that to the extent that this occurs the listener is liable to repeat the story. Having made this move Benjamin's argument takes a remarkable turn. He next suggests that the taking over of the story, its assimilation and hence possible repetition, demands 'relaxation'. What is intended by the reference to 'relaxation' and the one to 'boredom' can be seen later in the section when he invokes the 'rhythm of work'. 'Relaxation' and 'boredom' are not negative characteristics. It is rather that they denote a state of mind in which the activity of work demands less and less conscious attention and therefore the worker is open both to the hearing of stories and their repetition. The repetition of work involves a forgetting which allows the possibility of listening. Forgetting yields listening. This is why Benjamin can argue that when 'the gift for listening is lost . . . the community of listeners disappears. For storytelling is always the art of repeating stories and this art is lost when stories are no longer retained (*behalten*)'.[3] Memory (*Gedächtnis*) plays a fundamental role in the coherence of the 'community of listeners'. However, because listening and relaxation involve, as has been indicated, the 'self-forgetful (*selbstvergessener*) listener', it is essential to differentiate this type of forgetting from the forgetting that would stem from the unravelling of the community of listeners. It is in section XIII of 'The storyteller' that these points are to some extent clarified.

The section begins with the position already established: namely, that fundamental to the listener is the possibility of reproducing what has been said. A remembering, in other words, that will occasion repetition. It is the importance of both retaining and repeating that is signalled in the connection established by Benjamin between memory and epic.

Memory (*Gedächtnis*) is the epic faculty par excellence. Only by virtue of a comprehensive memory can epic writing absorb the course of events on the one hand and, with the passing of these, make its peace with the power of death on the other.[4]

Memory as *Gedächtnis* retains by absorbing 'the course of events' and in repeating and hence in the continual possibility of repetition it 'makes its peace with the power of death'. It should of course be added that this is an easy peace for it cheats death of its own power; the power to end, to preclude therefore the possibility of repetition. The epic is for Benjamin to be understood in relation to its muse, Mnemosyne. The relation introduces a distinction between memory (*Gedächtnis*) and remembrance (*Erinnerung*) because Mnemosyne, the muse of epic is also the rememberer. The epic in its origin contains both the story and the novel. However remembrance (*Erinnerung*) has a different form in each. The rest of section XIII is concerned with outlining this difference.

It is precisely at this point that Benjamin makes the important claim already cited above, that it is 'remembering' (*Erinnerung*) that 'creates the chain of tradition'. The form taken by storytelling within the epic involves taking over, retaining and repeating. The repeating is not simply the repetition of the same. It is not therefore simply a repetition on the level of narrative content. It is rather a repetition of the narrative form. Benjamin indicates this when he cites Scheherazade 'who thinks of a fresh story (*eine neue Geschichte*) whenever her tale come to a stop'.[5] The interplay of retention and repeating is described by Benjamin as 'epic remembrance' (*episches Gedächtnis*). It endures as the 'Muse-inspired element of the narrative'. Now the capacity to retain as well as repeat means that on one level the time of the story does not admit of death. Though on another level the story can end if it can no longer be passed on. The end of the story is the end of community. However the extent to which it is possible to hold these levels as separate remains an open question.

The origin of the novel is linked to memory (*Erinnerung*) in a different way. It involves that element in epic that necessitates and shows what Benjamin calls 'perpetuating remembrance' (*verewigendes Gedächtnis*). A conception of memory that Benjamin contrasts with the 'short lived reminiscences of the storyteller'. There is on the surface something odd about this distinction. Not only does the time scale proper to memory seem wrong – the novel as 'perpetuating' and the story as 'short lived' – the difficulties are compounded by his relating the novel to unity (it 'is dedicated to one hero, one odyssey, one battle') and the story to diversity ('to many diffuse occurrences'). It goes without saying that the conceptions of unity and diversity at work here do not lend themselves to any automatic or easy summation.

Each individual story – each telling – is a unique event within a general repetition. Repetition here is the work of tradition and that is why memory as *Erinnerung* is essential to the unfolding of tradition. The novel however is unique. It is not lodged within the process of taking over, retaining and repeating. This is why Benjamin approves of Lukács' description of it as 'the form of transcendental homelessness'. There is a very real sense in which, for Benjamin, the novel neither articulates nor continues the tradition. It clearly takes a place within it. However its place does not function to continue tradition. The story and the novel both demand memory and it is the different conceptions of each that are identified by Benjamin in his description of their initial unity in epic.

> It is . . . remembrance (*Eingedenken*) which as the muse-derived element of the novel, is added to reminiscence (*Gedächtnis*), the corresponding element of the story the unity

of their origin in memory (*Erinnerung*) having disappeared with the decline of the epic.[6]

Memory (*Erinnerung*) contains therefore both remembrance and reminiscence. They are combined in the epic though with its decline they separate, giving rise on the one hand to the novel and on the other to the story. The novel opens an enclosed world closed off from the world of repetition. The world it opens is self-enclosing and within it the novel is preoccupied with a unique happening. The novel finishes at the border of its own enclosure. The impossibility of repetition is therefore inscribed within the actual identity of the novel itself. The intricacy and complexity of its singularity demands what Benjamin has called 'perpetuating remembrance'. It is of course a remembrance that perpetuates within the self-enclosed world of the novel. The story on the other hand is brief. It passes with the moment and yet potentially its end is infinitely deferred. The story both in terms of form and content can be repeated *ad infinitum*, if the conditions for its reception also endure. Benjamin establishes this interplay of time and memory in both the novel and the story in the following way.

> There is no story for which the question of how it continued would not be legitimate. The novelist, on the other hand, cannot hope to take the smallest step beyond that limit at which he invites the reader to a divinatory realisation of the meaning of life by writing 'Finis'.[7]

As this passage makes clear the temporality of the novel differs profoundly from that of the story. It is of course commensurate with this difference that the concepts of memory also differ. The task at hand is to link these different conceptions to the initial problem raised by Benjamin; namely the growing impossibility of exchanging experiences. Towards the end of 'The storyteller' Benjamin makes a general claim about the nature of storytelling. It is a claim that is worth pursuing because not only does it forge an important distinction between the experience of the individual and what he calls 'collective experience' (*Kollectiverfahrung*), but it also introduces the concept of 'shock' (*Chock*) which, as we shall see, plays a vital role in his study of Baudelaire:

> All great storytellers have in common the freedom with which they move up and down the rungs of their experience as on a

ladder. A ladder extending downward to the interior of the earth and disappearing in the clouds is the image for a collective experience (*das Bild einer Kollectiverfahrung*) to which the deepest shock of every individual experience, death, constitutes no impediment or barrier.[8]

What is at stake here is a distinction between two different realms; a difference of kind. The ladder, the experiences of the storyteller, mark a type of totality. It is not the simple accretion of all the storyteller's experiences. A number of those experiences are no more than the result of having listened and therefore of having retained and repeated. The totality is tradition. Its past does not exist as a series of discrete events in themselves. Rather it endures as ritual. While Benjamin does not argue it as such, there is a distinction between the past proper to history and the past proper to ritual. It will be in relation to ritual that a conception of experience that involves allegory will emerge. Events are particularized and cannot be repeated. The continuity of ritual is the repetition of the storyteller. The ladder along which the storyteller moves could be seen as the repetition and living out of tradition.

The experience of the individual must be understood as not simply the opposite of collective experience but more importantly as the unique experience that takes place outside community. However even this formulation is not completely accurate. For in taking place outside of community it undermines the possibility of both the continuity of tradition and the community of listeners. The link between memory and experience that pertains to the individual differs fundamentally from the link within tradition, community and collectivity. Tradition and repetition do not unfold into an empty space. Nor are they merely taken over by passive subjects. (There is an enormous difference between boredom and passivity.) Tradition in Benjamin's sense demands and creates unity. Not only must the community of listeners be unified, the story and the storyteller must also refuse the possibility of fragmentation. The agent of repetition must repeat and be repeated. Community and collectivity can be seen as metaphors for a present that is fragmenting. It is one where it is no longer possible to understand the present as a unified site in which the unity of tradition is taken over and repeated. Fragmentation leads to a present that is not an envisaged end for tradition. The question – the philosophical question – to which this gives rise is how the present is to be understood without the singularity of tradition – in other words, in the absence of the unity of tradition; not of course in the absence of the plurality of tradition. Having traced some of the themes that emerge in 'The storyteller' it is now possible to return to the initial puzzling formulation of the present as that in which 'experience has fallen in value'. It is now clear that what is at play in this claim is the possibility of community itself. What has to be determined therefore is how this description of the growing impossibility of community is to be understood.[9]

Perhaps the most direct encapsulation of the problem of community is the claim of Benjamin that has already been noted, namely, that with the loss of the 'gift for listening . . . the community of listeners disappears'. The community therefore is structured by storytelling. But it is also the case that the community constructs the storyteller as storyteller. There is an identity-giving reciprocity between storyteller and community. The link between them, however, is not simply in terms of identity for it is also the case that they are both sites of repetition, and hence indispensable for the continuity of tradition. (The question that emerges here is how repetition is to be understood.) It could be the case, for example, that repetition continually returns and repeats the same. Or there could be a Nietzschean conception within which repetition involves the always *different*; a repetition where the eternal return of the same was always both same and different. At this stage the problematic nature of repetition can only be noted rather than resolved.

If emphasis is placed on tradition then continuity means that the repetition of tradition is to be understood in terms of repetition giving to tradition its mode of being as being present; as the always at hand. The fragmentation of community and hence the absence of the site of tradition gives rise to a number of specific problems. The first is the absence of the place of repetition. The second is the construction of the present as a site of loss. It is this construction which structures the nature of the task that Benjamin identifies as flowing from the present. There is therefore an important reciprocity between the way the present is construed and the task that is presented as at hand. The third is a cleavage in experience. In regard to the latter it is not simply that there is a growing impossibility to exchange experiences, it is that experience has become divided between the relatively unproblematic experience of that which is at hand and the problem of the possibility of experiencing that which has been lost. Fragmentation divides experience. There are therefore two distinct objects of experience and therefore the need for two different experiences. It is precisely these problems which may be traced in 'On some Motifs in Baudelaire'. Not only must their unfolding be noticed, their viability must also be questioned.

THE CLEAVAGE IN EXPERIENCE

It is tempting to begin any examination of Benjamin's writings on Baudelaire by commenting on their plurality and by noting developments as well as lacunae throughout texts as diverse as those gathered together to form the English language collection, *Charles Baudelaire: A Lyric Poet in the Era of High Capitalism* as well as the enigmatic *Zentralpark*[10] and of course the relevant section of *Das Passagen-Werk*.[11] The sheer diversity of these texts invites such an approach. Resisting it and thereby focusing almost exclusively on one text, seems to demand some type of justification. What needs to be identified here is therefore the specificity of 'On some motifs in Baudelaire'. It is to be found in the links that exist between the task already identified and established in 'The storyteller' and those at play in this particular text on Baudelaire. The links can be seen to take place in terms of a systematic reworking and development of the relationship between experience and tradition. The way this relationship unfolds in the earlier paper has already been noted. Furthermore what has also emerged is a number of questions. Taking them up opens the point of connection between these two texts. On a thematic level this connection is established by Benjamin himself in the opening section of 'On some motifs in Baudelaire': 'Experience (*Erfahrung*) is indeed a matter of tradition (*eine Sache der Tradition*) in collective existence (*Kollektiven*) as well as private life.' [12] The immediate question that arises here concerns the meaning of 'matter' (*Sache*). It will be in clarifying this 'matter' that the parameters for an understanding of the relationship between tradition and experience will begin to emerge.

For Benjamin the poetry of Baudelaire is attentive to a specific problem. It is apparent throughout Baudelaire's work, though most strikingly and with most dramatic force in poems such as 'Une Passante', 'Correspondances' and 'Le Soleil' amongst others. In them Benjamin notes Baudelaire's attempt to return to and to dwell on that which is no longer at hand. The '*correspondances*' established by

Baudelaire are Benjamin's continual point of reference. What these *'correspondances'* actually are remains the difficult question. That they are the focus of Benjamin's interest is exemplified thus: 'the *correspondances* record a concept of experience which includes ritual elements. Only by approaching these elements was Baudelaire able to fathom the full meaning of the breakdown which he, a modern man, was witnessing.' [13] The difficulty here is that the concept of experience in this text needs to be explained. The cleavage in experience is marked by the use of the words *Erfahrung* and *Erlebnis*. It must be added of course that merely explaining the difference will not capture what is at stake in it. It is vital, in this instance, to recognize that each brings with it a different temporality of experience.

Our task must be to trace the relationship between *Erfahrung* and *Erlebnis* in order then to go on and examine the important consequences that stem from the nature of their difference. Perhaps one of the most important moments in Benjamin's text that allows for an understanding of *Erfahrung* concerns the following description of the unskilled worker: 'The unskilled worker is the one most deeply degraded by the drill of the machines. His work has been sealed off from experience (*Seine Arbeit ist gegen Erfahrung abgedichtet*).' [14] Benjamin is alert to a possible response to this description, namely that the continuity of work – the rhythm of work itself – should construct the continuity of action that establishes itself as experience; as *Erfahrung*. His reply is the following: 'The manipulation of the worker at the machine has no connection with the preceding operation for the very reason that it is its *exact repetition*' (my emphasis). [15] At play here is a completely different conception of repetition than the one that was observed at work in 'The storyteller'. In that instance the importance of repetition was that it involved a repeating that took over and handed on. Repetition became that through which the tradition was continued. The same was never the same because it was supplemented by its own repetition. However the storytelling – the narrative practice – as the image of Scheherazade suggests, contains within it its own supplementarity. There is a sense in which the continuity of storytelling can only end, as has already been noted, if the site – the community – of storytelling becomes fragmented. The site is the unity constructed by and hence enabling the exchange of experience (*Erfahrung*).

The worker at the machine does not repeat by taking over. The repetition breaks the continuity because the act of repeating – the 'retelling' – is in each instance the same and therefore new. The logic of repetition within which the worker is locked means that he is, in Benjamin's words, 'sealed off' from *Erfahrung*. What is the force of being sealed off? How is this particular cleavage to be understood? A way of answering these questions is suggested by an intriguing passage that contains, in an abbreviated form, Benjamin's critical stance in relation to symbolism.

In his analysis of Baudelaire's sonnet 'La Vie antérieure' and before quoting the lines which he believes exemplifies the point he is trying to make, Benjamin states the following:

> The images of caves and vegetation, of clouds and waves which are evoked at the beginning of this second sonnet rise from the warm vapour of tears, tears of homesickness. . . . There are no simultaneous correspondences, such as were cultivated by the symbolists later. The murmur of the past may be heard in the correspondences, and the canonical experience of them has its place in a previous life.[16]

The 'previous life' is captured by Baudelaire's own use of the past tense, 'C'est là que j'ai vécu', 'Le printemps adorable a perdu son odeur'. What must be pursued is the connection between the critique of symbolism and the past tense, in order to develop an understanding of what is at play in the description of the worker as 'sealed off'. These interconnections will display the 'matter' of tradition.

The 'simultaneous correspondences' involve a conception of symbolism in which the symbol provides automatic access to the symbolized. The experience of one was the experience of the other. The at hand gave the not at hand. The cleavage was no sooner opened than it was sealed. The symbolized is therefore present within simultaneity. Symbolism does not raise the problem of memory. It is thus that they are not sealed off from the experiencing subject. Correspondence on the other hand marks the cleavage in experience. It involves the experience in the present which is the experience of that which can no longer be experienced. It is experienced as loss, the past tense marking that which is no longer present. There can be no return within present experience. What has been lost is no longer an object within memory. This accounts in part for Benjamin's interest in Proust. His conception of involuntary memory provides the possibility of access to the past – the past of the past tense, the 'that' from which the worker has been sealed off – that does not occur via an intentional act of memory.

At play here is the fundamental distinction between *Erfahrung* and *Erlebnis*. Benjamin connects the passer-by of Baudelaire's sonnet 'Une Passante' to the worker at the machine in the following way: 'The shock-experience (*Chockerlebnis*) the passer-by has in the crowd, corresponds to what the worker experiences (*Erlebnis*) at his machine.' [17] The worker at the machine does not experience *Erfahrung*. Each moment is new. A repetition of the same, of newness (novelty). The experience (*Erlebnis*) at the machine is not even noticed as it enters consciousness. It is located within memory without having been the object of conscious recognition. Modernity causes the forgetting of experience. Benjamin's reference to Freud is precisely in these terms. He uses psychoanalysis to argue for the possibility of an event entering into psychic life without the subject being aware of the event. What is at stake here is not the viability of Benjamin's reading of Freud but the conception of the subject proper to forgetting. It will be essential to return to this point.

The time of *Erlebnis* differs fundamentally from the time of *Erfahrung*. The first involves the temporality of the unique and fragmented moment while the second involves the sequential continuity within tradition. What is emerging here, of course, is a conception of alienation and hence of modernity as loss. It is moreover a loss which cannot be overcome, in other words that which has been lost, or that which has been fragmented cannot attain again its original status. It is none the less the case that access is provided; occurring either in terms of Proustian involuntary memory or Baudelaire's *correspondances*. Benjamin makes a significant reference to Baudelaire's rare use of what could be called temporal markers for example 'one evening';

> They are days of recollection (*Eingedenken*), not marked by any experience (*Erlebnis*). They are not concerned with other days but stand out from time. As for their substance Baudelaire has defined it in the notion of the *correspondances*, a concept that in Baudelaire stands side by side and unconnected with the notion of modern beauty. [18]

There is an important connection here with the distinction drawn in 'The storyteller' between the novel as 'perpetuating' and the story as 'short lived'. The novel is unique, a solitary and single event. It does not form part of the tradition. It is neither repeated nor handed down. It is the place of 'transcendental homelessness'. The days of recollection which stand out from chronological time are themselves situated within continuity and tradition. This is why 'correspondences record a concept of experience which includes ritual elements'. They overcome the results of fragmentation but without overcoming the fragmentation of the present. They do not return what has been lost but allow for an experience that is not jeopardized by the shocks of *Erlebnis*. That is why they are connected to a more original form of beauty, namely a conception that, 'one would define as the object of experience in the state of resemblance'. The reference to Plato is clear. However the important point here is that beauty pertains to *Erfahrung* – to that which is infused by ritual – but which cannot be experienced as such; hence correspondences and therefore resemblance. The importance of Baudelaire's poetry is that it has allowed *Erlebnis* to be enframed by *Erfahrung*. For Benjamin, Baudelaire's battling the crowd 'is the nature of something lived through (*Erlebnis*) to which Baudelaire has given the weight of experience (*Erfahrung*)'.[20] Baudelaire turned *Erlebnis* into *Erfahrung*. Perhaps this is Benjamin's final conclusion. It is of course a conclusion, the possibility of which, has already been gestured at in 'The storyteller'. There Benjamin attributes an aesthetic dimension to the death of the art of storytelling. He describes this death, not as modern but as secular, and therefore as part of the historical process of secularization. He then goes on to add that this death

> is . . . only a concomitant symptom of the secular productive forces of history, a concomitant that has quite gradually removed narrative from the realm of living speech and at the same time is making it possible to see a new beauty in its vanishing.[20]

Here is an aesthetic, not of decay, nor even of the modern, but one yielded by the growing incompleteness and fragmentation of the present. The new beauty is made possible by the cleavage in experience.

It is in Baudelaire's poetry however that the point of contact between these two forms of experience – the two sides of the cleavage – takes place. One is given the significance of the other. It is a relationship between them that differs fundamentally from the connection that Benjamin attributes to Bergson. Quoting Horkheimer to the effect that Bergson has 'suppressed death', Benjamin goes on to add that

> The durée from which death has been eliminated has the miserable endlessness of a scroll. Tradition is excluded from it. It is the quintessence of the passing moment [*Erlebnis*] that struts around in the borrowed garb of experience. The spleen on the other hand is exposing the passing moment in all its nakedness.[21]

In this passage and within the distinction between *Erlebnis* and *Erfahrung*, Benjamin has situated, albeit in a negative form, the 'matter' of tradition. Baudelaire's poetry – the spleen – reveals the reality of *Erlebnis*. Why is it that tradition is excluded from the endlessness of the scroll? The response is based on the fact that for Benjamin what Bergson has done is construct the lived – the passing moment – in terms of an unending continuity. It is of course continuity that is proper to tradition and therefore to *Erfahrung*. Hence the description of *Erlebnis* strutting 'around in the borrowed garb of experience'. The absence of death is the exclusion of history (and prehistory, the time of ritual). The scroll can be read as standing for the mechanical work that seals the worker off from tradition. It is therefore the continued repetition of the same. At play here is what must be seen as a fundamental aspect of Benjamin's understanding of tradition. It involves a particular form of repetition; one within which action plays a central role. Repetition is a handing on. Tradition is thus linked to a specific conception of action – a conception that is exemplified by the figure of the storyteller; who by telling a story (that is by acting) takes over and hands on. The storyteller emerges therefore as the figure within tradition. Action causes the tradition to endure and hence facilitates its continuity. It should always be remembered however that this action is only possible if the community in which it takes place is unified. Modernity renders this impossible because of the fracturing of the site of community.

Despite its initial attraction it should be remembered that Benjamin's conception of modernity is articulated within the distinction between *Erlebnis* and *Erfahrung*. It is only in terms of this distinction that it is possible to, say, characterize the worker as 'sealed off' from the possibility of a place within the continuity that is tradition, because he is 'sealed off' from *Erfahrung*. The consequence of this distinction is, as has been suggested, that it yields a conception

167

of the present as a place of loss. Clearly, of course, what is important here is the way in which loss is to be understood. Within any understanding of such a construction of the present it is vital to take account of the conception of subjectivity implicit within the cleavage in experience and thus which inhabits the present as the locus of loss.

In his discussion of beauty Benjamin quotes Goethe and then goes on to make the important additional point concerning *correspondances* and their role in understanding beauty: 'Beauty in its relationship to nature can be defined as that which remains true to its essential nature only when veiled. The *correspondances* tell us what is meant by the veil.' [22] They have allowed Baudelaire to give to the passing moment the 'weight' of an experience. Benjamin's conception of modernity does not sanction the possibility of a return or a recovery of what is no longer at hand. The aesthetic, here finding its most intense expression in beauty, is constrained to adopt resemblance. Benjamin uses Goethe's point that the aesthetic representation of nature must aim at resemblance and not an exact copy. It is to this extent that nature is unrepresentable. Once again the shadow of Plato can be seen haunting both Goethe and Benjamin. The additional point made by Benjamin is that it is Baudelaire's *correspondances* which allow for an understanding of the resemblance; an understanding that includes both its necessity and its function. It is at exactly this point that Benjamin and Goethe differ. Goethe is making a claim about representation within aesthetics, and hence the veil is simply an aesthetic category. Benjamin on the other hand gives to the veil an historical specificity. The veil emerges within – and hence also, in part, constructs – modernity. To redeploy the imagery of 'The storyteller' the veil marks the absence of 'the community of listeners'. The veil therefore smothers the 'matter' of tradition. It is the historical specificity introduced by Benjamin that further reinforces the argument that his position is both dependent upon as well as advancing a conception of the present as a place of loss.

The experiencing subject is no longer (and it is the 'longer' that must be emphasized) articulated within the continuity of tradition. The possibility of the 'no longer' – of what was identified before as Baudelaire's 'past tense' – necessitates the cleavage in experience. It is clear that at work here there is what could be called, a 'discursive reciprocity'. The 'no longer' and the cleavage in experience are mutually interdependent. The conception of alienation inherent in Benjamin's description of the worker at the machine is neither economic nor even overtly political. It is rather that modernity is the place of an alienation from the continuity of tradition. It is essential not to employ the language of causality. It is not as though, either implicitly or explicitly, alienation has its source in the development of technology. Implicitly, however, alienation is dependent upon the subject proper to the cleavage in experience. In other words a subject articulated within – and hence which articulates – the distinction between *Erfahrung* and *Erlebnis*.

The consequence of this interarticulation is that because it demands a conception of the present as a locus of loss it advances a related understanding of action that is itself based on the overcoming of loss. Such a conception of the present and therefore the particular orientation of the active is not unique to Benjamin. A similar conception is found, for example, in the work of Heidegger. The unique contribution made by Benjamin, however, is that instead of directing action in terms of a recovery or retrieval of that which has been lost (and where therefore the experience of that through which the lost can itself become the object of an experience emerges as central) Benjamin's position gestures toward the future. It is precisely this gesturing 'toward' that marks the Messianie in his work. It is a conception of the Messianic that can be politicized, as is found in some of his later writings. It is also however equally present as the conception of totality as the end of history that is found in *The Origin of German Tragic Drama*. This latter point emerges in Benjamin's argument that 'There takes place in every original phenomenon a determination of the form in which an idea will constantly confront the historical world, until it is revealed fulfilled, in the totality of its history.' [23] The revealed fulfilment of the idea is itself based on the impossibility of the idea to be actually present. Benjamin's argument is based on Plato and yet his conception of the future is Messianic. It is not that Benjamin reworks this precise formulation in his text on Baudelaire. It is rather that inherent in each is a futural dimension that necessarily depends upon a conception of the present either as incomplete or as the locus of loss.

In order to take these deliberations a step further it is necessary to return to what is in fact the central philosophical problem here, namely, the relationship between experience and the subject of experience. Consistent with both the cleavage in experience, and the present as loss and the resolution or overcoming of loss as futural, is a conception of the subject of experience as that which while modern (secular) – since it is located in the site of the fractured community – can at the same time see itself as a divided unity, and hence will be able to see itself as no longer alienated and therefore as reunited. The cleavage in experience demands the experience of the overcoming of that division. The important point here is that while the subject of experience may be divided, the nature of what may be antagonistic and perhaps even conflictual none the less gestures towards its own unity, in the same way as the idea is revealed as fulfilled 'in the totality of its history'.

When it is argued that alienation can be overcome, this must be understood as arguing that the present as the locus of loss can be overcome. Within the present it is the aesthetic which is privileged by Benjamin as providing access to the nature of the present as well as the possibility of redemption. However, what must be remembered is that the aesthetic takes place within – if not as – experience. Developing a critique of Benjamin should not involve taking the aesthetic as its object but rather the subject and place of aesthetic experience. Fundamental to such a task is the inherent unity that marks both the subject in the present and in the future. While it is true that the subject in the present is divided by the cleavage in experience, this division is the consequence of the process of loss. There is an interesting parallel here with tradition. When it is argued that modernity means that tradition is no longer a possible object of experience, it is presupposed that prior to this state of affairs there was a necessary communication between the subject of experience and tradition – a communication that is no longer present within modernity. The consequence of this is that the conception of the present and the conception of the subject of the present both derive their mode of existence – which could be described as a mode of self-irreconcilability – from there having been an original state of unity (perhaps this could also be called an original state of reconciliation). The cleavage in experience means that the subject is not reconciled with itself. The absence of community is a state of social irreconcilability where it is the image of the past which opens up the possibility of the future.[24]

What is emerging here is the negative characterization of the present that seems to dominate the philosophical orientation of modernity; a characterization, the overcoming of which is conditional upon accepting change as the overcoming of negativity, where negativity is the collapse of an initial unity. For Benjamin fragmentation, in subjectivity and within the social, must be sublated only because it is the mark of collapse. It is at this precise point that the limits of Benjamin's work can be traced. The problem is that if the present is understood either as incomplete or as a site of loss – where the designation of the incomplete or loss comes from the past and therefore demands a futural projection for either completion or the overcoming of loss – then this precludes any conception of the present as agonistic. If alienation, for example, is explained in terms of the relationship between the past and the present (it should of course be added that it is a past constructed by the present) such that it is also possible to argue that the difference between the past and the present is explicable in terms of alienation, then the agonistic moment is precisely the divide between the past and the present. In relation to the fragmentation of the community of listeners the agon becomes the moment of fragmentation. It is not located in the community as fragmented but in the distinction between the community as unity and its fragmentation; between the past and the present. The agon is not part of the present but merely the construction, and hence perhaps also the definition, of history.

Within Benjamin's work it is the relationship between the past and the present which gives rise to the possibility of conflict, the resolution of which is necessarily futural. Indeed the possibility of the future is the possibility of resolution. It is of course resolution as totality – not necessarily a return to the totality that was, but rather to a future totality. The consequence of this, of course, is that it both demands, as well as gives rise to, a conception of the future as a synthesized totality, where identity must always precede and ground difference. It is clear from this description the extent to which Benjamin's position is Messianic. However that is not the significant problem. It is rather the impossibility within the temporality of the scheme he presents of thinking the present as agon. It is only if the present can be thought as an agonistic plenitude that it is possible both to develop as well as situate critique. Furthermore, even if it is accepted that fragmentation is descriptive of both the subject and the social – and in sum therefore descriptive of the post-Enlightenment, that is the epochal present beyond synthetic unity – fragmentation in this sense demands neither an initial unity nor the need to define the present in terms of loss.

The philosophical challenge at the present – indeed of the present – is to map the interarticulation of the desire for unity with the necessity of differential plurality. The limiting element in Benjamin's conception of the interplay between tradition and experience is that it is unable to meet this challenge. The location of this limit is at the hinge separating the modern and the post-modern.[25]

NOTES

1 'On some motifs in Baudelaire', in *Charles Baudelaire: A Lyric Poet in the Era of High Capitalism*, trans. Harry Zohn (Verso, London, 1983), p. 110 (*GS*, 1, 608). All references to this text will be to this translation. I have also provided the volume and page number of the *Gesammelte Schriften* (abbreviated as *GS*), ed R. Tiedmann and Herman Schweppenhauser (Suhrkamp, Frankfurt, 1980).
2 References to this text will be to Harry Zohn's translation 'The story-teller' in *Illuminations* (Fontana, London, 1973).
3 'The storyteller', p. 91 (*GS*, 2, 446).
4 ibid., p. 97 (*GS*, 2, 453).
5 While it cannot be pursued here it is worth drawing attention to the link between *Geschichte* as story and *Geschene* as the 'happening' – though equally historicizing – that is passed from one generation to another in the 'chain of tradition' created by memory (*Erinnerung*).
6 'The storyteller', p. 98 (*GS*, 2, 454).
7 ibid., p. 100 (*GS*, 2, 455).
8 ibid., p. 102 (*GS*, 2, 457).
9 The problem of community is emerging as a central philosophical issue. The reason for this is in part due to the emergence of what I have called in this chapter the 'post-Enlightenment'. By this term I mean the relation-ship between on the one hand the desire for unity (indeed at times the need for unity) that is a direct result of the Enlightenment, and on the other the existence of a differential plurality that marks amongst other things contemporary multiracial societies.
10 *GS*, 1, 655–91.
11 For an important discussion of the issues that emerge from this text, see H. Wisman (ed.), *Walter Benjamin et Paris* (LeCerf, Paris, 1986).
12 'On some motifs in Baudelaire', p. 110 (*GS*, 1, 608).
13 ibid., p. 139 (*GS*, 1, 638).
14 ibid., p. 133 (*GS*, 1, 632).
15 idem.
16 ibid., p. 141 (*GS*, 1, 639–40).
17 ibid., p. 134 (*GS*, 1, 632).
18 ibid., p. 139 (*GS*, 1, 637).
19 ibid., p. 154 (*GS*, 1, 652–3).
20 'The storyteller', p. 87 (*GS*, 2, 442).
21 'On some motifs in Baudelaire', p. 145 (*GS*, 1, 643).
22 ibid., p. 140 (*GS*, 1, 639).
23 Walter Benjamin, *The Origin of German Tragic Drama*, trans. John Osborne (New Left Books, London, 1977), pp. 45–6 (*GS*, 1, 227).

24 Richard Wolin in *Walter Benjamin. An Aesthetic of Redemption* (Columbia University Press, New York, 1982) also uses the expression reconciliation. While recognizing the importance of Wolin's position I have however tried to deploy the term in a different way.

25 I wish to thank Peter Osborne for the many valuable comments he made on an earlier draft of this chapter.

11
DESCARTES' FABLE: THE
DISCOURS DE LA METHODE

INTRODUCTION

Philosophy conceives of itself as continually involved in a search for truth in which truth is envisaged as an end in itself. This self-conception is, of course, usually mirrored in the expectations held for philosophy. The search, evident throughout the texts comprising philosophy's history, is for our concerns more than adequately exemplified in the title of Descartes' philosophical dialogue, *La Recherche de la vérité*. However despite philosophy's proclaimed goal being the uninterrupted enactment of a will to truth, it is our contention that this is in fact the articulation of a different and indeed more subtle strategy, one which could be described as a will to overcome error, or perhaps to be more precise, as the will to overcome the possibility of deception. Part of the aim of this chapter is to trace both the unfolding as well as some of the consequences of this strategy.[1]

If truth is no more than that which ensues from a strategy that establishes two inherently incompatible domains – one being the domain of error and characterized by temporality and the other the domain of truth that is in turn characterized by universality – then truth itself has the appearance of remaining unquestioned and unexamined in regard to the truth. If truth is the result of a will to overcome deception then this leaves unposed, albeit almost as a matter of necessity, the question of the true *qua* true.

Philosophy's search for truth can be described, therefore, as involving these two interrelated components, that is truth as the consequence (but no more than the consequence) of having overcome the possibility of deception, and the unexamined status of truth. This is of course not to deny that the various ways in which truth is

175

thought to be established are not themselves always the subject of constant scrutiny; rather it is to suggest that what remains unexamined is the essence of truth. It is as though the status of the true *qua* true was simply a given.

There are three areas for further investigation that are delimited by this particular construal of philosophy's concern with truth, and even though they vary in their relevance for a study of Descartes' *Discours de la méthode* it is none the less advisable to outline them.

Accepting the assumption that the ascription of truth signifies the claim to have overcome the possibility of deception, and in so doing to have driven a wedge between the domains of error and truth, then the first area of investigation must concern whether or not the possibility of deception can be continually overcome. Furthermore, can these two domains be rendered incommensurable, as they would have to be if truth is to be both secure and secured? The possibility of an intermingling, let alone an interdependence between them, would mean that the sign of truth was no more than the site of truth's self-deception. In other words truth could be based on that which could bring about the destruction of the basis of truth.

The second area of inquiry stems from the fact that, as has been mentioned, the status of the true *qua* true (that is truth itself) is left unresolved. The problem and thus the area to be exploded concerns how to interpret this unposed question. Probably the most intriguing response comes from the work of Heidegger, in which it is consistently argued that the refusal of western philosophy to raise and thus to confront the question of the essential marks a continual and significant absence which does itself reveal the way in which philosophy has worked hitherto. This position is argued in 'Vom Wesen der Wahrheit' [2] in relation to truth; however the absence of the essential as an area of inquiry is discussed in texts as seemingly diverse as 'Vom Wesen des Grundes' [3] and *Nietzsche.* [4]

In the suggestion that this absence must be examined Heidegger is committed to the position that not only do concepts have an essence, but furthermore that the unfolding of history has obscured this essence, and hence he views their recovery as one of the tasks incumbent on philosophy. Whatever viability Heidegger's position has, it does of course lie in there actually having been an original, and now thwarted, will to truth. Part of the aim of this study of Descartes is to call the basis of Heidegger's position into question, for another response to Heidegger's claim that the essential remains unques-

THE JESSOP GROUP LIMITED
LONDON CENTRAL
TEL: 0171-240-6077
VAT REG. No. GB 350 3281 86

11/02/99   18:04   Inv.No: 663431
CASH   S/Man No: 1195

DNPE635PO   1 P   2.49
E6 35MM PROCESS ONLY   2.49
DOCKET NOS: 065222
STUDENT
DNP0436200   2   4.99
D+P 4" 36EXP +JESPHR2003536   9.98
DOCKET NOS: 065223

TOTAL VALUE   12.47

CASH TENDERED: 20.00 CHANGE: 7.53

*** 'P' DENOTES PRICE CHANGE   ***

tioned would be to argue that this is no more than the inevitable consequence of the way in which truth is established. While the force of Heidegger's observation is not in doubt, it should not, as it does in his case, give rise to a search for lost essences driven on by a redemptive nostalgia, but rather it should be recognized that the question of the essential cannot be posed since all that divides truth and falsity is their incommensurability. There is nothing called truth (or falsity) that has a discrete identity and therefore of which there can be an essence. The search for essences is just one more example of philosophy's sedulous fascination with origins.

The third domain concerns what may be loosely called the ethical. An ethics based on the possibility of avoiding error can only be expressed in terms of imperatives. If the domain of error (and thus sin) is the world of lived experience, then it is quite clear that the ethical can be neither based on nor grounded in the world. The guarantee of the ethical will have to be transcendental in nature as it is only the transcendental which, in being beyond the domain of error, is itself beyond reproach. This sketch indicates that the ethical is embroiled in the same problem as truth. In other words, the problem alluded to earlier, namely the question of whether or not the epistemological division between the temporal and the transcendental can be maintained, is here reflected in the division which itself yields the ethical. Kant, for example, in wanting to ground the possibility of ethics in a universal conception of duty, had to leave unposed the question of the basis of duty itself. There is no obvious answer to this question, or at least not one that avoids the potential circularity that would result from an attempt to resolve the difficulty by resorting to an argument based on the need for such a conception of duty.

The specific importance of the *Discours de la méthode* is that there Descartes tries to establish a methodology which both necessitates, and depends upon, forging a radical distinction between the domains of error and truth. The articulation of this position involves the use of the language of ethics, especially in framing the relationship foreseen between the text and reader. What will be traced here is the text's intentional logic.

THE CRITIQUE OF COMMON SENSE

Early in what proved to be a prolific correspondence, Descartes wrote a letter to Mersenne in which one of the principal subjects of discussion was the aesthetic.[5] The problem posed by the aesthetic was that it did not lend itself to scientific study. Not only was pleasure to be divorced from truth, it could not even be spoken of in the same breath. Pleasure was to be relegated to the domain of opinion, imagination and the non-universalizable. Pleasure in relation to the aesthetic lends itself to diversity, to what are called in the *Discours*[6] the 'diversity of our opinions', which stand in opposition to a method which 'teaches us to follow the true order'. The clash is between the multiplicity of opinion and the unitary nature of truth. The multiplicity of opinion cannot be allowed to impinge upon the singularity of truth. The distinction between multiplicity and unity is not imported into the *Discours*, but rather flows within it. Descartes in Part Two suggests that the advantage of method lay in the fact that, 'there being only one truth about each thing whoever discovers it knows as much about the thing as can be known'. The distinction between the one and the many is not unique to Descartes for it is precisely in these terms that Plato adumbrates his own epistemology in the *Republic*. Diversity was and is the domain of error, sin and temporality. The inclusion of temporality is of course a consequence of Platonism in so far as things are temporal while the forms are eternal.

The dream of philosophy is, as has been mentioned, to overcome the deception stemming from the interplay of diversity, sin and temporality and thus to lay a firm foundation in terms of which truth, in Descartes' sense, and morality, in Kant's, can be guaranteed.[7] In the case of Descartes, the method which consists in following 'the true order' is that which 'contains everything that gives certainty to the rules of arithmetic'. The question that must be asked is that of how successful this has been. This is not to ask whether or not philosophy thinks itself to have dismissed or excluded the fictive. Rather, philosophy must be taken at its word, and the cost of the dismissive gesture must be evaluated in terms of its consequences for that particular conception of philosophy.

As a preliminary step toward an evaluation of Descartes' autobiographical attempt to give philosophy a foundation in method, it is essential to trace his critique of common sense. It is from this critique that the importance and necessity of a methodological basis for certain emerges, because fundamental to Descartes' strategy is the recognition that common sense cannot of itself yield certainty. In order to trace the critique I shall examine in some detail a number of passages from the *Discours* which will pave the way toward an understanding of a fundamental moment in the text, namely Descartes' estimation and evaluation of his own intellectual training. This will create a position from which to assess what it is that the *Discours* is attempting and therefore how it should be understood.

The first passage to be examined is the conclusion of Part One of the *Discours*, which can be viewed as a justification by Descartes of his approach.

It is true that while I only considered the customs (*les moeurs*) of other men, I hardly found anything to assure myself and I noticed almost as much diversity as I had previously among the opinions of the philosophers. The greatest profit that I derived from them was that, seeing several things which, even though they seemed to us extravagant and ridiculous, were still commonly accepted and approved by other great nations, I learnt not to believe anything too firmly of which I had only been persuaded by example and by custom, and thus I gradually freed myself from many errors which can obsure our natural light and render us less capable of responding to reason.[8]

This important passage begins with the assertion that mere empirical observation cannot provide certainty. Descartes cites two reasons why this is the case. The first is that observation on its own is ill-informed and not of itself systematic. This is a position advanced by Descartes throughout his philosophical writings; namely, that while all knowledge is based on observation and is thus empirical in nature, error is also based in observation. Observations therefore must be ordered and dealt with systematically in order to avoid the possibility of deception. The second reason is that the 'customs of other men' are diverse.

Diversity may and probably will mean that various groups of people will hold conflicting attitudes in relation to the same activity or thing. Clearly, if truth is unitary in nature, then diversity strikes at the heart of truth itself. Consequently, Descartes argues, a thing cannot be true simply in respect of its being believed to be true. Belief, even if held by a majority, does not provide a thing with its truth. As Descartes states, the 'extravagant and ridiculous' are accepted by some as true. The consequence of this position was Descartes' decision to believe no longer those things where the basis of the belief was either custom or example. As he realized, to abandon such beliefs was in fact

179

to abandon the world, for not only was the world the source of error, it also restricted the operation of the understanding. Descartes is not suggesting that knowledge is or ought to be *a priori*, but simply that knowledge of the world is only possible if method both instructs and guides claims about the world. The universality of method would yield unitary truths and thereby would give knowledge of the world a firm and secure foundation.

The critique of custom is joined to an intriguing use of the image of the one and the many in Part Two of the *Discours:*

> it is custom and example that persuade us rather than any certain knowledge; nevertheless the plurality of voices is worth-less as a proof for truths that are slightly difficult to discover, thus it is much more likely that a man on his own will find them than an entire people.[9]

This passage is of great strategic importance in the *Discours*, for it provides part of the foundation for the autobiographical nature of Descartes' project. If one person is more likely than the majority to discover difficult truths, then there is no reason why Descartes should believe anyone apart from himself. The autobiographical component, while important, should not in this passage be overestimated, for it is conditioned by and thus emerges from the distinction between the one and the many. In other words, the emergence of the importance of the solitary voice is part of the strategy involved in overcoming the possibility of deception, in so far as error is related to the many and truth to the one. This passage need not be interpreted therefore as an argument for the centrality of the *cogito* in the determination or discovery of truth, for it indicates that a more complex manoeuvre is at work.

Descartes has once again dismissed habit and example as them-selves being able to furnish the basis of truth and goes on to suggest that the reason why 'popular beliefs' are held is best accounted for in terms of habit and example. The important aspect of error is that it is linked to 'popular belief' and sometimes has its origin in such beliefs. The consequence of this link is that the overcoming of error must involve a twofold strategy. The first component of this strategy would be to give up 'popular beliefs', while the second would involve a search for a method in terms of which those popular beliefs that are true can be shown to be true. Descartes wants in the end to be able to distinguish between a set of beliefs that are only believed because of habit and custom, and a set of beliefs the certainty of which has been established, and are thus not held to be true in respect of being believed, but are held to be true because truth has been given a transcendental guarantee. In Descartes' words a 'man' on his own is more likely to overcome the impetus of popular assent than a crowd. Knowledge is not phronesis but legislation. Method and the knowing subject act in unison but the method that establishes certainty pre-exists and post-exists any one instance of its use and is therefore that which allows the legislator to act. The certainty of the *cogito* is grounded in the certainty of method. The problem of the foundation of method itself remains unresolved.

The final passage that must be noted concerns a description of error that is advanced in Part One of the *Discours:*

> However, it may be that I am wrong, and it may be only a bit of copper and glass that I take for gold and diamonds.[10]

Descartes' claim is that we are often mistaken about that which is at hand or which concerns us, in other words by things *'qui nous touchent'*: the important point is why this is so. On what is this particular form of error based?

The possibility of a relationship, let alone a confusion, between copper and glass on the one hand and diamonds and gold on the other, could only be provided by resemblance. 'I' may be mistaken only because one resembles the other. The imagination moves from one to the other along a chain of resemblances. The theme of resemblance is well known in Descartes' philosophical work. It is continually cited as a cause of error and is often invoked in explanations of how the imagination works. There are however two aspects of resemblance that need to be emphasized here. The first resemblance can be described as a chain of interconnections where metonymy provides the possibility of movement along the chain, then this movement has the consequence of robbing the thing of its specific identity. The reason why metonymy accounts for this movement is that resemblance differs from representation in that the connection between two things is established by an element in each. The possibility of substitution belongs to shared elements rather than to the thing itself. Clear and distinct perception can be understood, therefore, as an intervention into a sequential chain which breaks it into separate identifiable links and thus re-establishes the identity of each specific thing. The links re-established as discrete identities mean that they have acquired

181

the self-identity envisaged in the definition of thing (*la chose*) in *La Logique du Port-Royal*. 'I call a thing what one can conceive as subsisting by itself and as the subject of all that can be conceived of there'.[11] The thing existing in itself can be represented. The importance of representation is outlined in the *Second Responses* where Descartes argues that the knowing subject represents the world to itself in the form of an idea. If it were not the case that clear and distinct perception overcame resemblance, knowledge of the world would be impossible, since the coextensivity between sign and thing that characterizes Cartesian representation would itself be impossible. Knowledge therefore is premised on the possibility of overcoming not simply the threat of the imagination, but more importantly the interrelationship between resemblance and metonymy, in other words the basis of fiction itself.

The second aspect on which I want to comment concerns elements of the historicity of resemblance. The need to overcome resemblance is a constant theme in the history of philosophy. St Augustine in *De Trinitate*[12] suggests that one of the ways in which 'mind' (*mens*) goes astray in its attempt to respond to the demand 'know thyself' was to think that it resembled the contents of mind and thus conceived of itself as a physical object.

The problem of resemblance and therefore of error, as Augustine indicates, cannot be divorced from the general question of mimesis and thus of fiction. Mimesis or imitation is itself inextricably linked to, if not originating in, the distinction drawn by Plato between the 'idea' and the physical instantiation of the 'idea'. In the *Republic*, in his treatment of the activity of the cabinet-maker Plato draws a distinction between the Form of the bed and a particular bed, and goes on to say that the cabinet maker,

> does not make what *is*, the product is not that which is, rather it
> is like what is without *being* it.   (section 597a, lines 3–5)

The distinction between 'what is' and that which is similar to 'what is' is not restricted to the category of physical objects and the 'idea' of the particular object, as it is this distinction which makes problematic one particular mimetic activity, namely poetry.

In sections 598–601c of the *Republic* Plato's preoccupations centre around his claim that the poet (here Homer) 'has no hold on truth' (section 600e, line 7). The inability of the poet to control the truth of what is said will allow the 'poetic' interchangeability of glass and diamond, for this does not necessitate knowledge of either. The other important aspect is that the initial likeness opens up the possibility that glass could be believed to be diamond. It is the possibility of being deceived about the exact nature of material objects that Plato is in general attempting to point out, though in this instance he is making the further claim that poets make use of the way in which there is the potentiality for deception in their creation of poetry. While Plato does not express it thus, it can none the less be argued that not only does poetry involve mimesis, it also makes use of, if not depends for its poetic quality on, metonymy. The consequence is that overcoming deception will involve a necessary reciprocity between the specific ontology of the object of knowledge (namely an ontology of stasis) and knowledge itself. Plato establishes this connection in the *Republic*, sections 477a–b, where he states, 'Knowledge is related to what is, and knows what is as it is' (section 477b, lines 8–9). This does of course commit Plato to the existence of a fundamental reality of things both temporal and eternal about which deception is possible. It is the retention by Descartes of this ontological structure that situates the concerns of Cartesian thought within the ontologico-epistemological framework that commences with Plato. The relationship between truth and fiction is here envisaged as taking place within this framework.

For Descartes to think that glass and copper were diamond and gold would be to engage in a fiction that was only possible because of resemblance, though this could be overcome by that particular form of cognition which would secure and ensure genuine knowledge of the world. Related to this is the fact that the threat of resemblance and imitation concerns the domain of 'common sense', and that therefore the guide of method is needed to steer knowledge of the world away from resemblances and towards things themselves. The existence of deception entails that the search for the foundations of knowledge is imperative.

The critique of 'common sense' involves, therefore, the importance of method; the knowing subject's subordination to method; the recognition that custom and example cannot provide the basis of truth; the necessity of the destruction of the chain of resemblances by clear and distinct perception (for this alone will facilitate the form of perception central to truth, namely of seeing one thing apart from the other);[13] and finally, the triumph by method over the continual threat

183

of fiction. These themes are also at play in Descartes' evaluation of his own school life.

THE FABLE OF OVERCOMING FABLES

Descartes' assessment of the training he received at Le Collège des Jésuites de la Flèche forms part of his general argument in favour of abandoning old educational procedures. The argument is in part based on his recognition that certainty and truth could not be based on anything that he was taught. He did suggest that some value could be gleaned from his lessons. 'I knew that the languages learned there are necessary in order to understand the books of the ancients; that the charm of fables awakens the mind.' [14] In the end he decided, however, that such a diverse range of subjects and the knowledge to be gained from them were unnecessary for the task at hand. 'But I thought I had already given enough time to languages and also to reading the books of the ancients, and their histories (*histoires*) and their fables (*fables*).' [15] Not only were such subjects diversions, in the case of fables there was a greater problem; 'fables make us imagine many events as possible which are not'.[16] In other words, fables introduced not just the threat of fiction and therefore deception, but its actual presence. The methodological was intended to triumph over the fabulatory. The instantiation of method was understood therefore as at the same time announcing the demise of fiction, in so far as it was a threat to truth, while opening an untraversable gulf between the possibility of error and the possibility of truth. Error's link to the imagination and thus to the fictive was to be permanently sealed off from the interrelationship between understanding and knowledge. The consequence would be that the actual existence of error could no longer threaten the presence of truth, and also that which brought it about, namely method.

Having sketched some of the prerequisites for a discourse on method as well as having indicated some of the elements presupposed in such a discourse, it is essential to examine Descartes' own understanding of the *Discours de la méthode*. This is not a recourse to intentionality and thus to viewing the *Discours* as a mere consequence of intentions; rather it is to respond to the autobiographical component of it in which it is argued, as we have already noted, that the solitary individual is more likely to discover complex truths than the multitude. If Descartes is able to claim, as a consequence of the critique of common sense, that the individual rather than the crowd is more likely to discover the truth, then it seems reasonable to take this conception of the *Discours* as itself presenting the frame within which the *Discours* may be interpreted.

In order that this be achieved we need to return to Part One of the *Discours* in which Descartes advances three different though inter-related conceptions of what the text actually is. In each case there are additional factors which make these comparisons of special interest. The first comparison is the following:

> I shall be very pleased to show in this discourse the ways that I have followed and to represent my life in it as in a painting (*un tableau*), so that everyone may judge it and that, learning from public response the opinions they have of it, this will be a new means (*moyen*) of instructing myself that will add to those which I am accustomed to using.[17]

According to Descartes the *Discours* will have the same status as a painting (*un tableau*) and in addition not only will it be judged by the many, the author now sees himself as constrained to respond to the many. The crowd's response will serve the author as a means of self-instruction, thus almost inverting the way in which the relationship between the one and the many had previously functioned in relation to the search for truth. This comparison and the related inversion will have to be explained in detail. However, prior to setting out on this task, it will be best to set in motion the other two comparisons made by Descartes, both of which occur in the same passage:

> [but] only proposing this work as a history (*une histoire*) or if you prefer as a fable (*une fable*) in which among other examples that can be imitated (*on peut imiter*) you will perhaps also find several that it would be correct not to follow.[18]

In this passage Descartes' claim is that the *Discours* is proposed not only as a story or history (*une histoire*) but also as a fable (*une fable*). However, implicit in this claim is the further point that the reader's response is delimited by imitation, as all possible responses centre around the question of whether or not to imitate the story being told. In other words, the writer of an autobiography is suggesting that after having read his life the reader may choose to live (or not) in the 'same' way. The problem of the 'same' is of course vast. Indeed it is this 'same' that is at the heart of Plato's final condemnation of the practice of imitation in the *Republic* (section 602a–b). Even though we shall return to the problem of the 'same' it is worth noting that part of Plato's objection is simply that imitation is possible independently of any real knowledge of what it is that is being imitated. It is after all the 'same' that plays into the hands of deception via resemblance.

The first problem concerns examining those things which are at play in the comparison of the *Discours* to a painting. The complicating factor is that Descartes is interested in the public's response to this specific painting. It is to another text, the first draft of which had been written at the time of his writing the *Discours*, that we can turn to see what is at play in the comparison between text and *tableau*. In the first *Meditation*, one of Descartes' initial moves is to prepare the way for the argument that the possibility of deception need not stand in the way of attaining truth and certainty. Part of these preparatory procedures involves establishing a distinction between the idea or thought, and the content of the idea or thought. The result of this is to provide Descartes with the conceptual manoeuvrability to overcome the threat posed to truth by dreaming. Establishing this distinction involves Descartes in a detailed consideration of painters whose paintings contain imaginary events or animals.

> At the same time it must at least be acknowledged that things which are represented to us in sleep are like the tableaux of painters which can only have been formed from the resemblance of something real and true (*de réel et de véritable*) and it is thus for at least these general things, namely eyes, heads, hands and all the rest of the body, are not imaginary but true and existent. For painters even during the careful construction of Sirens and Satyrs by bizarre and extraordinary forms cannot attribute to them entirely new natures but only make a certain mixture or composition of the limbs of various animals; or if their imagination is extravagant enough in order to invent something so new that the same thing had never been seen before and thus their work represented a thing purely fictitious and absolutely false (*une chose purement feinte et absolument fausse*) then at least the colours of which they are composed must be real (*véritables*).[19]

In this important passage Descartes' first move is to compare the reality of the contents of dreams with that of paintings whose reality is completely dependent upon their content resembling something that is real and true. The existence of a non-fictional element in both dreams and paintings is based on there being a resemblance between all or some of their content and something outside of the dream or painting whose existence could be assured. As the passage indicates, resemblance is enacted via representation, for resemblance furnishes paintings with their reality to the extent that what is represented resembles that of which it is a representation. Descartes forsees that the immediate objection to this characterization would be to argue that some paintings have contents that are so fabulous, there could be no possibility of a resemblance between what is represented in the painting and something '*réel*', let alone '*véritable*'. This argument is summed up in the question of how something can be represented in a painting when there is no apparent resemblance between the fabulous content and a reality beyond the *tableau*. It is essential to notice here that this objection depends upon a necessary and functional reciprocity between resemblance and representation.

Descartes responds to this already foreseen objection with the claim that even within fictions there are elements that are not fictional, that is, elements which both resemble and represent something '*réel*'. Even in the extreme case where the painting presents 'a thing purely fictitious and absolutely false', there is still an element that is true, for there remains a resemblance between, for example, the colours in the painting and the colours themselves.

Without having to dwell on every aspect of Descartes' argument it is clear that one of the inevitable consequences of the attempt to divorce fiction from reality is that the reality of the painting (or the representation) can no longer be said to lie in the representation *tout court* but only in the relationship between the elements and what they resemble. The difficulty is of course that even if the *tableau* were not fictional and there appeared to be a resemblance between the *tableau* and the *réel*, this could never be established with certainty so long as the reality of the painting depended upon resemblance. It is, after all, precisely resemblance that is at the heart of error, and thus it is that which needs to be replaced by clear and distinct perception. The problem is compounded by the fact that the reality of the painting does not lie exclusively in the painting but only in the elements of the representation. The truth of the *tableau* can be neither pinned down nor guaranteed for it is at every moment neither completely false nor completely true. The *tableau* is the exemplar of fiction.

The two questions that arise from this conclusion are, firstly, whether or not the *Discours de la méthode* is a fiction, and the related question of what would secure the truth of an autobiography? The answers revolve around the possibility that the text truly represents the life as it really happened. Any other configuration would entail a displacement between life and representation with the consequence that the representation no longer represented, and as such the *Discours* would indeed be a fiction.

There needs to be a coextensivity between the representation and what is represented. It is not surprising that the definition of 'sign' advanced in *La Logique du Port-Royal* is couched in terms of this coextensivity. That the sign is a metaphor for the way in which the *Discours* can be true and not a fiction, can be seen in the definition of sign: 'the sign encloses two ideas: one of the thing which represents: the other of the represented thing'.[20] From the definition it is clear that to the extent that the text remains a sign, it eludes fiction. The dilemma is that the conditions that the *Discours* must fulfil to be a sign are exactly those that it cannot. While there is an inter-dependence between representation and resemblance in so far as the relationship between 'the thing which represents' and 'the represented thing' cannot be based on resemblance, representation must involve more than resemblance. The structure of the sign demands coextensivity, and therefore the necessity to exclude resemblance is due to its connection with metonymy. The result of the connection between them is the blurring of the identity of those things within a metonymic chain and it is the aim of representation to represent the actual identity of 'the represented thing'. In this instance therefore, resemblance undermines the possibility of the *Discours* remaining a sign because the necessity of its presence undermines the coextensivity inherent in the structure of the sign. In other words, the necessary presence of resemblance means that the structure of the sign is never secure. The result of the need to exclude resemblance is that the *Discours* is irreparably divided from the possibility of its own truth. What would make it true is what removes it from the position where it could attain its own truth.

The other important consequence is that the method which is represented in the *tableau* and whose province is the discovery of truth is robbed of its certainty, not just by the fiction of the *tableau*, but also by the presence of the method in the *tableau*. The reality of the painting is provided by resemblance, and therefore the painting cannot both contain and present the truth. What is true in the *tableau* is true for reasons that are found beyond the frame, namely in the resemblance between the representation and the real. The *tableau* is literally unable to contain the truth.

It is, however, only in terms of the *Discours* understood as *tableau* that it is possible to understand the way that Descartes expects his readers to respond to the text. The peculiarity of the envisaged response is that it stands in contradistinction to his initial formulation of the relationship between the one and the many. The initial formulation was based on the fact that because people can and do hold false beliefs, it is more likely that an individual working on his or her own will discover the truth. The consequence of this is that the untutored response of the many should count for little in the search for truth. In the passage under consideration Descartes states that his response to public judgement will amount to another 'means' (*moyen*) by which he can instruct himself. Public opinion is on the one hand diverse, not grounded in method, not advanced from a position that ensures accurate judgement, and is thus that which should be excluded from the domain of truth. On the other hand, however, the response of the many is to be taken at face value as itself comprising a legitimate response, and moreover a response that is instructive in the general search for truth. It must be remembered that the second response is to a *tableau* and therefore it is the *tableau* that introduces the paradoxical position of public opinion. Indeed, this position is only possible if the initial structure of the one and the many is inverted. The reason that the inversion has this result is based on the function and necessity of resemblance in the contents as well as in the understanding of the *tableau*. The necessity of resemblance in order that the *tableau* be a *tableau*, coupled with the incommensurability between a unitary conception of truth and resemblance, combine to result in the abnegation of unity. The inversion dislodges the centrality of a unitary truth in so far as this conception of truth is structurally similar to the sign in *La Logique du Port-Royal*. It also dislodges the centrality of the solitary individual in pursuit of truth. In this regard, the inversion has the effect of casting doubt on both the efficacy as well as the centrality of the subject, that is, the 'I' of the *cogito ergo sum*.

As the inversion means that potential diversity is no longer excluded, the possibility of error is reincluded, and therefore the strategy that was intended to divorce truth from the possibility of error has resulted in uniting them. The comparison between text and *tableau* has the consequence of dividing the text, turning it into a paradox that could only ever be overcome by suppressing those moments within the text that gave rise to the division, and hence the paradox. It is thus that the unity of the text is contingent upon the suppression of the logic of paradox.

Not only did Descartes suggest a comparison between the *Discours* and a *tableau*, he went further and suggested that it could be understood as *une histoire* (a story or a history) or *une fable* (a fable). I will not dwell on the suggestion that the *Discours* can be read as *une histoire*, but only point out that Descartes' subsequent criticisms of *l'histoire* are usually seen as an attempt to set the limits of Virgil's *Aeneid*; in other words, to set the limits of fiction. It is perhaps sufficient to note that the term *l'histoire* in the context of its appearance in the *Discours* implicates the text, yet again, within philosophy's constant struggle to overcome fiction and to do more than merely tell stories.

Of more direct importance are the elements at play in reading the *Discours* as a fable. The first problem is how we are to understand the fable. While it is important to realize that the moral of a fable is practical in nature, it should be remembered that the fable can never present an obligation, that is, it cannot present anyone with a duty to act in one particular way rather than in another. In part this forms the basis of Rousseau's objection to the fable. The reading of fables to children, he argued, could result in their being as easily attracted to vice as to virtue. The fable does therefore lack the force of an imperative. This absence will emerge as being of great importance; however at this stage we must remain with the question of the relationship between the fable and philosophy. La Fontaine in the preface to his *Fables* wrote of the connection between philosophy and literature in the presentation of his version of the death of Socrates, as recounted in the *Phaedo*.

Socrates had been condemned to death but his execution had been postponed because of holidays. Cebes went to see him on the day of his death. Socrates said to him that the Gods had advised him several times during his sleep to apply himself to music before he died. First of all he had not understood what the dream meant: for, as music did not make men better what good could be derived from such an application? There must have

190

been some mystery involved especially as the Gods had not tired of sending him the same message. . . . he had noticed that there was music and poetry without harmony: but there was none without fiction; and Socrates only knew how to tell *the truth*. Finally he found a solution which was to choose fables that contained something of the truth, such as those of Aesop. He used therefore the last moments of his life putting them into verse.[21]

If, as La Fontaine suggests, a fable contains something of the truth, then its success in conveying it must involve fiction; for there is no good poetry 'without fiction'. The consequence of the link between poetry and fiction is that poetry and fiction depend for their communicative power on *persuasio*. In other words it is *persuasio* rather than *scientia* that is fundamental to the way in which fables convey truth. The difficulty is of course that while *scientia* is the mode of knowledge proper to method, and thus that which the *Discours* must impart, it is exactly this mode which is excluded in order that the fable can function effectively as the conveyor of truth. A fable depends upon persuasion rather than on the recognition of truths which are the consequence of clear and distinct perception.

This, however, is not the whole of the matter, for Descartes has also said that the reader may respond to the fable by imitating (or not) its content. The aspects that readers find of value may be imitated while others can be ignored. There are many areas of further discussion opened by imitation, but the most important concerns the relationship between imitation and the failure of a fable to present an imperative.

It has already been noted that fundamental to the critique of common sense is the position that resemblance cannot provide the basis of knowledge. Knowledge involves knowing the thing as it is, and it is to that extent that the object of knowledge is unitary in nature. Linked to this conception of knowledge is what could be called an epistemological imperative, in that, since neither truth nor knowledge admit of degrees, the true as a consequence has to be recognized as true. This point is further reinforced by the fact that as the 'natural light' is universal, the truths which are the consequences of the application of method and recognized as such by the 'natural light' are also universal. Universal truths have to involve an epistemological imperative.

An important aspect of such an imperative is that it be recognized as an imperative. Responding to it must involve, therefore, the full recognition both of the imperative *qua* imperative as well as those elements essential to establishing the imperative *qua* imperative. Two of the most important of these other elements are the recognition of the failure of resemblance to ground knowledge and the necessary overcoming of the threat of fiction. Both are essential in order that the epistemological imperative be recognized.

The problem is obvious. This *Discours* is not just described as a fable by Descartes; it has already been noted that it is constrained to adopt the figure of fiction. It is not, therefore, that there is an incompatibility between the claim made by Descartes that the *Discours* can be read as a fable, and the need to establish a discourse on method. If it were, then the only difficulty would be that the text contained a contradiction. The difficulty is more complex because the text, in order that it be a methodological treatise, has to adopt a fictional mode of presentation. The problem, therefore, is not contradiction, but paradox. It is the paradoxical element that emerges in relation to the imperative. A fable, which the fictionalized *Discours* has become, cannot advance that which it must to be a discourse on method, namely an epistemological imperative. The *Discours* has become the site of the paradox stemming from philosophy's attempt to rid itself of fiction.

As a fable cannot present its readers with imperatives and as the *Discours*, in order to be a methodological text, must be followed to the letter, its only possibility of surviving as the presenter of methodological imperatives is by the suppression of the fictive within it. It is this question, of suppression and therefore of reading suppression, that will serve as a conclusion.

The reason why this kind of concluding comment is needed is simply that the *Discours* is seldom read as a text which is in the end forced to relate philosophy's fabulous end. The question emerges, therefore, of the relationship between a conventional reading of Descartes' text, which reads it *à la lettre*, and therefore as a discourse on method, and the reading deployed in the preceding pages.[22] This is by no means an easy question to answer, and all that will be attempted is to offer an indication of a fuller response.

The major point of divergence concerns the way in which the emergence of a philosophical argument or position is interpreted or understood. The difference centres on the importance attributed to textuality. The conventional reading seems in some way to rely on what it takes to be a non-textual outside that provides the means or reasons for interpreting the text. The outside could be context, or perhaps even an investigation of the viability of the arguments at play in the text under consideration. In each instance it is the purportedly non-textual that provides access to the text. The proof that the outside is thought to be of a fundamentally different nature to the textual inside is that it is not itself subjected to any form of analysis. It is as though the use of contexts or the investigation of arguments were themselves beyond interpretation. The claim being made is not that contexts are beyond interpretation, but rather that the process of having recourse to them is. The consequence of subjecting both contexts and the use made of them to interpretation, and thus of emphasizing their textuality, is not that philosophy becomes ahistorical and no longer interested in historically delimited intertextual studies; it is rather that the claims of history and historicity lose their automatic privilege, and the conditions that govern the emergence of the text become of central importance. History is reinscribed within the practice of interpretation and is no longer in the untenable position of attempting to remain outside, governing interpretation. The position of government moves from the outside to the inside, and in so doing dissolves the inside/outside opposition. The other consequence is that history becomes textual. It is more than simply concerned with texts, for it is itself a textual event.

The emphasis on textuality means that the text cannot be given or attributed an organizing principle from outside the text itself. The direct result is that the text is no longer a simple unity but rather is the site where the interplay of the conditions governing its existence takes place, where those conditions are deployed in relation to a text's intentional logic. There can be therefore no general statement concerning the conditions at play in all texts. Once again, this would be to erect a governing theory which sought to establish an outside that would control the inside. The absence of a general theory of texts (as opposed to a description of texts) means that what is at issue is a reading of a particular text. In this instance the text in question was Descartes' *Discours de la méthode* and its attempt to forge a radical distinction between truth and fiction. In focusing on the unfolding of the text, what emerged was the impossibility of this task. It is at this stage possible to offer an interim conclusion, namely that the *Discours* is indeed a fable, one recounting philosophy's oldest aspiration. The moral of the fable is practical, in so far as it suggests, though no more than suggests, a way of reading texts.[23]

NOTES

1 As the major concern of this chapter is Descartes' *Discours de la méthode* I have not attempted to provide a justification for this reworking of philosophy's goal. I have however provided some justification in my 'Wisdom and science in Augustine and Descartes', *Ideas and Production*, 2, 1984.

2 This paper is collected in M. Heidegger, *Wegmarken* (Klostermann, Frankfurt, 1967). English translation in *Martin Heidegger: Basic Writings*, ed David Farrell Krell (Routledge & Kegan Paul, London) 1978.

3 This paper is also collected in Heidegger, *Wegmarken*, see in particular pp. 23–5.

4 The passage I have in mind is the following and it does I think show the importance Heidegger attaches to the 'oversight'. The translation comes from the English edition by David Farrell Krell, *Nietzsche, Vol. 1: The Will to Power as Art* (Routledge & Kegan Paul, London, 1981), p. 149.

> That the question of the essence of truth is missing in Nietzsche's thought is an oversight unlike any other; it cannot be blamed on him alone, or him first of all – if it can be blamed on anyone. The 'oversight' pervades the entire history of Occidental philosophy since Plato and Aristotle.

Clearly more needs to be said about Heidegger's own position if only because of his special understanding of the term 'essence'. On this latter problem see George A. Ghanotakis, 'Unscrambling Heidegger's notion of "essence": a consideration of some topographical and thematic difficulties', *Journal of the British Society for Phenomenology*, 15, 1984.

5 Descartes, *Oeuvres Philosophiques*, ed F. Alquié, vol. 1 (Garnier, Paris, 1963–7), p. 251. This letter is also discussed by Peter France in *Rhetoric and Truth in France* (Oxford University Press, Oxford, 1972), p. 41. France's analysis of Descartes follows a different path to the one pursued here.

6 All references to the *Discours de la méthode* are to the edition established by Étienne Gilson (Vrin, Paris, 1967).

7 For a discussion of this point that follows a similar though not the same line, see Richard Rorty, *Philosophy and the Mirror of Nature* (Blackwell, Oxford, 1980).

8 Gilson (ed.), *Discours*, p. 10. All translations are my own.

9 ibid., p. 16.

10 ibid., p. 3.

11 A. Arnauld and P. Nicole, *La Logique ou l'art de penser* (Flammarion, Paris, 1970), p. 73. The value of the *Logique* is that its Cartesian nature and the fact that it was continually modified between 1660 and 1683

means that it provides a contemporary commentary on Descartes' own writings.

12 For a further discussion of this point see my paper mentioned in note 1 above.

13 This point is made by Descartes in *La Recherche de la vérité* in *Oeuvres Philosophiques*, ed Alquié, vol. 2, p. 1140.

14 Gilson (ed.), *Discours*, p. 5.

15 ibid., p. 6.

16 ibid., pp. 6–7.

17 ibid., pp. 3–4.

18 ibid., p. 4.

19 The text of the *Meditations* that I have used is *Meditationes de Prima Philosophia. Méditations Métaphysiques*, Texte latin et traduction du Duc de Lyons. Introduction et Notes par Geneviève Rodis-Lewis (Vrin, Paris, 1966), pp. 20–1. The virtue of this edition is that it provides both the Latin and the French text on opposite pages. The important claim of the representation of something both fictitious and false is borne out in the French, quoted in the text; and in the Latin 'fictium sit & falsum'.

20 Arnauld and Nicole, *La Logique*, p. 80.

21 La Fontaine, *Fables* (Flammarion, Paris, 1966), pp. 27–8.

22 I do not wish to pretend for a moment that this chapter is a complete departure from all other interpretations. Indeed, it is indebted, as are all current reinterpretations of Descartes, to Jean-Luc Nancy's important collection, *Ego Sum* (Flammarion, Paris, 1979). Another important recent interpretation of Descartes is that by Sylvie Romanowski, *L'Illusion chez Descartes* (Editions Klincksieck, Paris, 1974). The question of imitation receives an interesting discussion in John D. Lyons, 'Subjectivity and imitation in the *Discours de la Méthode'*, *Neophilologus*, 66, 1982.

23 I wish to acknowledge the help given by John Christie and Sarah Richmond who provided extremely valuable comments on an early draft of this chapter.

12

THE REDEMPTION OF VALUE: LAPORTE, WRITING AS *ABKURZUNG*

The value of writing resides in its increasing resistance to the question of value. This resistance has elicited a number of different responses. However the form they usually take invariably involves that specific attempt to redeem value that necessitates its having been reworked by investments stemming from a variety of sources all of which are, in the end, inimical to the essential heterogeneity of the literary text.[1] The attempt to reassert value is thought to be essential in order to avoid the problems raised by the relationship between heterogeneity and evaluation. It is of course a futile attempt. It is also unnecessary. There is no reason why these problems need give rise either to a celebration of kitsch or to an unending and proliferating relativism. If the interpolation of conventional ethical and moral positions (guided by truth) into the literary text is no longer a viable move within interpretation, how then is evaluating possible? Any attempt to answer this question can only begin after it has been recognized that a redemption of value must be predicated upon the actuality of a revaluation of value itself. Revaluation, here, concerns the move from homogeneity to heterogeneity. The temporality of the move is complex. It does not involve progression but rather the temporality at work within the psychoanalytic conception of *Nachträglichkeit*. It is the original site that comes to be reworked. (Its being the 'original' is thereby put in question.)

The first move to be made in the revaluation of value involves dwelling on the complex interplay between tradition, repetition and the plural. The tradition within which value – both aesthetic and moral – is situated is repeated in and as the dominant tradition within the history of thought. Fundamental both to tradition and to what makes the repetition of tradition possible is the articulation of these different conceptions of value within the terms set by the conceptions

197

of unity that figure within them. Unity here is, at the very least, twofold. On the one hand the intentional logic[2] of any theory of value assumes the essential unity of that theory. On the other hand it constructs the object of interpretation in terms of what can be described as its self-image. Here the construction involves the construal of the object of interpretation in terms of the essential homogeneity assumed by the intentional logic of the mode of interpretation. The homogeneity of the object of interpretation is therefore a consequence of its having been thus determined by the intentional logic of the mode of interpretation. The assumption of homogeneity constructs the relationship between object and interpretation in terms of an ontological homology. The distinction between object and interpretation is thereby bridged. The ontological homology does not restrict the range of interpretations except in so far as interpretation must assume the twofold conception of homogeneity.

Interpretation becomes flat and mechanistic: the dull drive toward truth taking place in the absence of intensity. Furthermore it is the complex interrelationship between the ontological homology, intentional logic and the self-image that provides what in Derrida's terms would be the site of deconstruction. As within any site interest may often lie beyond the borders. It is precisely the multitude of border relations – that which is situated within them, what cannot be situated within them, what must be situated beyond them, etc., – that is at stake here.

Border relations not only figure within Laporte's work, they also provide the dominant form in which the critical writings take place. Mathieu Bénézet writing about *Fugue* argues that:

> *L'écriture de* Fugue *évide les métaphores, elle les rend exsangues, elle fait de leur vide la condition de son œuvre: immense désœuvrement de* Fugue *qui ainsi ruine la figure romancière dans sa régence.*[3]
> (The writing of *Fugue* hollows metaphors, leaving them bloodless. It turns their emptiness into the precondition of the work itself: the vast unworking of *Fugue* which thus ruins the novelistic figure in its regency.)

Bénézet has not simply identified the disruptive force of *Fugue*. He is making far more important claims, two of which need to be noted. The first is that the emptying of metaphor is not the consequence of

198

Laporte's work but its precondition, one which then comes to be enacted, if not acted out, in the text. The second is that *Fugue*, as a consequence of the enactment of the precondition, 'ruins' the regency of the novelistic figure.

In the first instance both the border and contents of metaphor have been undone. Metaphor as a semantic site constituted a complex but none the less identifiable relationship between signifier and signified. The function of metaphor within *Fugue* is no longer determined in advance – plotted out, the borders already established – and yet metaphor still figures. In addition the border delimited by *'la figure romancière'* has been ruined, its power overthrown from within. The border, now, barely borders. The strategy for the redemption of value has become a border question.

It is within the ambit opened by the play of borders that it is essential to pose the question of how Laporte's work is to be understood. In a sense this is already to ask a secondary question. The initial, and more perplexing one, is: how is it to be presented? Will citation not flatten rather than flatter? The gap between text and interpretation is both closed and opened by citing Laporte.[4] The work resists citation and yet any argument advanced to secure this claim would have to involve citation. In the place of an attempt to resolve this paradox, further headway into the work itself will need to be made. Rather than trying to bridge the gap between interpretation and text via an almost anonymous citation that would exemplify the difficulty in advance of any interpretation, a different approach will be taken. Emphasis will be directed to the borders and their construction. The place of limits and the delimited place of interpretation are opened by – in addition to opening up – the two paths of music and biography.

The presence of music and biography does not involve marking out an interpretive thematics. On the contrary they are deployed within work, marking out the work's terrain (its work). Music and biography are, in part, an unscripted *mise-en-abyme*. The music in question resists incorporation into either the progression preordained by a teleological and prescriptive patterning, or an artful showing where mimesis operates within music in order to show music's outside. Resisting mimesis is at the same time to resist teleology. The incorporation of teleology into the interpretation of art, writing, etc. – and thereby with the object construed in teleological terms – reduces resistance to a simple refusal or negation of tradition. Resistance, however, is that moment of tension opened up by an incorporation of tradition (or elements of tradition) but where that incorporation no longer provides the dominant logic of the object of interpretation. Resistance is diverse and resists a synthetic thematization.

The study of *Fugue* is the study of repetition: a form of repetition, repeated within *Fugue* as the fugal form. Therefore within *Fugue* (and within the fugal form), the text (and the texture) become the site of their own recitation. A written text – a written fugue – instantiates itself within itself as its own subject: writing as the expression of writing. The instantiation, repetition, takes place within the medium to which writing subjects itself. The written fugue writes writing and as such provides no way out:

> *J'ai longtemps cru que l'acte d'écrire était le lieu d'une guerre entre le dedans et le dehors, l'intimité et la sauvagerie, l'écriture conservatrice et la contre-écriture destructrice, mais il y a le jeu d'écrire et rien d'autre, singulière machine de combat qui lutte amoureusement avec elle-même . . .*[5]
> (I thought for a long time that the act of writing was the space of a war waged between the inside and the outside, intimacy and savagery, the writing which conserves and the counter-writing that destroys, but there is the game/gamble of writing and nothing else, a strange war machine that struggles lovingly with itself . . .)

The interplay of writing itself sets the parameters of *Fugue*. What takes place within it takes place within a fugue.

Fugue begins with a quotation from the *Dictionnaire Robert* giving a definition of fugue, and within which there is a quotation from Rousseau. The quotation suggests that the elements of the fugue are meant to '*se fuir et se poursuivre l'une l'autre*' (run from and pursue one another). Identified here is Laporte's work. The '*poursuivre*' (pursue) not only names part of one of his texts. It is alluded to in the titles *Supplément, Codicille, Suite*. The continuity, the addition, the supplement, the pursuit, unfold in the titles and in the fugal form as well as in *Fugue*. The move from *fuga* and *fugare* (perhaps from Dufay to Bach) involves the move from a musical imitation enacted by one voice following another to an imitation based on a reworking and repetition. The temporality of each form is different.

While it is tempting to dwell on the force of Laporte's citation from the *Dictionnaire Robert*, it raises, in addition to its own interpretive potential, the problem of describing a writing that may involve imitation but cannot be said to involve mimesis. This may seem a straightforward contradiction in so far as imitation has to involve a type of mimesis. The complexity of the problem and the appearance of a contradiction marks the need to reconsider the role played here by the relationship between the inside and the outside.

Mimesis in its classical sense must involve a relationship between the expression and that which is outside the expression but which comes to be expressed within it. Within Platonism this involved a transgression of the form (ἰδέα/εῖδος) if it were thought that an artistic mimetic presentation could present the form itself. However in moving from mimesis within art to mimesis in language the transgressive element is no longer either as apparent let alone as dominant. In the *Cratylus*, for example, a fundamental part of Socrates' argument is premised upon the possibility of mimesis; it provides the criterion for both correctness and truth. Indeed in the following passage artistic mimesis appears less problematic than it does in the *Republic*. It concerns the assigning of likeness in which the correct attributes of something are used in its mimetic presentation. Of these assignments Socrates states that:

in the case of both imitations [τοῖς μιμ ήτασιν] – painting and names – [they are] correct [ὀρθὴν] and in the case of names not only correct but true [ἀληθὴ] and the other kind that applies the unlike imitation, I call incorrect and in the case of names false.   (430d)

For Plato therefore, and for the tradition to which Platonism gave rise, the intentional logic within which mimesis is articulated concerns the relationship between an outside and inside. It is furthermore a relationship that can express the truth as well as falsehood. The consequence of this is that mimesis must be understood not as a simple showing but as definitional of any relationship (structured in terms of a presentation or showing) that involves the distinction between an inside and an outside, where that which is inside intends to present the outside. Mimesis need not involve success, accuracy, or truth. Mimesis names a relationship between, as has already been suggested, that which is outside the mode of mimetic presentation and its subsequent presentation within that mode. (The mode may be a painting, a name, a poem, a play, etc.)

Now, within fugal form what comes to be repeated – imitated – is what is presented within the fugue itself. Within the fugue, while there is a general threefold division, its potential for variation within that division cannot be delimited in advance. Laporte's reference/use/allusion/deployment of fugue and fugal form, not just in *Fugue*, but in other titles suggested by the term, or the form, unfolds both within repetition and expression. It is in relation to both these points that the question of value can be re-posed.

Expression in taking place beyond those borders delimited by the relationship between the inside and the outside – in involving what Laporte called '*le jeu d'écrire*' (the game/gamble of writing) – is situated within the writing of heterogeneity:

> *l'écriture est toujours agie au cœur de son activité.*[6]
> (Writing is always being acted at the heart of its activity).

The important element here is the identification of writing being the acting of writing. The subject introduces itself. It repeats and reworks itself. The fugal form becomes a writing that resists the opposition between the inside and the outside and is therefore situated beyond the possibility of its own incorporation into mimesis. It is not 'outside' mimesis. It is simply that it is not enacted in mimetic terms and therefore cannot be evaluated within them. The question that emerges here concerns the relationship between the impossibility of mimesis and heterogeneity. Laporte in reaffirming what had *always already been there* opens up a writing that can no longer be incorporated within the reign of the Same and thus within the dominant tradition within the history of thought, philosophy and writing.

This is not to deny that the character of what has *always already been there* is difficult, if not elusive, if what is being sought is an all-encompassing designation and description. Any description of this ontologico-temporal concatenation has to take the intentional logic of the work into consideration. If the intentional logic decrees that the work is enacted within semantic homogeneity, then the heterogeneous is that which is already there, despite the decree, in spite of the logic, but then only for that mode of interpretation that is itself enacted within heterogeneity. This is interpretation as redemption.

The more interesting case – indeed the one that is both more important and disruptive – concerns the attempt within writing to affirm heterogeneity. This affirmation is, of course, plural. It involves a particular relation to tradition, to the traditional *telos* of writing, to

202

mimesis, etc. Rather than being read within the terms set by *always already there*, it is to be understood as 'there', as the text, *'le jeu d'écrire'*. However, and this is to locate a limit in Laporte's work that will need to be explored elsewhere, in greater detail, there is no need to restrict the affirmative dimension to writing (in the narrow sense of the term), let alone to literature. When, for example, Jean-François Lyotard argues against the 'pedagogical' interpretations of Cézanne, he does so because they fail to acknowledge what has been called thus far the affirmative. In Lyotard's terms such as interpretation

laisse dans l'ombre le principe souterrain de déreprésentation qui opère en permanence dans l'approche de l'objet par Cézanne.[7]

(leaves in the shadows the underground principle of derepresentation which is permanently at work within Cézanne's approach to the object.)

The affirmative, here, is that which is 'there' in Cézanne's work and which therefore demands that particular form of interpretation that, to use Lyotard's formulation, allows it to appear. There is clearly more at play here than interpretation since the denial of heterogeneity by homogeneity – the denial of difference by the reign of the Same – has both political and ethical considerations.

The fugal form, *Fugue* and writing itself open onto the path of biography. The complexity of biography within Laporte's writings is presented by him in the following terms. The element of danger, of intensity, involves the recognition that both the exclusion of a meta-commentary on writing/biography, as well as the comment itself (the length of the citation cannot be avoided) are the work of writing:

Je préfère ... réserver le terme de Biographie, voire celui d'écrire, à l'entreprise littéraire où écrire constituant le seul sujet: ce dont on traite, le seul objet: ce que l'on cherche, et la seule pratique, est par conséquent inséparable de sa 'mise en abyme'. Il ne s'agit pas d'écrire un Traité, d'énumérer les opérations qui seraient effectuées par un praticien inconnu dans un autre lieu et dans un autre temps, mais il faut instituer un texte practico-théorique. Ecrire, nous le savons, provoque une série indéfinie de remaniements et même, de loin en loin, une refonte radicale qui engendre une série d'opérations, jamais exactement les mêmes, mais qui justement ne peuvent être exécutées sans être inventées, explorées, décrites comme telles et par conséquent inscrites dans le texte.[8]

(I prefer . . . to reserve the term Biography, even that of writing itself, for the literary enterprise where writing by constituting the sole subject – what it is about – the sole object – what is being searched for –, and the sole practice, is consequently inseparable from its *'mise-en-abyme'*. There is no question of writing a Treatise, of enumerating the operations which would be carried out by an unknown practitioner in another place and at another time, but it is necessary to institute a practico-theoretical text. Writing, as we know, provokes an indefinite series of revisions and even, on occasion, a radical reorganization which produces a series of operations, which are never exactly the same, but which cannot be carried out without being invented, explored, described as such and consequently inscribed within the text.)

To begin with, it is essential to note that biography is linked, not to the life of writing as opposed to the life of the writer, but rather to the life of the writer which is the life of writing and which has via this subtle variation become the writing: the writing itself.

The particular citation – the one cited above – is not from *Fugue*, but from the next volume included in *Une Vie*, namely *Supplément*. The interpretive difficulty here is straightforward. It concerns the relationship between the passage dealing with biography and which delimits it in terms of writing (and thereby overcoming the trap posed by the opposition between life and writing), its place within a book entitled *Supplément*, and the place of both of these elements within a larger book entitled *Une Vie*. Unpicking this interrelated tangle necessitates returning to that which was originally held in suspense, that is the bracketed relationship between life and writing.

The relationship between life and writing involves a repetition of the relationship between life and art. In other words this is not a simple relationship, an arbitrary bringing together of two random counters. The relationship enacts an opposition – an either/or – in which one term works to exclude the other. The exclusion is linked to the relationship – once again an either/or – discussed above, between the inside and the outside. Biography involves the written form, expression, of that which is outside writing. Life as the outside receives its mimetic presentation, via writing, as biography. It is not difficult to see here what, in terms of the interpretation enacted thus far, would count as the interconnection between biography, mimesis and the opposition between the inside and the outside. It is precisely this interconnection that makes Laporte's claims about biography explicable in terms of both resistance and redemption, and which will in turn open up the way for a more general understanding of redemption. Both of these are central to any revaluation of value.

If resistance is the tension of a repetition that involves innovation, experimentation, etc., then an interpretation that identifies such an event is redemptive. The reason why this is the case is that it is an interpretation that does itself resist the ontological homology demanded by the assumed homogeneity within the object of interpretation and the mode of interpretation. What becomes redeemed is either an affirmation, or the heterogeneity that has *always already been there*. Redemptive interpretation highlights in both instances the 'there'. While this thread will need to be pursued, it does, at the very least, allow for a way of understanding the distinction as well as the connection between affirmative (and therefore avant-garde) texts and affirmative (and therefore avant-garde) interpretations. The revaluation of value will involve the affirmative and hence will be a redemption of value inscribed within the very practice to which it gave rise.

The presentation of biography within Laporte's *Supplément* involves the attempt to repeat biography beyond the oppositions in which it is usually presented. Biography as the writing about, or of, self enacts, as was suggested above, the opposition between the inside and the outside. However for the sake of accuracy it would also have to be added that it was enacted within that opposition. In other words the opposition life/art (writing) and inside/outside are, *qua* oppositions, interarticulated. They involve therefore an ontological homology. The repetition of biography beyond these oppositions allows for the presentation of biography, as well as the inter-articulated oppositions, but where that interarticulation no longer dominates the presentation of biography. In more general terms it is this form of repetition that is marked by the 'beyond'. Within interpretation 'beyond' means that what presents itself to be interpreted resists interpretations that stem from and thus would take place within the categories, oppositions, concepts, etc., that are handed down within the dominant tradition. The 'beyond' therefore is neither utopian, nor Hegelian, nor the outside of that which is inside.

The 'beyond' is the actuality of resistance. It is also present – and presented – within and as redemptive interpretation.

The repetition at work within *Supplément* is not a simple following or re-presentation in which the repetition is the repetition of the Same. The Same figures within repetition but in this instance the repetition is new. There is however a striking and disturbing element in this work. Its mode of address moves between an 'I' (*Je*) which, for example, recognizes (*'N'ai-je pas déjà reconnu'* [Have I not already recognized]), or one that names/calls (*'je l'ai appelé'* [I called/named it]) and the 'I' (*Je*) that is almost instantiated as an object within the text.

> *J'aurais voulu désigner Je du seul nom de scripteur ou de scriptographe, mais il est aussi joueur et enjeu d'une partie qu'il commente, et comment oublierais-je que Je est corps, matière qui porte et supporte la rature de toute scription!* [9]
> (I would have wanted to designate 'I' with the sole name of scriptor or scriptographer, but he/it is also a player and the object of play in a game on which he/it is a commentary, and how could I forget that 'I' is a body, matter bearing and sustaining the erasure of all scription!)

It is clear both from the loss emerging from any attempt to translate this passage, as well as its own internal (French) semantic combinations, that the *Je* unfolds in a plurality of forms. The *Je* has become the pluralized site of its own reflection on itself. In a sense, therefore, it does not matter that the identification established between *Je* and body (*corps*) results in the possible erasure of scription. The significant element is that this identification takes place in writing (in scription). Writing the possibility of the impossibility of writing can only serve both to affirm its power while denying it any essential nature. Writing has no essence.

Writing and the *Je* have become plural. The presentation of this plurality takes place within the interplay between '*Je*', '*je*', '*joueur*', '*enjeu*', '*il commente*'/'*comment*', '*oublierais-je que Je*', '*porte*'/'*supporte*'. The I (*je*) writes but the 'I' (*Je*) resists precisely that reduction. Indeed the possibility of biography, in the sense that the term is deployed by Laporte, is based on exactly the impossibility of reducing the *je* to the *Je*. There is however more at stake.

At play here are two specific – though of course related – moments of disruption and even though they cannot be followed in detail they need, none the less, to be noted. The 'I' reflecting on itself so that it comes to 'see' itself as itself marks a fundamental moment within the philosophy of reflection. It is this possibility that, amongst other things, marks the distinction between Fichte on the one hand and Hegel on the other. The Hegelian conception of absolute self-consciousness necessitates the unity of consciousness in order that consciousness be present to itself. Once the 'I' and consciousness become a pluralized site, then that plurality is no longer explicable in Hegelian terms. The impossibility of reducing the *je* to the *Je* opens up a philosophical, literary and interpretive field beyond Hegelianism. The other element concerns the disruption of the Cartesian subject. In sum this involves the impossibility of *scribo ergo sum* securing the unity of the 'I' of consciousness. The 'I' of the *sum* has, because of and within writing, become the mark of its own plurality. It is not just that the 'I' of writing and the 'I' of the existence are split, it is rather that the split takes place both 'within' as well as 'between'. Laporte's *Une Vie* refuses any straightforward interpolation either into the philosophy of reflection or Cartesianism.

It is possible via a close and scrupulous reading to trace the non-reductive presentation and unfolding of the many levels of *je/Je*. The point that emerges in this instance however is the way in which what appeared as a personal reflection – personal and hence biographical in the traditional sense – became in the end the enactment of the impossible possibility of the personal. Any claim within the text, within *Supplément*, that appears to privilege the voice of the authorial 'I' is, as soon as it is proffered, called into question by that which presented it in the first place, namely writing. The *'enjeu'* of writing, what is at stake in writing, checks the power of both the *je* and the *Je* (as well as the heritage of Cartesian thought). Further elements need to be taken into consideration given that this personal and complex interplay of *je* and *Je* also touches upon the difficult problems of translation and signatures. In each case what is at play is authorship and authorization. The heterogeneous text can, within that mode of interpretation that does not attempt to still it, allow interpretation (though clearly interpretations) to proliferate. The end of interpretation is called into question by the absence of dominance of teleology. Such is the end of interpretation. The object of interpretation, here, has yet to be clarified. The inclusion of all the texts either mentioned or discussed thus far, in a larger and all-encompassing text called *Une Vie*, is therefore the dimension that must now be explored.

207

As Laporte's writings are traced throughout *Une Vie*, biography is continually repeated anew. It is reworked, sometimes in relation to signatures, other times in relation to psychoanalytic considerations, and even within the terms set by a confrontation, in writing, as writing, with Roger Laporte. The two latter elements are most apparent in *Codicille*, a supplement to a work that can never finish. What then is a life? What is *Une Vie*? Perhaps the only way of beginning to answer this question is to re-ask it in terms of naming. In other words, what does the title *Une Vie* name? What is grouped beneath the name? Does the name name no more than the totality of texts grouped and named *Une Vie*?

All of these questions turn on the impossibility of securing continuity in writing. The 'I' deployed through these texts, the subject of biography, 'thanatographie', the 'I' that has been wounded, the 'I' that suffered, the 'I' that entitled the last section of *Une Vie*, the entire book, *Poursuivre*, is at the same time both the same and not the Same. It is this quality that appears in fugal form. The voices, here introduced as each 'I', come to be repeated and reworked throughout *Une Vie*. There can be no end to *Une Vie*, not because the book cannot end, the book does end and in addition fugal form posits not just an ending but its introduction within the stretto. None the less, fugal form is open to an infinite repetition. It is impossible to limit, except in so far as the threefold internal structure is concerned, what can take place within the form. The plural 'I' is the same because it involves a repetition that is continually different and hence not the Same. The 'I' of biography because it is the 'I' of writing cannot be limited, hence the impossibility of unified and unitary consciousness emerging from *scribo ergo sum*. Within writing there is no border. *Une Vie* names this continual reworking of borders.[10] In philosophical terms this means that Becoming holds sway over Being. Here is the Nietzschean gesture. *Une Vie* cannot end because of its refusal to let teleology dominate the temporality of its progression. Repetition refuses the temporality of ends which is the end of Being. The radical separation of Becoming and Being – a separation enacted and affirmed within *Une Vie* – is captured by Nietzsche in fragment 708 of *Der Wille zur Macht*.

Das Werden hat keinen Zielzustand, mündet nicht in ein Sein.
(Becoming has no final state of rest, does not flow into a Being.)

It is at this juncture – this border – that the question of value can be allowed to reappear. It has already been suggested that value, rather than involving ethical or aesthetic considerations, can be reconsidered in terms of affirmation and resistance. If redemption within interpretation is the recognition of heterogeneity, then what is the redemption of value? The first aspect of an answer to this question necessitates the recognition that the heterogeneous is not simple difference. It is not the difference which is the same as that which is opposed to identity. The heterogeneous demands an understanding of difference as differential. The differential is ontological in form but has implications within semantics and interpretation. The second aspect is that value will come to be deployed within the site of resistance. In other words that general repetition in which a term, concept, etc., is present but not dominated by the logic within which tradition hands it down will also incorporate value.[11]

The redemption of value leading to a revaluation of value means, in the first instance, that the repetition of value is a repetition beyond (in the sense that the term has been used above) the dominance of the dominant tradition. The revaluation of value therefore is the affirmation of and within that beyond. This is the reason why, as has already been suggested, the redemption of value is at work within the practice to which it gives rise. It is now possible to go a step further. Value is the recognition and enactment of affirmation. It is not to be expressed in evaluative terms. It involves a particular relation to, and understanding of, tradition. Value becomes linked to experimentation, to resistance and to the plural. The revaluation of value – its redemption – is an artistic, literary, philosophical and interpretive practice unfolding, in its plurality as the avant-garde. Value – the affirmation of value – is delimited by a concern to attribute value. The fact that it cannot be automatically attributed stems from an interpretive practice that is itself structured by the attempt to interpret that which resists tradition and hence which opens up the site of tension.

Perhaps the only way to end is in terms of citation: completion as citation. Bénézet describes *Fugue* in the following way. It should be noted that it is a description opened by the affirmative:

> *Tout le livre est la reprise d'un commencement impossible, immense phrase qui désespère de son sens et de commencer enfin, lors même que le livre s'achève.*[12]
>
> (The entire book is the continuation of an impossible beginning, an immense sentence which despairs of its meaning and of finally starting, even when the book is about to finish.)[13]

NOTES

1 As will be seen, the text in question is not reducible simply to the literary text. What is at stake here is both textuality in general and the nature of that generality.

2 I am using the expression in order to provide the interpretive means by which to identify the dominant logic of a particular text or object of interpretation. I have deployed it within the field of painting in Chapter 3 'Betraying faces: Lucian Freud's self-portraits'.

3 Mathieu Bénézet, *Le Roman de la langue* (Union Générale d'Editions, Paris, 1973), p. 82. Bénézet's excellent book is both a study of the novel as a form of writing as well as a presentation of some of the most significant writers and texts of the period 1960–75.

4 There is, of course, not only just the problem of citation but also the question of where the citation is from. Laporte's work – his writings – over the past twenty years (*La Veille, Une voix de fin silence, Pourquoi?, Fugue, Supplément, Fugue 3, Codicille, Suite, Moriendo*) is gathered, now, in one volume, entitled *Une Vie* (POL, Paris, 1986). It is not that works located in the overall text are so different that reference cannot be made to more than one. It is rather that rereading them in the light of each other brings to the fore concerns and differences that were not initially apparent. This is most striking in the case of *La Veille*, originally published by Gallimard in 1963. While writing figures within the text, its presence both as act and figure is mediated by the third-person 'Il':

> Il *vient pour que j'écrive: voilà ce que j'ai toujours naïvement cru et, depuis que j'ai commencé ce travail, je suis allé jusqu'à prétendre qu'écrire correspondait à son désir préalable de je ne sais quelle expression. . . . Sans* lui, *jamais je n'aurais eu à écrire; s'il n'y avait l'œuvre,* il *demeurerait inconnu, pourquoi est-*il *donc détaché de toute œuvre? – Comment écrire ne m'aurait-il point paru une énigme?*
> (He comes so that I write: that has always been my naive belief and, since I began working, I have been so far as to claim that writing corresponded to his prior desire for I know not what expression . . . Without him, I would never have had to write, if the work did not exist, he would remain unknown, why therefore is he divorced from any work? – How could writing not have appeared to me as an enigma?)

It is also not just that the concern with an unnamed – and unnamable – element disappears in the latter writings, it becomes reworked. 'Il' is the third term. It is that which is neither subject nor object and yet it figures, haunting and producing writing. It is there within the denial of both parts of the either/or. It is neutral. It bears on Blanchot's *'neutre'* (the neuter). The strategy of *La Veille* is condemned to operate within a tripolar oscillation between the subject, the object and the neuter: the self, the other and the other than. Writing becomes the response to a call. The ethics of Lévinas figure here. The writing – the works – within and after *Fugue* deploys, enacts, a thinking, a writing, of repetition. However, the repetition in which writing, the ethical, value, can be placed is itself a dwelling on repetition, etc., but from within repetition: Nietzsche.

5 Roger Laporte, *Une Vie*, p. 315.

6 ibid., p. 273.

7 Jean-François Lyotard, 'Freud selon Cézanne', in *Des dispositifs pulsionnels* (Union Générale d'Editions, Paris, 1973), p. 82.

8 Roger Laporte, *Une Vie*, p. 391.

9 ibid., p. 347.

10 There is much that remains undone. One of the most intriguing questions is that of the relationship between Blanchot and Laporte. What needs to be pursued is not just their writings on each other but the unstated connections within the work themselves. Finally, whatever merit the preceding discussion may have, it resides in the influence exerted on it by Derrida's remarkable paper on Laporte, 'Ce qui reste à force de musique', in Jacques Derrida, *Psyché* (Galilée, Paris, 1987), pp. 95–104. For a discussion of *Abkürzung*, see J. G. Albrechtsberger, *Gründliche Anweisung zur Composition* (Leipzig, 1790).

11 This is not to deny that affirmation has both ethical and political dimensions.

12 Mathieu Bénézet, *Le Roman de la langue*, p. 267.

13 This chapter is dedicated to Jacques Collin in recognition of his friendship, help and support over a number of years.

SELECT BIBLIOGRAPHY

Arendt, H., 'Aufklärung und Judenfrage', in *Die verborgene Tradition*, Suhrkamp, Frankfurt, 1976.

Barthes, R., 'Le Troisième Sens', in *L'Obvie et l'obtus*, Editions du Seuil, Paris, 1982.

Bénézet, M., *Le Roman de la langue*, Union Générale d'Editions, Paris, 1973.

Benjamin, A., 'Wisdom and science in Augustine and Descartes', *Ideas and Production*, 2, 1984.

—— 'Time and interpretation in Heraclitus', in A. Benjamin (ed.), *Post-Structuralist Classics*, Routledge, London, 1988.

—— *Translation and the Nature of Philosophy: A New Theory of Words*, Routledge, London, 1989.

Benjamin, W., *Gesammelte Schriften*, ed. R. Tiedmann and H. Schweppenhauser, Suhrkamp, Frankfurt, 1980.

—— *Illuminations*, trans. H. Zohn, Fontana, London, 1973.

—— *The Origin of German Tragic Drama*, trans. J. Osborne, New Left Books, London, 1977.

—— *Charles Baudelaire: A Lyric Poet in the Era of High Capitalism*, trans. H. Zohn, Verso, London, 1983.

Bennington, G., 'Lyotard: from discourse and figure to experimentation and event', *Paragraph*, 6, 1985.

Buck-Morss, S., *The Origin of Negative Dialectics*, MIT Press, New York, 1977.

Burke, E., *A Philosophical Enquiry into the Origin of our Ideas of the Sublime and the Beautiful*, ed. J. Boulton, University of Notre Dame Press, Notre Dame, 1968.

Derrida, J., 'Signature événement contexte', in *Marges de la philosophie*, Editions de Minuit, Paris, 1972.

—— 'Ce qui reste à force de musique', in *Psyché*, Galilée, Paris, 1987.

—— 'Point de Folie', trans. K. Linker, *AA Files*, no. 12, 1988.

Descartes, R., *Oeuvres Philosophiques*, ed. F. Alquié, Garnier, Paris, 1963.

—— *Discours de la méthode*, ed. E. Gilson, Vrin, Paris, 1967.

Eisenman, P., *Houses of Cards*, Oxford University Press, New York, 1987.

—— 'The Blue Line Text', *Architectural Design*, vol. 58, no. 7/8, August 1988.

ART, MIMESIS AND THE AVANT-GARDE

[4] [4][4][4]
Fuller, P., *Images of God*, The Hogarth Press, London, 1985.
Gablik, S., *Has Modernism Failed?*, Thames & Hudson, London, 1984.
Heidegger, M., *An Introduction to Metaphysics*, trans. R. Mannheim, Yale University Press, New Haven, 1959.
—— *Wegmarken*, Klostermann, Frankfurt, 1967.
—— *Being and Time*, trans. J. Macquarrie and E. Robinson, Basil Blackwell, Oxford, 1972.
—— *On Time and Being*, trans. J. Stambaugh, Harper & Row, New York, 1972.
—— *Martin Heidegger: Basic Writings*, ed. David Farrell Krell, Routledge & Kegan Paul, London, 1978.
—— *Nietzsche, Vol. 1. The Will to Power as Art*, Routledge & Kegan Paul, London, 1981.
Husserl, E., *Experience and Judgement*, trans. J. S. Churchill and K. Ameriks, Routledge & Kegan Paul, London, 1973.
Johnson, P. and Wigley, M., *Deconstructive Architecture*, Museum of Modern Art, New York, 1988.
Laporte, R., *Une Vie*, POL, Paris, 1986.
Lyotard, J.-F., *Discours Figure*, Editions Klincksieck, Paris, 1971.
—— 'Freud selon Cézanne', in *Des dispositifs pulsionnels*, Union Générale d'Editions, Paris, 1973.
—— 'Histoire universelle et différences culturelles', *Critique*, May, 1985.
Malevich, K., *Essays on Art. Vols 1 and 2*, trans. X. Glowacki-Pros and A. McMillin, Rapp & Whiting, London, 1969.
—— *The World as Non-Objectivity*, trans. X. Glowacki-Pros and E. T. Little, Burgen, Copenhagen, 1976.
—— 'Chapters from an artist's autobiography', *October*, Fall 1985.
Nancy, J.-L., *Ego Sum*, Flammarion, Paris, 1979.
Nietzsche, F., *On the Genealogy of Morals*, trans. W. Kaufman, Vintage Books, New York, 1966.
—— *The Birth of Tragedy*, trans. W. Kaufman, Vintage Books, New York, 1967.
—— *The Gay Science*, trans. W. Kaufman, Vintage Books, New York, 1974.
Puppe, H. W., 'Walter Benjamin on photography', *Colloquia Germania*, XII, 3, 1979.
Sallis, J., *Spacings – of Reason and Imagination*, University of Chicago Press, Chicago, 1987.
Wolin, R., *Walter Benjamin. An Aesthetic of Redemption*, Columbia University Press, New York, 1982.
Zhadova, L. A., *Malevich. Suprematism and Revolution in Russian Art, 1910–1930*, trans. A. Lieren, Thames & Hudson, London, 1982.

INDEX

215